FIREARMS & VIOLENCE IN AMERICAN LIFE

A STAFF REPORT
SUBMITTED TO THE
NATIONAL COMMISSION ON THE
CAUSES & PREVENTION OF VIOLENCE

George D. Newton, Jr.
Director

Franklin E. Zimring
Director of Research

NATIONAL COMMISSION
ON THE CAUSES AND PREVENTION OF VIOLENCE

For sale by the Superintendent of Documents, U.S. Government Printing Office
Washington, D.C. 20402 - Price $1.25

Library of Congress Catalog Card Number: 70-601932

STATEMENT ON THE STAFF STUDIES

The Commission was directed to "go as far as man's knowledge takes" it in searching for the causes of violence and the means of prevention. These studies are reports to the Commission by independent scholars and lawyers who have served as directors of our staff task forces and study teams; they are not reports by the Commission itself. Publication of any of the reports should not be taken to imply endorsement of their contents by the Commission, or by any member of the Commission's staff, including the Executive Director and other staff officers, not directly responsible for the preparation of the particular report. Both the credit and the responsibility for the reports lie in each case with the directors of the task forces and study teams. The Commission is making the reports available at this time as works of scholarship to be judged on their merits, so that the Commission as well as the public may have the benefit of both the reports and informed criticism and comment on their contents.

Dr. Milton S. Eisenhower, *Chairman*

TASK FORCE ON FIREARMS

GEORGE D. NEWTON, JR.
DIRECTOR

FRANKLIN E. ZIMRING
DIRECTOR OF RESEARCH

STAFF:
HARRY BARNETT
E. ASA BATES, JR.
JOAN A. BURT
LEIGH S. HALLINGBY
WILLIAM HELMER
JAMES G. HUNTER
JOEL KOFORD
CLAIRE WHITAKER
HARRY G. SKLARSKY

VIVIAN BULLOCK
MARGARET S. ENRIGHT
JEAN M. HORAN
ELIZABETH F. KOURY
SUSAN WATTS
SECRETARIES

COMMISSION STAFF OFFICERS

LLOYD N. CUTLER
EXECUTIVE DIRECTOR

THOMAS D. BARR
DEPUTY DIRECTOR

JAMES F. SHORT, JR.
MARVIN E. WOLFGANG
CO-DIRECTORS OF RESEARCH

JAMES S. CAMPBELL
GENERAL COUNSEL

WILLIAM G. McDONALD
ADMINISTRATIVE OFFICER

JOSEPH LAITIN
DIRECTOR OF INFORMATION

RONALD WOLK
SPECIAL ASSISTANT TO CHAIRMAN

NATIONAL COMMISSION
ON THE CAUSES AND PREVENTION OF VIOLENCE

Dr. Milton S. Eisenhower
CHAIRMAN

iv

By . . . our readiness to allow arms to be purchased at will and fired at whim; by allowing our movie and television screens to teach our children that the hero is one who masters the art of shooting and the technique of killing . . . we have created an atmosphere in which violence and hatred have become popular pastimes.—*Dr. Martin Luther King, November 1963.*

* * *

We have a responsibility to the victims of crime and violence. . . . It is a responsibility to put away childish things—to make the possession and use of firearms a matter undertaken only by serious people who will use them with the restraint and maturity that their dangerous nature deserves—and demands.—*Robert F. Kennedy, July 11, 1967.*

PREFACE

From the earliest days of organization, the Chairman, Commissioners, and Executive Director of the National Commission on the Causes and Prevention of Violence recognized the importance of research in accomplishing the task of analyzing the many facets of violence in America. As a result of this recognition, the Commission has enjoyed the receptivity, encouragement, and cooperation of a large part of the scientific community in this country. Because of the assistance given in varying degrees by scores of scholars here and abroad, these Task Force reports represent some of the most elaborate work ever done on the major topics they cover.

The Commission was formed on June 10, 1968. By the end of the month, the Executive Director had gathered together a small cadre of capable young lawyers from various Federal agencies and aw firms around the country. That group was later augmented by partners borrowed from some of the Nation's major law firms who served without compensation. Such a professional group can be assembled more quickly than university faculty because the latter are not accustomed to quick institutional shifts after making firm commitments of teaching or research at a particular locus. Moreover, the legal profession has long had a major and traditional role in Federal agencies and commissions.

In early July a group of 50 persons from the academic disciplines of sociology, psychology, psychiatry, political science, history, law, and biology were called together on short notice to discuss for 2 days how best the Commission and its staff might proceed to analyze violence. The enthusiastic response of these scientists came at a moment when our Nation was still suffering from the tragedy of Senator Kennedy's assassination.

It was clear from that meeting that the scholars were prepared to join research analysis and action, interpretation, and policy. They were eager to present to the American people the best available data, to bring reason to bear where myth had prevailed. They cautioned against simplistic solutions, but urged application of what is known in the service of sane policies for the benefit of the entire society.

Shortly thereafter the position of Director of Research was created. We assumed the role as a joint undertaking, with common responsibilities. Our function was to enlist social and other scientists to join the staff, to write papers, act as advisers or consultants, and engage in new research. The decentralized structure of the staff, which at its peak numbered 100, required research coordination to reduce duplication and to fill in gaps among the original seven separate Task Forces. In general, the plan was for each Task Force to have a pair of directors: one a social scientist, one a lawyer. In a number of instances, this formal structure bent before the necessities of available personnel but in almost every case the Task Force work program relied on both social scientists and lawyers for its successful completion. In addition to our work with the seven original Task Forces, we provided consultation for the work of the eighth "Investigative" Task Force, formed originally to investigate the disorders at the Democratic and Republican National Conventions and the civil strife in Cleveland during the summer of 1968 and eventually expanded to study campus disorders at several colleges and universities.

Throughout September and October and in December of 1968 the Commission held about 30 days of public hearings related expressly to each of the Task Force areas. About 100 witnesses testified, including many scholars, Government officials, corporate executives as well as militants and activists of various persuasions. In addition to the hearings, the Commission and the staff met privately with scores of persons, including college presidents, religious and youth leaders, and experts in such areas as the media, victim compensation, and firearms. The staff participated actively in structuring and conducting those hearings and conferences and in the questioning of witnesses.

As Research Directors, we participated in structuring the strategy of design for each Task Force, but we listened more than directed. We have known the delicate details of some of the statistical problems and computer runs. We have argued over philosophy and syntax; we have offered bibliographical and other resource materials, we have written portions of reports and copy edited others. In short, we know the enormous energy and devotion, the long hours and accelerated study that members of each Task Force have invested in their labors. In retrospect we are amazed at the high caliber and quantity of the material produced, much of which truly represents, the best in research and scholarship. About 150 separate papers and projects were involved in the work culminating in the Task Force reports. We feel less that we have orchestrated than that we have been members of the orchestra, and that together with the entire staff we have helped compose a repertoire of current knowledge about the enormously complex subject of this Commission.

That scholarly research is predominant in the work here presented is evident in the product. But we should like to emphasize that the roles which we occupied were not limited to scholarly inquiry. The Directors of Research were afforded an opportunity to participate in all Commission meetings. We engaged in discussions at the highest levels of decisionmaking, and had great freedom in the selection of scholars, in the control of research budgets, and in the direction and design of research. If this was not unique, it is at least an uncommon degree of prominence accorded research by a national commission.

There were three major levels to our research pursuit: (1) summarizing the state of our present knowledge and clarifying the lacunae where more or new research should be encouraged; (2) accelerating known ongoing research so as to make it available to the Task Forces; (3) undertaking new research projects within the limits of time and funds available. Coming from a university setting where the pace of research is more conducive to reflection and quiet hours analyzing data, we at first thought that completing much meaningful new research within a matter of months was most unlikely. But the need was matched by the talent and enthusiasm of the staff, and the Task Forces very early had begun enough new projects to launch a small university with a score of doctoral theses. It is well to remember also that in each volume here presented, the research reported is on full public display and thereby makes the staff more than usually accountable for their products.

One of the very rewarding aspects of these research undertakings has been the experience of minds trained in the law mingling and meshing, sometimes fiercely arguing, with other minds trained in behavioral science. The organizational structure and the substantive issues of each Task Force required members from both groups. Intuitive judgment and the logic of argument and organization blended, not always smoothly, with the methodology of science and statistical reasoning. Critical and analytical faculties were sharpened as theories confronted facts. The arrogance neither of ignorance nor of certainty could long endure the doubts and questions of interdisciplinary debate. Any sign of approaching the priestly pontification of scientism was quickly dispelled in the matrix of mutual criticism. Years required for the normal accumulation of experience were compressed into months of sharing ideas with others who had equally valid but differing perspectives. Because of this process, these volumes are much richer than they otherwise might have been.

Partly because of the freedom which the Commission gave to the Directors of Research and the Directors of each Task Force, and partly to retain the full integrity of the research work in publication, these reports of the Task Forces are in the posture of being submitted to and received by the Commission. These are volumes published under the authority of the Commission, but they do not necessarily represent the views or the conclusions of the Commission. The Commission is presently at work producing its own report, based in part on the materials presented to it by the Task Forces. Commission members have, of course, commented on earlier drafts of each Task Force, and have caused alterations by reason of the cogency of their remarks and insights. But the final responsibility for what is contained in these volumes rests fully and properly on the research staffs who labored on them.

In this connection, we should like to acknowledge the special leadership of the Chairman, Dr. Milton S. Eisenhower, in formulating and supporting the principle of research freedom and autonomy under which this work has been conducted.

We note, finally, that these volumes are in many respects incomplete and tentative. The urgency with which papers were prepared and then integrated into Task Force Reports rendered impossible the successive siftings of data and argument to which the typical academic article or volume is subjected. The reports have benefited greatly from the counsel of our colleagues on the Advisory Panel, and from much debate and revision from within the staff. It is our hope, that the total work effort of the Commission staff will be the source and subject of continued research by scholars in the several disciplines, as well as a useful resource for policymakers. We feel certain that public policy and the disciplines will benefit greatly from such further work.

* * *

To the Commission, and especially to its Chairman, for the opportunity they provided for complete research freedom, and to the staff for its prodigious and prolific work, we, who were intermediaries and servants to both, are most grateful.

James F. Short, Jr.   Marvin E. Wolfgang

Directors of Research

ACKNOWLEDGEMENTS

The work of this Task Force in the short period available has been made possible only by the diligent efforts of many persons.

Hans Zeisel of the University of Chicago had a pervasive influence on this report, understated by his title of general consultant. We are grateful for the guidance and assistance provided by Quinn Tamm and R. Dean Smith of the International Association of Police Chiefs; Jerome J. Daunt and Robert H. Haynes of the Federal Bureau of Investigation; Thomas F. Casey, William D. Behan, and Cecil M. Wolfe of the Alcohol and Tobacco Tax Division of the Treasury Department; Jack W. Osburn, Jr., and Mary A. Chorba of the Bureau of Defense Services of the Commerce Department; the staff of the Senate Subcommittee on Juvenile Delinquency; Jack J. Basil of the National Rifle Association; Peter Rothenberg of the Office of General Counsel of the Army; Barnes Ellis and Lawrence Margolis of the Department of Justice; Richard Hellman of the Small Business Administration; and Frederick S. York of the State Department. We are also grateful for the assistance provided by John M. Linsenmeyer and C. David Anderson.

We also acknowledge the assistance of the firearms manufacturers and their attorneys and the police departments of many cities for invaluable help in accumulating data and the Detroit Police Department, the Medical Examiner of Wayne County, Mich., and the Los Angeles Suicide Prevention Center for collaboration in our research.

CHAPTER SUMMARIES

1. *The Number of Firearms in Civilian Hands*

Of the estimated 90 million firearms in civilian hands in the United States, 24 million are handguns, 35 million are rifles, and 31 million are shotguns.

2. *Patterns of Firearms Ownership*

About half of all American homes have a firearm, and many have more than one. Firearms ownership is highest in the South and lowest in the East. Ownership of rifles and shotguns is higher in rural areas and towns than in large cities, but handgun ownership is highest in towns and large cities.

3. *How Firearms are Acquired*

Almost half of all long guns, and more than half of all handguns, are acquired secondhand. New firearms and a large number of used firearms are purchased from sporting goods stores, hardware stores, or other firearms dealers. But, about half of secondhand firearms are acquired from friends or other private parties.

4. *Recent Trends in Firearms Sales*

Sales of long guns doubled from 1962 to 1968; in the same period sales of handguns quadrupled. In the last decade, about 10 million handguns were sold in this country, more than one third of all handguns produced or imported for the civilian market since the turn of the century.

Growing interest in shooting sports may explain much of the increase in long gun sales, but it does not account for the dramatic increase in handgun sales. Fear of crime, violence, and civil disorder, and perhaps the anticipation of stricter firearms laws, appear to have stimulated sales of handguns in recent years.

5. *Firearms and Accidents*

Americans are currently dying from firearms accidents at a rate of about 2,900 per year; another 20,000 persons suffer accidental injuries each year from firearms. Firearms accident rates follow the pattern of firearms ownership; they are highest in the South and lowest in the East. Over half of all fatal firearms accidents occur in or around the home, and about 40 percent of accident victims are children and teenagers.

6. *Firearms and Suicide*

For persons who seek to end their lives, firearms are a speedy and effective method. There is some evidence that, if persons who now use firearms were forced to resort to other means where there is a higher chance of intervention and rescue, some would not die. But there is little reason to expect that reducing the availability of firearms would cause a significant reduction in suicides. A person who really wants to die will find a way of doing so.

7. *Firearms and Crime*

Homicide is seldom the result of a single-minded intent to kill. Fatal injuries most often occur from an attack growing out of an altercation and committed in a rage. Firearms were used in 65 percent of homicides in this country in 1968. When a gun is used, the chances of death are about five times as great as when a knife is used. In the last 5 years the number of firearms homicides has increased by almost 50 percent.

Aggravated assault differs from homicide only in its outcome—the victim survives. Although the knife is still the No. 1 weapon used in aggravated assault, the share of gun attacks is increasing, and in 1968 nearly one in four aggravated assaults involved firearms.

One third of all robberies are committed with guns. The chances of the victim's being killed increase substantially if the robber uses a gun.

8. *The Firearms Used in Crime*

The criminal's primary firearm is the handgun. Although only about one quarter of all firearms in this country are handguns, they are used in three quarters of the homicides involving firearms. Of the handguns used in crime in the District of Columbia, nearly half are imported. Samples of firearms manufactured in this country and used in crime reveal that a surprising number are more than 50 years old and one in six is a military weapon. Many of the handguns used in crime were owned by legitimate users at one time but appear to have been sold privately or to have been stolen without the theft having been reported.

9. *Firearms and Collective Violence*

The availability of firearms at relatively low cost makes it easy for extremist groups and individuals to obtain such weapons; the possession of firearms by some groups encourages opposition groups and individuals likewise to arm themselves; and possession of firearms by any group invites quicker and deadlier response on the part of rival armed groups and law enforcement agencies.

10. *Firearms and Self-Defense*

Owning a gun for self-defense and protection of homes and businesses is deeply rooted in American tradition. Guns may be of some utility in defending businesses, but householders may seriously overrate the effectiveness of guns in protection of their homes. In our urbanized society the gun is rarely an effective means of protecting the home against either the burglar or the robber; the former avoids confrontation, the latter confronts too swiftly. Possession of a gun undoubtedly provides a measure of comfort to a great many Americans, but, for the homeowner, this comfort is largely an illusion bought at the high price of increased accidents, homicides, and more widespread illegal use of guns.

11. *More Firearms—More Firearms Violence*

Data from three sources document that the proportion of gun use in violence rises and falls with gun ownership. Statistics from Detroit show that firearms violence increased after an increase in handgun acquisitions. Regional comparisons show that the percentage of gun use in violent attacks parallels rates of gun ownership. A study of guns used in homicides, robberies, and assaults in eight major cities shows that cities with a high proportion of gun use in one crime tend to have high proportions of gun use in the other crimes.

12. Strategies of Firearms Control

Different strategies of firearms control—regulation of the place and manner in which firearms can be used, regulation of who may possess firearms, permissive and restrictive licensing, registration and transfer notice—can be combined in a variety of ways to produce a comprehensive system of control. Since handguns and long guns do not contribute equally to firearms misuse, it may be appropriate to use different strategies for different types of firearms.

13. State and Local Firearms Laws

State and local firearms regulation in the United States is a patchwork quilt of more than 20,000 laws, many of them obsolete, unenforced, or unenforceable. Serious efforts at state and local regulation have consistently been frustrated by the flow of firearms from one state to another. Attempts to establish uniform state and local firearms laws have failed.

14. Federal Firearms Laws

Public opinion in this country has favored regulation of firearms since the 1930's. Yet, from the enactment of the first federal firearms possession law in 1934, federal gun laws have been passed in this country only after sensational episodes of gun violence. The Gun Control Act of 1968, which followed the assassinations of Dr. Martin Luther King, Jr., and Senator Robert F. Kennedy, commits the federal government to support state and city gun control laws by reducing the interstate flow of firearms which has long frustrated local control efforts. Proposals for a federal system of screening firearms owners have not been enacted.

15. Firearms Control and the Constitution

The second amendment raises no legal barrier to federal or state firearms legislation. The fifth amendment, however, could be invoked against enforcement of such laws. Fifth amendment problems might be minimized by exempting from licensing, registration, or transfer notice requirements all persons in those categories prohibited by law from possessing firearms. This exemption of illegal possessors would not decrease the effectiveness of firearms control because other parts of the control system could allow prosecution of such persons without requiring them to incriminate themselves.

16. *Foreign Firearms Laws*

Most countries have passed national firearms control laws. The great majority of these laws appear to be more stringent than the laws of most states in the United States, although many of the foreign laws may not be effectively enforced. Many countries regulate handguns more stringently than long guns, and rough estimates of handgun ownership in 10 countries are all far below the rate of handgun ownership in the United States.

17. *Can We Reduce Firearms Violence?*

The gun control controversy has often involved comparisons of crime statistics from states with firearms control laws with statistics from states with no such laws and comparisons of the United States to foreign countries. These comparisons are never wholly satisfactory, but when care is exercised to focus not upon the number of crimes committed but solely upon the proportion of crimes involving guns, an inference can be drawn that control systems that substantially reduce the number of guns are effective in reducing the level of gun violence. Since handguns are the major problem, a nationwide restrictive licensing system for handguns promises a more certain and more substantial reduction of gun violence in this country than a permissive system.

18. *The Costs of Firearms Control*

The costs of any firearms control system include both the funds needed to administer the system and the effect on opportunities for legitimate firearms use. The monetary cost of an efficiently administered permissive or restrictive licensing system would not be excessive. Restrictive licensing, however, would significantly reduce the legitimate use of the controlled firearms.

19. *Technology and Firearms Control*

Technological advancements in tracing of firearms to owners, in detecting firearms in public places, and in development of nonlethal weapons or ammunition would help reduce firearms misuse by making firearms control systems more effective. Government and private industry should engage in a concerted program of scientific research and development to promote such technological advancements.

FIREARMS AND VIOLENCE IN

AMERICAN LIFE

CONTENTS

FIGURES

TABLES

FIREARMS OWNERSHIP IN THE UNITED STATES

Firearms have long been an important part of American life. For many years the armed citizen-soldier was the country's first line of defense; the "Kentucky" long rifle opened the frontier; the Winchester repeater "won the West"; and the Colt revolver "made men equal."

Firearms no longer play a significant role in keeping food on American tables, yet Americans own and use firearms to a degree that puzzles many observers. If our frontier has disappeared, our frontier tradition remains. In addition to this tradition, however, our national enthusiasm for firearms derives from the genuine pleasures of hunting, sport shooting, and gun collecting and, to some degree, from fear for personal and family safety—a fear of guns in the hands of others.

Part I considers general patterns of firearms ownership in order to gain perspective on the misuse of firearms in this country. The analysis addresses four questions:

(1) How many firearms are privately owned in the United States?

(2) What types of firearms are owned, who owns them, and where?

(3) How are firearms acquired?

(4) What are the current trends in firearms sales?

Chapter 1

THE NUMBER OF FIREARMS
IN CIVILIAN HANDS

Any meaningful study of the relationship between firearms and violence in the United States should begin with an effort to determine the number of serviceable firearms—handguns, rifles, and shotguns[1] —currently in the hands of civilians. Estimates have ranged from 50 to 200 million.[2] The Task Force has attempted to reduce this margin of error. The ideal estimate would be based on domestic firearms production, plus imported firearms, less the number of guns that have disappeared through wear, loss, breakage, or confiscation and destruction by the police.

Table 1-1 shows domestic production and reported imports of handguns, rifles, and shotguns for civilian use. The domestic production figures cover the years since 1899, and the import figures

---

[1]Handguns, rifles, and shotguns are the three common types of civilian small arms. Handguns include both revolvers (cartridge chambers in a rotating cylinder separate from the barrel) and pistols (single chamber contiguous with the barrel) designed to be fired with one hand. Shotguns and rifles are sometimes classified "long guns" or "shoulder arms" because their longer barrels and stocks are designed for firing from the shoulder.

Shotguns fire a burst of lead pellets from a paper or plastic "shell." Rifles and handguns fire a bullet from a metallic cartridge. Shotguns have smooth bores, while rifle and handgun barrels have spiral grooves or "riflings" which impart a spinning motion to the bullet. The distinction sometimes made between centerfire and rimfire weapons stems from the difference in the location of the primer at the base of the cartridge. Generally, rimfire guns are of relatively small caliber and low power, while center-fire guns are of larger caliber and greater power.

Throughout this report, the three main types of guns will be represented by the following symbols:

Handguns   Rifles   Shotguns

Other firearms, such as machineguns, antitank guns, and similar large caliber weapons, are described in App. B.

[2]See "The Challenge of Crime in a Free Society," a report by the President's Commission on Law Enforcement and the Administration of Justice, p. 239; Alan S. Krug, Assistant to the Director, The National Shooting Sports Foundation, Inc., 114 Cong. Rec. 1, 90th Cong., 2d sess. (Jan. 29, 1968).

3

Table 1-1–U.S. domestic production and imports of firearms for civilian use.
[in thousands]

	Handguns	Rifles	Shotguns	Total
Domestic production since 1899 . .	22,568	36,345	32,349	91,262
Reported imports since 1918	5,363	3,200	2,562	11,125
Total	27,931	39,545	34,911	102,387

Source: Task Force study (App. C).

cover the years since 1918.[3] Studies of firearms confiscated by
the police show that some guns manufactured before 1899 are still
in use,[4] although their numbers are probably small.[5] The total
number of firearms produced or imported for the domestic civilian
market is approximately 100 million–27 percent handguns and 73
percent rifles and shotguns.

The estimate of imports is not yet complete, however, since it
does not reflect firearms brought into the country but not reported as imports. There are two ways in which firearms have
been brought into this country without being reflected in import
or production statistics. First, considerable numbers of military
firearms have been brought into the country by returning servicemen. The Department of Defense cannot advise us of the number
of firearms sold within the United States as military surplus, but
it is known that firearms purchased by the military since 1940,
less those in current use, total approximately 14 million. Approximately 2 million of these have been supplied to foreign countries
since 1950 under military assistance programs. Many of the remaining 12 million were lost in combat or scrapped, but a significant number, together with foreign-made firearms taken as souvenirs, have found their way back to the United States in packages
or duffel bags of returning servicemen.[6] These guns, plus the domestic military small arms sold as surplus in this country after
every wartime mobilization, constitute a sizable portion of the
firearms in civilian hands in this country.

FBI records reveal that, of nearly 185,000 firearms reported
stolen as of November 1968, 23 percent originally were military

---

[3] A description of the methods used in compiling this data is contained in App. C.
[4] Of 328 confiscated handguns traced by the Task Force, for instance, seven were manufactured in 1898 or before. (See ch. 8, infra.)
[5] Information supplied the Task Force by four existing manufacturers indicates production by these manufacturers of about 4 million firearms from 1856 to 1898. These
firearms are now classified as antiques by the Gun Control Act of 1968. (See ch. 14,
infra.)
[6] Some indication of the extent of uncounted imports of military firearms is revealed
from the high ownership of handguns by veterans. (See Fig. 2-3 in ch. 2, infra.)

firearms. Similarly, records of several police departments indicate many firearms confiscated by the police are former military firearms.

Another source of uncounted imports are foreign visitors and returning tourists who have been allowed to bring as many as three handguns and a thousand rounds of ammunition into this country without a formal declaration.[7] Millions of tourists enter or re-enter the United States every year,[8] but the Bureau of Customs has no records with which to estimate the number who have brought in firearms.

On the other side of the ledger, many of the firearms included in the totals in Table 1-1 have been lost, destroyed, or are no longer serviceable. Firearms manufacturers have advised the Task Force that a firearm can be expected to last indefinitely if given proper care.[9] However, a substantial number of firearms produced since the turn of the century have been taken out of circulation through loss or neglect.

A considerable number of firearms are confiscated each year by law enforcement agencies. Only a few states, however, require the police to destroy confiscated firearms; in other states these firearms are auctioned off to the highest bidder and returned to circulation.[10]

This leaves our computation with an unknown number of military firearms sold as surplus or brought into the country as souvenirs by servicemen, an unknown number of firearms brought through customs from abroad, and an unknown number of firearms that have been worn out, lost, or confiscated and destroyed. One method of completing our estimate of the number of firearms is to assume that these unknown entries and disappearances cancel each other and that the total number of firearms in civilian hands is about 100 million.

---

[7] 22 C.F.R. 123.52.

[8] The Immigration and Naturalization Service has advised the Task Force that nearly 5 million Americans visited abroad last year and another 86 million visited Canada and Mexico. About 6 million foreign visitors came to this country.

[9] The small number of firearms that are worn out through use is confirmed by the fact that manufacturers advise that the useful life of a gun, in terms of rounds fired, ranges from 10,000 to 100,000 rounds, depending on the quality and type of gun. Information from the manufacturers of ammunition indicates that 4.4 billion rounds of ammunition were made in 1967. If all this ammunition were expended, this would amount to an average of only 43 rounds per year, assuming 100 million firearms. Although all firearms are not used equally, it is unlikely that any significant number of firearms are worn out through use.

[10] In New York, for instance, firearms confiscated in crime must be destroyed (New York State Penal Code, Sec. 400.05). But North Carolina, on the other hand, auctions such weapons off to the highest bidder and thus returns them to circulation (N.C. Stats. Sec. 14-269-1). In other states the police apparently have discretion to destroy or sell confiscated firearms.

National public opinion polls also provide insight on the number of firearms in civilian hands. A 1968 Harris poll conducted for
this Commission, and discussed in detail in the next chapter,
showed that 49 percent of the 60.4 million American households
reported firearms ownership and that the average number of firearms owned was 2.24. These data allow a projection of 66 million
firearms (49 percent of 60.4 million households times 2.24). A
1966 Gallup poll showed that 59 percent of American households
possess firearms. Using the 1968 Harris figure of 2.24 firearms for
each firearms-owning household allows a projection of 80 million
serviceable firearms (59 percent of 60.4 million households times
2.24).

Two factors at least partially account for the discrepancies between the calculated and projected totals. There is evidence that
many persons are increasingly reluctant to disclose ownership of
firearms in a door-to-door survey.[11] Also, wives or children who
are interviewed may not always know about all the weapons owned
by other members of the household.

Survey results thus indicate ownership of approximately 80
million firearms, while production and import totals indicate approximately 100 million . We can do no better than average these
two figures and conservatively estimate the number of firearms
now in civilian hands in this country to be 90 million. A more
precise estimate must await the availability of more precise data.

The 90 million estimate is divided in Figure 1-1 into the three
main types of firearms according to the percentage reflected in the
production and import totals.

Figure 1-1—Estimated number of firearms in civilian hands.
(United States, 1968)

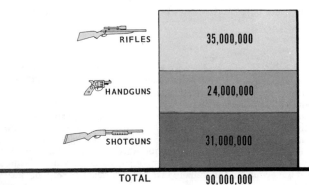

RIFLES	35,000,000
HANDGUNS	24,000,000
SHOTGUNS	31,000,000
TOTAL	90,000,000

[11]The discrepancy between the Harris and Gallup polls can be interpreted as evidence of
this reluctance. Fifty-nine percent of the sample households conceded firearms ownership in 1966, but only 49 percent did so in 1968 despite a dramatic increase in firearms sales since 1966. (See ch. 4.)

Whether one accepts the figure of 80 million firearms indicated by the public opinion polls, the figure of 100 million indicated by production and import figures, or an intermediate figure makes little difference to any public policy question about firearms. By whatever measure, the United States has an abundance of firearms.

Summary

There are an estimated 90 million firearms in civilian hands in the United States today: 35 million rifles, 31 million shotguns, and 24 million handguns—in 60 million households.

Chapter 2

PATTERNS OF FIREARMS OWNERSHIP

Public opinion surveys conducted for firearms manufacturers and a Harris survey conducted for this Commission[1] provide data on the ownership of firearms in this country. Because people are reluctant to answer questions about firearms ownership, the polls give us an incomplete picture of firearms ownership. However, the public opinion polls are the best source of information available about patterns of ownership in the United States.

Table 2-1 shows the distribution of firearms among the 60 million households in the United States as revealed from the Harris poll data:

Table 2-1—Number of firearms per household.
(United States, 1968)

Firearms owned	Households (millions)	Percent
None	30.8	51
1	12.1	20
2	7.9	13
3	3.6	6
4 or more	6.0	10
Total	60.4	100

Source: 1968 Harris poll (App. D).

About one half of the approximately 60 million households in the United States have one or more firearms. The average number of firearms for each firearms-owning household is 2.24.[2]

The geographical distribution of firearms is shown in Figure 2-1.

---

[1]A description of the methods used in the Harris poll is contained in App. D.
[2]Even though, as noted in ch. 1, these figures probably underestimate the firearms in civilian hands in this country, the data are valid to see how firearms are distributed.

Figure 2-1—Percent of U.S. households owning various firearms, by region*.
(United States, 1968)

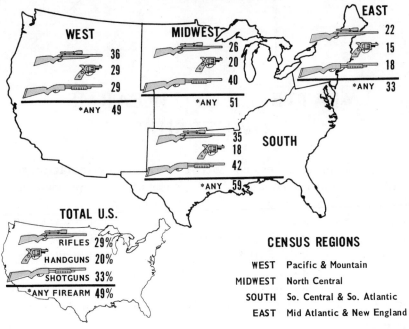

*Any firearm = households having any firearm at all.
Source: 1968 Harris poll.

Firearms ownership is highest in the South (59 percent of all households) and lowest in the East (33 percent). Ownership in the Midwest and West is close to the national average. The type of firearm
owned varies considerably by region. Rifle ownership is highest in
the West (36 percent) and the South (35 percent); shotguns are
more frequently owned in the South (42 percent) and the Midwest
(40 percent); and handgun ownership is highest in the West (29
percent) and lowest in the East (15 percent).[3]

Firearms ownership varies significantly with density of population, a fact already reflected to some extent in the geographic dis-

---

[3]Similar regional patterns are reflected in a manufacturer's survey in 1963, when total
firearms ownership was apparently lower.

	Percent households with—			
		Rifles		
	Shotguns	Low power	High power	Handguns
Nationally	33	25	13	16
By region:				
Northeast. . . .	23	18	12	11
North Central .	37	27	11	14
South	41	29	10	20
West.	26	29	23	21

tribution. It is highest in rural areas and lowest in the large cities, as indicated in Figure 2-2.[4]

Figure 2-2—Percent of households with firearms, by city size.
(United States, 1968)

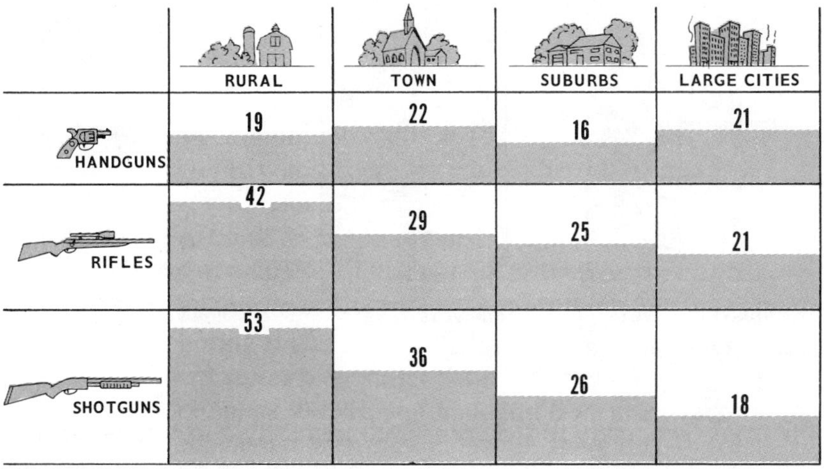

	RURAL	TOWN	SUBURBS	LARGE CITIES
HANDGUNS	19	22	16	21
RIFLES	42	29	25	21
SHOTGUNS	53	36	26	18

Source: 1968 Harris poll.

Shotgun ownership declines most rapidly as the population becomes denser—from 53 percent in rural areas to 18 percent in large cities. Rifle ownership declines less sharply—from 42 percent. Handgun ownership, on the other hand, is slightly higher in the large cities. Rifle ownership declines less sharply—from 42 percent to 21 percent.. Handgun ownership, on the other hand, is slightly higher in the large cities than in rural areas and suburbs.

Finally, veterans are more likely to own firearms than nonveterans, as seen in Figure 2-3.

---

[4]The 1963 manufacturer's survey again reflects a similar pattern.

Community size	Percent households with—			
	Shotguns	Rifles		Handguns
		Low power	High power	
Rural	52	40	20	19
Metropolitan areas:				
2,500-49,999.	45	32	17	18
50,000-499,999 . . .	30	22	11	16
500,000-1,999,999 .	22	17	9	13
2,000,000 and over .	11	11	7	11

Figure 2-3–Firearms ownership: veterans and non-veterans, by type of weapon.
(United States, 1968)

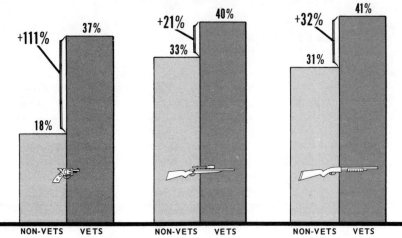

Source: 1968 Harris poll.

Firearms ownership for veterans is consistently above the ownership level for non-veterans. Compared to non-veterans, 21 percent
more veterans own rifles, 32 percent more veterans own shotguns,
and 111 percent more veterans own handguns.[5]

Summary

About half of all American homes have a firearm, and many have
more than one. Firearms ownership is highest in the South and
lowest in the East. Ownership of rifles and shotguns is higher in
rural areas and towns than in large cities, but handgun ownership
is highest in towns and large cities.

---

[5]Rifle ownership by veterans is 7 percent higher than non-veterans, shotgun ownership
10 percent higher, and handgun ownership 19 percent higher. It seems unlikely that all
of the 19 percent differential for handguns can be accounted for by veteran familiarity
with firearms, since it far exceeds the margin for rifles and shotguns. These data suggest
that many veterans have returned from service with one or more military handguns.

Chapter 3

HOW FIREARMS ARE ACQUIRED

Firearms, as noted in Chapter 1, are generally quite durable and can be expected to last indefinitely when given proper care. It is therefore not surprising that the secondhand market in firearms is almost as important as the new market, as indicated in Figure 3-1.

Figure 3-1 —How firearms were acquired.
(United States, 1968)

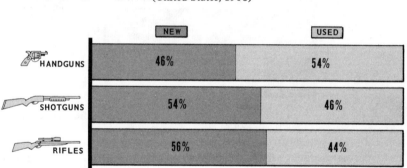

Source: 1968 Harris poll

Almost half of all rifles and shotguns and slightly more than half of all handguns were acquired used by their present owners.

New firearms are normally sold by manufacturers and importers to wholesalers, who sell to dealers, who in turn sell to consumers. In 1967, the Treasury Department issued 102,041 licenses to firearms dealers and wholesalers, many of them large businesses.

In 1967, 10 wholesalers each purchased more than a million dollars' worth of firearms from major manufacturers; 30 other wholesalers each purchased over $500,000 worth of firearms. Wholesalers vary widely in the products they handle and the territories they cover. Some operate in many states, but most sell primarily in a handful of states surrounding their location and have only a few customers in other states.

The largest share of the approximately 100,000 federal firearms licenses are issued to an estimated 70,000 retail dealers[1] ranging from gunshops and sporting goods stores to hardware stores, department stores, and pawnshops.[2]

Most of the remaining 32,000 federal firearms licenses are held by private individuals who paid the $1 fee to allow them to buy firearms at wholesale prices and transport firearms through the mails.[3]

The market for secondhand firearms is somewhat different, as noted in Figure 3-2.

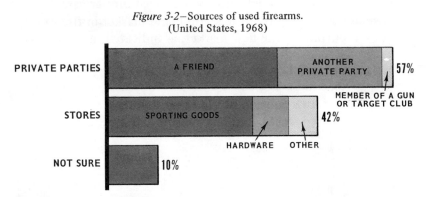

Figure 3-2–Sources of used firearms.
(United States, 1968)

Percents add to more than 100: Some respondents acquired firearms from more than one source. Source: 1968 Harris poll

Just over 40 percent of the buyers surveyed bought a used firearm from a retail firearms dealer. Over half of all secondhand guns are obtained from a "friend" or another "private party." Figure 3-3 breaks down these firearms acquisitions by income group.

---

[1]Joseph W. Barr, Under Secretary of the Treasury, Hearings before the Senate Subcommittee To Investigate Juvenile Delinquency, 90th Cong., 1st sess., p. 40 (1967).

[2]A 1966 survey of nearly 14,000 retail outlets handling rifles and shotguns showed 44 percent are sporting goods stores, 21 percent hardware stores, and 11 percent department and general merchandise stores (1966 Manufacturer's Market Survey, App. D). On the other hand, information submitted to the Task Force by firearms wholesalers indicates that a large percentage of retail outlets handling firearms, particularly handguns, are pawnshops. The 300 accounts of one major wholesaler, engaged almost exclusively in selling domestically manufactured handguns, included 70 pawnshops or loan companies, representing 16 percent of its business.

Many firearms are sold by chain store merchandisers. One such chain store increased its firearms sales approximately 50 percent from 1963 to 1967. Another had mail-order and over-the-counter sales of more than $10 million from 1963 to 1967. A major chain store discontinued sales of handguns in 1963 and mail-order sales of rifles and shotguns in 1968, as well as the listing of firearms in its catalog.

[3]See footnote 1, *supra*. The Gun Control Act of 1968, discussed in ch. 14, *infra*, raised the dealer's license fee to $10 and also provided for a license for gun "collectors" for the same fee. See 82 Stat. 1221.

Figure 3-3—Used guns acquired from a friend or other private party, by income group.
(United States, 1968)

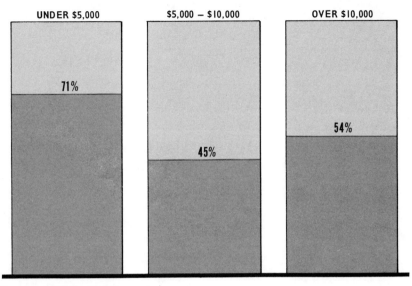

| UNDER $5,000 | $5,000 – $10,000 | OVER $10,000 |

71%

45%

54%

Source: 1968 Harris poll

Of persons earning under $5,000 per year who acquired a gun,
more than 7 out of 10 made the acquisition from a friend or other
private party.

Summary

Almost half of all long guns, and more than half of all handguns,
are acquired secondhand. New firearms and a large number of
used firearms are purchased from sporting goods stores, hardware
stores, and other firearms dealers. But about half of secondhand
firearms are acquired from friends or other private parties.

Chapter 4

RECENT TRENDS IN
FIREARMS SALES

In Chapter 1 an estimate was made of the total number of firearms presently owned by civilians in the United States. In this
chapter, production and imports of civilian firearms over time are
examined, with particular attention being given to what has occurred in the last 10 years.

Table 4-1 shows the long-range trends in domestic production.
and imports of firearms for the civilian market.[1]

Table 4-1—*Firearms introduced into the
U.S. civilian market—1899 to 1968.
[In millions for every 10-year period]*

Period	Total	Rifles	Shotguns	Handguns
1899-1948 (average)	10.6	4.7	3.2	2.7
1949-58	20.0	6.4	9.4	4.2
1959-68	29.2	9.6	9.4	10.2
Accumulated total in 1968. . .	102.3	39.5	34.9	27.9

Source: Task Force study(App. C).

The number of rifles added to the civilian firearms market grew
from an average of 4.7 million per decade through 1948 to 6.4 million in the 1950's. For the decade ending in 1968, the increase was
9.6 million. Shotguns increased sharply in the 1950's (3.2 to 9.4
million per decade) but leveled off in the 1960's (9.4 million). The
number of handguns added to the domestic market shows the most
substantial increase. The average increase of 2.7 million per decade
in the first 50 years rose to 4.2 million per decade in the 1950's
and to 10.2 million for the decade ending in 1968.

---

[1]Tabulations of annual firearms domestic production and imports from 1946 to 1968
and a description of the methods used in compiling figures on domestic production and
imports are contained in App. C.

A more detailed examination of domestic production and imports for the last decade reveals that the greatest expansion of the firearms market has occurred during the last 5 years.

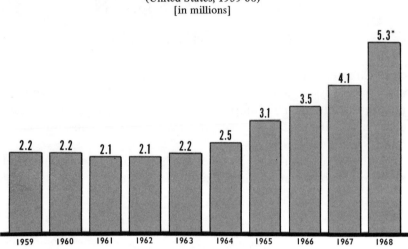

Figure 4-1–Firearms added to the civilian market.
(United States, 1959-68)
[in millions]

*Projection based on 1st 6 months' production and imports.
Source: Task Force study.

During the first half of this decade, the figures remained stable. After 1964 they rose sharply to an all-time high in 1968, about 2½ times the earlier level.

Of even greater significance are the market trends for each of the three major types of firearms over the last 7 years, as seen in Figure 4-2. Rifle sales doubled from 1962 to 1968, and shotgun sales nearly doubled, while handgun sales in the same period quadrupled. The 1968 annual level was nearly equal to the average

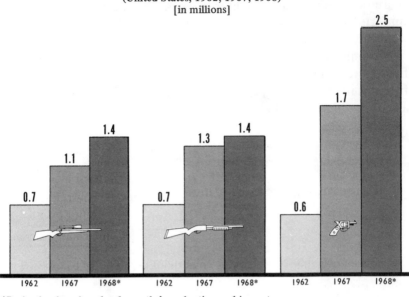

Figure 4-2–Production and imports of major types of firearms.
(United States, 1962, 1967, 1968)
[in millions]

*Projection based on 1st 6 months' production and imports.
Source: Task Force study.

decade in the first half of the century (Table 4-1).

Figure 4-3 shows the increase in the last 6 years in the proportion of imported firearms to all firearms sold in the domestic market.

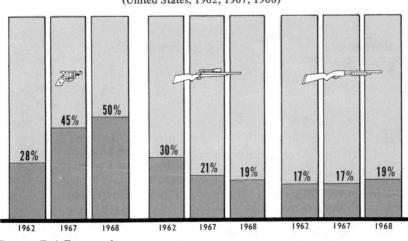

Figure 4-3–Imports as percent of all firearms sold.
(United States, 1962, 1967, 1968)

Source: Task Force study.

While the share of rifle imports has declined since 1963 and the share of shotgun imports has grown slightly, the share of handgun imports has climbed steadily since 1963 and in 1968 was equal to domestic handgun production.[2]

To some extent these dramatic increases in gun sales merely reflect increased shooting sports activity. Information supplied by firearms manufacturers, indicates production of clay targets has about doubled since 1962.

Table 4-2–Manufacturers' shipments of clay targets.
(United States)

	Millions of units
1955	113
1960	169
1961	185
1962	216
1963	238
1964	267
1965	297
1966	333
1967	403

Source: Sporting Arms and Ammunition Manufacturers Institute.

The number of members of skeet and trapshooting clubs, although only a small proportion of all gun owners, has more than doubled in the last decade, as shown in Table 4-3.

Table 4-3–Trap and skeet association membership.
(United States)

National Skeet Shooting Association:	*1957*	*1968*
Membership	4,792	15,521
Amateur Trap Association:	*1964*	*1968*
Membership	23,000	50,000+

Source: National Skeet Shooting Association and Amateur Trap Association.

However, the number of licensed hunters, which unlike the number of trap and skeet shooters is in the millions, has remained relatively stable since 1958.

---

[2]See ch. 13, *infra*, for a discussion of the probable impact of the Gun Control Act of 1968 on firearms imports.

Table 4-4—Individual hunting licenses, 1938-68.
(United States)

Year	Licenses issued (millions)	Rate per 100,000
1938-47 (average)	8.4	5.8
1948-57 (average)	13.5	8.5
1958	14.8	8.5
1959	11.9	6.7
1960	11.8	6.5
1961	11.8	6.4
1962	13.8	7.4
1963	14.0	7.4
1964	14.1	7.4
1965	14.3	7.3
1966	14.4	7.3
1967	14.7	7.3
		7.4

Source: Bureau of Sport Fisheries and Wildlife, U.S. Department of the Interior,
Washington, D.C.

At the same time, hunters now have longer seasons, more shooting preserves, and more leisure time and income to spend on sports and hobbies. For instance, between 1960 and 1966, the last year for which comparable data are available, expenditures for sporting arms and ammunition increased 72 percent—the same as the increase in expenditures for fishing equipment.[3]

Yet increases in hunting and sport shooting only partly account for the spiraling sale of firearms and can have little to do with handguns. Firearms purchases in recent years have often been motivated by fear of crime, violence, and civil disorder, as well as the fear that stricter firearms laws may make guns harder to obtain in the future.

The acquisition of firearms for defensive purposes is indicated both in public opinion surveys[4] and in studies of the trends of handgun permits issued in the last 3 years. Figure 4-4, adapted from a report submitted to the National Advisory Commission on Civil Disorders, shows the timing of civil disorders and the demand for handgun permits in the City of Detroit.[5]

---

[3]"Trends in the Purchase and Use of Sporting Shoulder Arms" (Sept. 1968), submitted to this Commission by Winchester-Western Division of Olin Mathieson Chemical Corp. and contained in the Hearings of this Task Force as Exhibit IV. See, also, Philip H. Burdett, Vice President and Assistant General Manager, Remington Arms Co., Inc., Commission Hearings (Executive Session), Oct. 10, 1968, Tr. 72-74.

[4]Self-defense is the most frequently given reason for owning a handgun. See ch. 10, infra.

[5]This subject is discussed in detail in ch. 11, infra. The utility of firearms in defending homes and businesses is discussed in ch. 10, infra.

Figure 4-4—New permits to purchase firearms in Detroit, Mich. (by quarter).
(1965-1968)

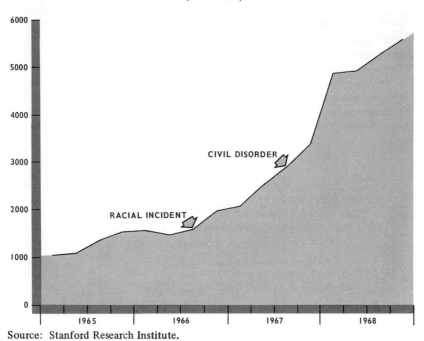

Source: Stanford Research Institute.

Summary

Sales of long guns doubled from 1962 to 1968; in the same period, sales of handguns quadrupled. In the last decade, about 10 million handguns were sold in this country, more than one third of all handguns produced or imported for the civilian market since the turn of the century. Growing interest in shooting sports may explain much of the increase in long gun sales, but it does not account for the dramatic increase in handgun sales. Fear of crime, violence, and civil disorder, and perhaps the anticipation of stricter firearms laws, appear also to have stimulated sales of handguns in recent years.

PART II

FIREARMS AND VIOLENCE– CAUSE, CONTRIBUTION, OR COINCIDENCE?

In 1967, firearms were involved in approximately 73,000 robberies, 53,000 aggravated assaults, 9,000 suicides, 7,000 homicides, and 2,900 accidental deaths in this country. Although firearms used in these deaths and crimes represent only a small fraction of the total guns in the United States, some relationship clearly exists between firearms and violent death and crime.

Three propositions might explain this relationship. First, firearms may be a *cause* of violence. Second, if firearms do not cause violence, their availability may be a *contributing* factor to the rate or seriousness of violence. Third, firearms and violence may be related only by *coincidence,* since firearms are only one of many weapons that can be used in violence.

The following chapters discuss the use of firearms in accidents, suicides, and crime; the age, origin, and prior history of firearms used in crime; the use of firearms in civil disorders; the arms policies of extremist organizations; the utility of guns as defensive weapons; and the apparent consequences of increases in the number of firearms in civilian hands.

Chapter 5

FIREARMS AND ACCIDENTS

Firearms accidents are but a small fraction of all accidental deaths in our country. The 2,896 known firearms deaths in 1967 ranked only fifth among all accidental deaths in the United States, as shown in Figure 5-1.

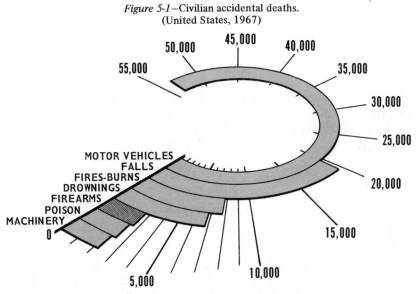

Figure 5-1—Civilian accidental deaths.
(United States, 1967)

Source: "Accident Facts," National Safety Council, 1968 edition.

The rate of accidental deaths by firearms per 100,000 people in the United States declined steadily from the 1930's until the 1960's, when a slight upward trend began.

Figure 5-2—Rate of fatal firearms accidents per 100,000 U.S. civilian population.*

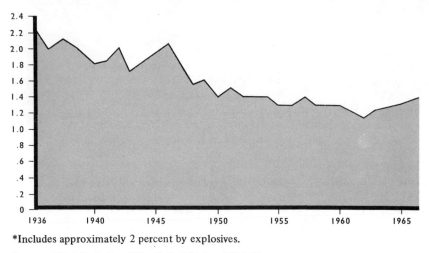

*Includes approximately 2 percent by explosives.

Source: Vital Statistics of the United States, 1936-66.

Until 1965 the declining rate of deaths from firearms accidents per 100,000 people and the increase in population balanced each other to produce a fairly steady number of deaths from firearms accidents in the United States. The rate hovered around 2,400 per year until 1967, when there were about 2,900 deaths from firearms accidents.

Figure 5-3—Civilian deaths from firearms accidents.

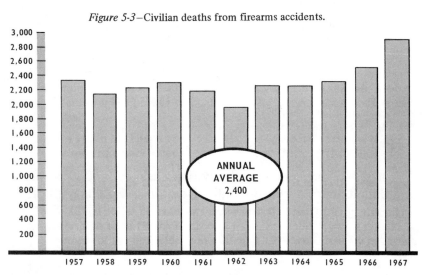

Source: Vital Statistics of the United States, 1957-67.

Table 5-1 shows the distribution of firearms death rates by race and sex in 1967, the last full year for which detailed statistics are available.

Table 5-1—Civilian fatal firearms accidents by race and sex.
(United States, 1966)

	Accidents %	U.S. population %
Sex:		
Male............	85	48
Female.........	15	52
	100	100
Race:		
White...........	77	88
Nonwhite........	23	12
	100	100

Source: Vital Statistics of the United States, 1966. Unpublished data.

Men are more likely to be victims of fatal firearms accidents than women, and nonwhites are almost twice as likely to be victims of firearms accidents as are whites.

The victims of fatal firearms accidents are young. The average life expectancy in this country is about 70 years. As Figure 5-4 shows, the average age of people who die in accidents is 41 years; for automobile accidents it is 32, and for firearms accidents it is 24.

Figure 5-4—Median age at death from firearms and other accidental causes.
(United States, 1967)

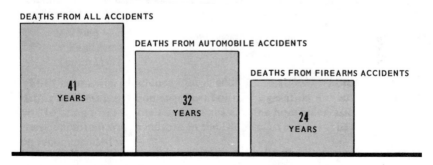

DEATHS FROM ALL ACCIDENTS

DEATHS FROM AUTOMOBILE ACCIDENTS

DEATHS FROM FIREARMS ACCIDENTS

41
YEARS

32
YEARS

24
YEARS

Source: Vital Statistics of the United States, 1966.

Figure 5-5 shows, in greater detail, the distribution by age of firearms accident victims in 1966.

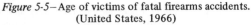

Figure 5-5– Age of victims of fatal firearms accidents.
(United States, 1966)

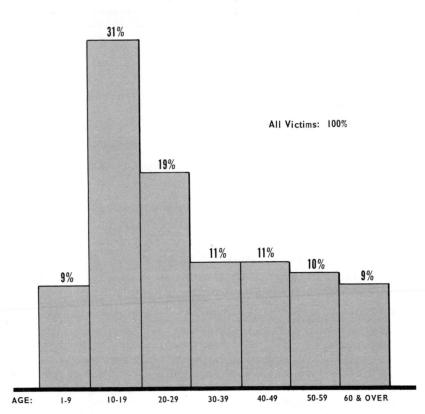

Source: Vital Statistics of the United States, 1966.

Nine percent are children under 10, and by far the largest group of firearms accident victims are children between 10 and 19 years of age.

Fatality statistics, however, are only part of the picture. Firearms accidents also inflict nonfatal injuries. One informed source estimates the annual number of such injuries at over 100,000.[1] A projection from hunting accident deaths indicates that about 20,000

---

[1] Albert P. Iskrant and Paul V. Joliet, "Accidents and Homicide" (Cambridge: Harvard University Press, 1968), p. 93.

accidental firearms injuries can be expected annually,[2] suggesting that for all firearms accidents the 100,000 figure may be too high.

In addition to age, sex, and race, some information is available on the background of persons involved in firearms accidents. A recent study showed that persons causing firearms accidents in Vermont were also prone to disproportionate involvement in traffic accidents and offenses, criminal violence, and heavier than average drinking.[3]

Figure 5-6 shows the rate of accidental deaths from firearms for the last available year (1966) by region of the country.

Figure 5-6—Accidental civilian firearms deaths by region.
(United States, 1966)
[annual rate per 100,000]

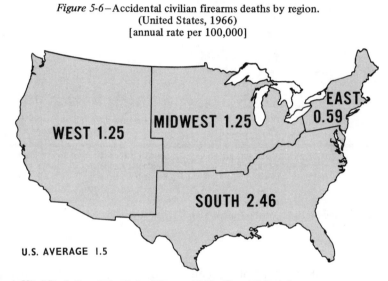

Source: Vital Statistics of the United States, 1966. Unpublished data.

Although the level of death from firearms accidents is relatively low, the fluctuation of rates from region to region parallels the pattern of firearms ownership.[4] The simple truth is that more gun accidents happen where more guns are.

---

[2]The 1966 Uniform Hunter Casualty Report of the National Rifle Association shows, for instance, 289 fatal firearms casualties compared to 1,967 nonfatal casualties, approximately a 7 to 1 ratio. Applying this ratio to the 2,900 accidental firearms injuries for 1967 would indicate about 20,000 firearms injuries for that year. The same method is applicable to homicides. In 1967, the Uniform Crime Reports show nonfatal attacks with firearms totaled 53,000, compared to 7,700 fatal firearms attacks—approximately the same ratio of 7 woundings for each fatality. Since many such nonfatal attacks and woundings probably go unreported, the true ratio of nonfatal-to-fatal injuries is probably substantially higher.

[3]Waller, "Accidents and Violent Behavior: Are They Related," a report prepared for this Commission.

[4]See ch. 2, Fig. 2-1.

Another point of interest is how and where firearms accidents occur. Some insight into these questions is provided in Figure 5-7.

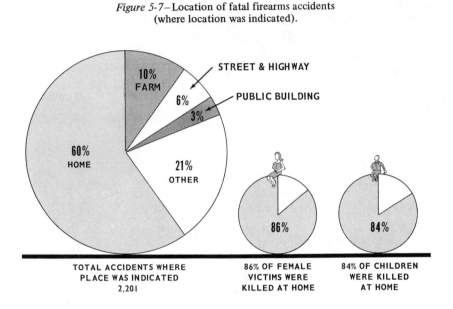

Figure 5-7—Location of fatal firearms accidents (where location was indicated).

STREET & HIGHWAY

PUBLIC BUILDING

10% FARM

6%

3%

60% HOME

21% OTHER

86%

84%

TOTAL ACCIDENTS WHERE PLACE WAS INDICATED 2,201

86% OF FEMALE VICTIMS WERE KILLED AT HOME

84% OF CHILDREN WERE KILLED AT HOME

Source: Vital Statistics of the United States, 1966. Unpublished data.

Figure 5-7 shows that 60 percent of accidental firearms deaths occur in the home. For women and children, the percentages are 86 and 84 percent, respectively.

The place and manner in which firearms are used also affects the accident rate. Figure 5-8, taken from a life insurance company study, shows the types of activity that lead to fatal firearms accidents around the home. More than half of all the accidents in the home are not the result of normal shooting activity.

Figure 5-9 sets forth information on the types of firearms involved in the activities leading to fatal accidents. Although many firearms accidents occur during shooting activities or while cleaning weapons after such activities, others arise from activities that have little to do with proper firearms use. Handgun accidents are more likely to fall into the latter category of accidents which are *not* directly related to the shooting sports.

Figure 5-8–Activities leading to fatal firearms accidents around the home.

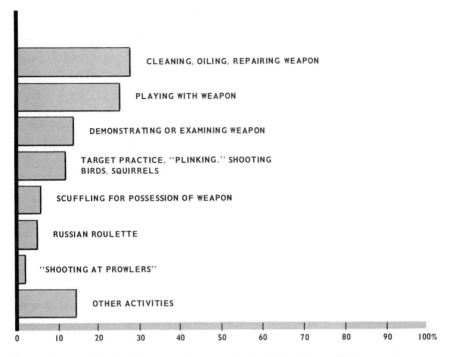

CLEANING, OILING, REPAIRING WEAPON

PLAYING WITH WEAPON

DEMONSTRATING OR EXAMINING WEAPON

TARGET PRACTICE, "PLINKING," SHOOTING BIRDS, SQUIRRELS

SCUFFLING FOR POSSESSION OF WEAPON

RUSSIAN ROULETTE

"SHOOTING AT PROWLERS"

OTHER ACTIVITIES

0   10   20   30   40   50   60   70   80   90   100%

Source: Metropolitan Life Insurance Co., Statistical Bulletin, July 1968.

Figure 5-9–Accidental deaths by type of firearm.

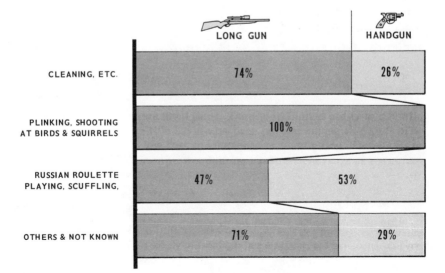

	LONG GUN	HANDGUN
CLEANING, ETC.	74%	26%
PLINKING, SHOOTING AT BIRDS & SQUIRRELS	100%	
RUSSIAN ROULETTE PLAYING, SCUFFLING,	47%	53%
OTHERS & NOT KNOWN	71%	29%

Source: Metropolitan Life Insurance Co., Statistical Bulletin, July 1968.

Summary

Americans are currently dying from firearms accidents at a rate of about 2,900 per year; another 20,000 persons suffer accidental injuries each year from firearms. Firearms accident rates follow the pattern of firearms ownership; they are highest in the South and lowest in the East. Over half of all fatal firearms accidents occur in or around the home, and about 40 percent of accident victims are children and teenagers.

Chapter 6

FIREARMS AND SUICIDE

Every year over 20,000 Americans commit suicide. Since almost half of these suicides (47 percent) are commited with firearms,[1] it behooves the Task Force to investigate whether firearms contribute to the number of suicides. The question is simply whether those who seek to end their lives would find other equally effective methods of suicide if all or some of them did not have firearms. Our inquiry begins with an examination of the available data on suicides and attempted suicides. Tables 6-1 and 6-2 give, separately for men and women, the suicide statistics for 1957 in the County

Table 6-1—*Methods of suicide attempts and completed suicides for men.*
(Los Angeles, 1957)

	Percent attempts	Percent attempts ending in death	Percent of all completed suicides
Barbiturates	26	20	14
Firearms	19	84	42
Cut wrist	12	3	1
Hanging.	8	83	17
Poisoning	7	23	4
Cut throat	4	9	1
Gas	3	25	2
Jumping	2	67	3
Carbon monoxide (automobile) . .	1	82	2
Stabbing	1	38	1
Drowning (jumping)	*	100	10
Others and unknown	10	11	3
Total	93	38**	100

*Less than ½ percent.   [Number of cases: 1,368]
**The average success rate for all attempts by men.

Source: Norman L. Farberow and Edwin S. Schneidman, *The Cry for Help* (New York: McGraw-Hill, 1961), p. 35.

---

[1] In 1966, 48 percent of the suicides in this country involved firearms or explosives; explosives can be estimated to account for about 2 percent of these suicides. Vital Statistics of the United States, 1966.

33

Table 6-2–*Methods of suicide attempts and completed suicides for women.*
(Los Angeles, 1957)

	Percent attempts	Percent attempts ending in death	Percent of all completed suicides
Barbiturates	53	9	36
Firearms	3	69	17
Cut wrist	10	0	0
Hanging	2	47	7
Poisoning	9	8	6
Cut throat	2	16	3
Gas	3	8	3
Jumping	1	33	2
Carbon monoxide (automobile) . .	1	5	*
Stabbing	1	10	1
Drowning (jumping)	*	100	5
Others and unknown	15	16	19
Total	100	13**	100

*Less than ½ percent   [Number of cases: 2,068]
**The average success rate for all attempts by women.

Source: Norman L. Farberow and Edwin S. Schneidman, *The Cry for Help*
(New York: McGraw-Hill, 1961), p. 35.

of Los Angeles.[2] While these figures do not represent the national picture in every respect, they are the most comprehensive information available for a major U.S. city.

For males, firearms are the second most frequent means of attempting suicide (19 percent) and account for almost half (42 percent) of all completed suicides. The picture for women is quite different. Only in 3 percent of all attempts do women use firearms. But when they do, firearms produce a high death rate—though not quite as high as for men (69 percent versus 84 percent).[3]

Although firearms are a highly successful means of committing suicide, a few other methods—hanging, carbon monoxide, jumping, and drowning by jumping—are almost equally effective. The question, therefore, is whether persons attempting suicide, if they had no firearms, would turn to equally effective methods that are now used by only a small proportion of those attempting suicide—or whether some would turn to the more frequently used, but less effective, alternatives such as barbiturates.

[2]There is no reason to believe that more recent information would be significantly different.

[3]Note that the overall success rate for women attempting suicide (13 percent) is only one third of that for men (38 percent). This is partly because of women using, on the whole, less deadly methods (e.g., barbiturates) than men, but also because of the lower success rate for females for every method (except drowning and throat cutting).

Stated differently, the question is whether the 19 percent of all men who attempt suicide by shooting are so determined to kill themselves that they would find another effective way if firearms were not available.

A tentative answer comes from Table 6-3 which shows the suicide rates in 1966 for 16 countries and the percentage of those suicides committed with firearms.

Table 6-3—Suicide rates and suicide with firearms in 16 countries.

Country	Suicide rates per 100,000[1]		Percent of suicides committed with firearms[2]	
	Rate	Rank	Rank	Percent
Sweden	20.1	1	7	12
Germany	20.0	2	13	4
Denmark	19.3	3	11	5
France	15.0	4	8	12
Belgium	15.0	5	10	6
Japan	14.7	6	16	1
Australia	14.1	7	4	20
United States	10.9	8	1	46
England and Wales	10.4	9	12	4
New Zealand	9.2	10	5	15
Canada	8.6	11	2	37
Scotland	8.0	12	14	3
Norway	7.7	13	3	25
Netherlands	7.1	14	15	1
Italy	5.4	15	6	13
Ireland	2.4	16	9	8

Sources:
[1] 1967 Demographic Year Book, 19th edition, New York, 1968.
[2] World Health Statistics Report, Vol. 21, No. 6, 1968.

The data in Table 6-3 show great variation in the suicide rates from one country to another. The rates range all the way from 20 per 100,000 population in Sweden and Germany to 5 and 2 per 100,000 in Italy and Ireland. The United States, with 10 suicides per 100,000, holds a middle position among these 16 countries in reported rates of suicide.

The different rank orders of the overall suicide rates and the suicide rates by firearms show that no significant relationship exists between the frequency of suicide and the frequency of suicide by shooting. The German suicide rate, for instance, is almost the highest (20 per 100,000 and second among the 16 countries), but with respect to suicides by shooting, it ranks 13th (4 per 100,000), or almost last. And Norway, which ranks 13th in suicides (7.7 per 100,000) ranks third in suicides by shooting (25 per 100,000).

Cultural factors appear to affect the suicide rates far more than the availability and use of firearms. Thus, suicide rates would not seem to be readily affected by making firearms less available.

While firearms may not be a major factor in suicides, there is some evidence that they might be a minor one, In Los Angeles, physicians who treated persons who failed in their attempts at suicide were asked to rate the seriousness of the survivors' intention to end their lives. These ratings are reproduced in Table 6-4.

Table 6-4–*Seriousness of intention to die of survivors of attempted suicide.*
(Los Angeles County, 1957)

	Men (percent)	Women (percent)
Really wanted to die	36	27
Left survival up to chance	23	19
Did not intend to die	25	40
Unknown.	16	14
Total suicides	100	100
Number of cases	828	1,825

Source:
> Norman L. Farberow and Edwin S. Schneidman, *The Cry for Help* (New York: McGraw-Hill, 1961), p. 36.

Because many of those who survived really wanted to die (36 percent of the males and 27 percent of the females), it would seem that any method of suicide which would allow time for intervention would reduce the chances of death, however serious the intent of the person attempting suicide.[4] This is particularly true for women. The number of women survivors who really wanted to die (493) was over twice the number who succeeded in their attempt (228).[5]

Thus, the high suicide rates in countries in which guns are not as readily available as in the United States show that persons seriously intent on dying find other ways, such as hanging. Yet if some persons would use slower methods of self-destruction instead of firearms, some lives might be saved.

Also, the possibility that the presence of a gun is in some instances part of the causal chain that leads to an attempted suicide cannot be dismissed. With a depressed person, the knowledge of having a quick and effective way of ending his life might precipitate a suicide attempt on impulse.

---

[4]Intervention by a third party was involved in the case of 72 percent of the male survivors and 64 percent of the female survivors. Farberow and Schneidman, *The Cry for Help*, p. 36.
[5]Farberow and Schneidman, *The Cry for Help*, p. 36.

Summary

For persons who seek to end their lives, firearms are a speedy and effective method. There is some evidence that, if persons who now use firearms were forced to resort to other means where there is a higher chance of intervention and rescue, some would not die. But there is little reason to expect that reducing the availability of firearms would cause a significant reduction in suicides. A person who really wants to die will find a way of doing so.

Chapter 7

FIREARMS AND CRIME

Firearms are commonly involved in three of the four major categories of crime causing injury or death[1]—homicide, aggravated assault, and armed robbery.[2]

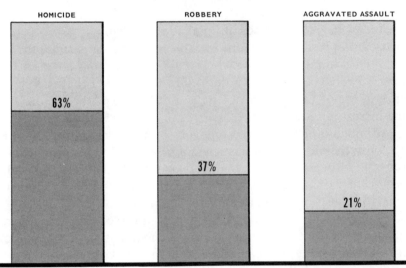

Figure 7-1—Role of firearms in crimes against the person.
(United States, 1967)

Source: 1967 Uniform Crime Reports.

Two out of every three homicides, over a third of all robberies, and one out of five aggravated assaults are committed with a gun, usually a handgun.[3]

---

[1]The use of firearms in rape in all probability is not substantial.
[2]Firearms are, of course, also used in other crimes. In 1968, for instance, firearms were used in at least 16 airplane hijackings, a crime difficult to commit without firearms or explosives. (Information from Federal Aviation Administration.)
[3]See ch. 8, *infra.*

Homicide

Although firearms are the principal weapon used in homicides
in the United States. knives are used in one out of four homicides,[4]
as shown in Table 7-1.

Table 7-1 — Weapons used in homicide.
(United States, 1967)

Weapon	Percent
Firearms	63
Knives	25
Other	12
Total.......	100

Source: 1967 Uniform Crime Report.

Since 1963, the number of homicides involving firearms has increased 48 percent in the United States. At the same time, the
number of homicides committed with other weapons has risen
only 10 percent. We shall point out in this chapter that the increased use of firearms in violent assaults is one of the reasons for
the increase in homicides.

Although other weapons are involved in homicide, firearms are
not only the most deadly instrument of attack but also the most
versatile. Firearms make some attacks possible that simply would
not occur without firearms. They permit attacks at greater range
and from positions of better concealment than other weapons.
They also permit attacks by persons physically or psychologically
unable to overpower their victim through violent physical contact.
It is not surprising, therefore, that firearms are virtually the only
weapon used in killing police officers.

The policeman, himself armed, is capable of defending against
many forms of violent attack. He is trained and equipped to ward
off attacks with blunt objects, knives, or fists, and his firearm is usually sufficient to overcome his attacker, even if surprised at close
range. It is, therefore, the capacity of firearms to kill instantly and
from a distance that threatens the lives of police officers in the
United States.

---

[4] Knives are also the most frequently used substitute for firearms in armed robbery. In
aggravated assault, the situation is reversed — knife attacks are more frequent than gun
attacks. (1967 Uniform Crime Report.)

From 1960 through 1967, 411 police officers were killed in the course of their official duties, 76 of them in 1967 alone.[5] In 96 percent of these fatal attacks, firearms were used.

Firearms also play a major role in assassination. Of the nine assassination attempts on Presidents or presidential candidates, all involved handguns except the rifle assassination of President Kennedy.[6] Another task force of this Commission will present information on these and other attacks on prominent persons.

In addition to providing greater range for the attacker, firearms are also more deadly than other weapons. Table 7-2 sets forth illustrative data for the City of Chicago.[7]

Table 7-2—Percentage of reported gun and knife
attacks resulting in death.
(Chicago, 1965-67)

Weapons	Deaths as percentage of attacks
Knives (16,518 total attacks)...	2.4
Guns (6,350 total attacks)....	12.2

Source: Chicago Police Department.

The fatality rate of firearms attacks is about five times higher than the fatality rate of attacks with knives, the next most dangerous weapon used in homicide.[8]

---

[5]1967 Uniform Crime Report, p. 47. Police officers are the victims of criminal homicide four times as often as ordinary citizens:

Homicide rate per 100,000 (1964-66 average):

Police 21.1
General population 5.7

Source: Analysis prepared by Robert Silverman,
Department of Sociology, University of Pennsylvania, 1968.

[6]These attempts were on Andrew Jackson (1835); Abraham Lincoln (1865); James Garfield (1881); William McKinley (1901); Theodore Roosevelt (1912); Franklin D. Roosevelt (1935); Harry S. Truman (1950); John F. Kennedy (1963); Robert F. Kennedy (1968).

[7]Data for Chicago are based on research conducted in cooperation with the Chicago Police Department. See Zimring, "Is Gun Control Likely To Reduce Violent Killings," 35 U. Chi. L. Rev. 721 (1968).

[8]Knife and firearms fatality rates in Chicago have remained fairly stable over the years:

	Firearms (percent)	Knives (percent)	Ratio
1965	13.0	1.9	6.8:1
1966	12.4	2.8	4.4:1
1967	11.6	2.3	5:1

Source: Chicago Police Department.

The circumstances that lead to homicides also bear on the relationship between the use of firearms and the homicide rate. Table 7-3 sets forth the circumstances of homicides in Chicago in 1967 based on information obtained from the Chicago police.

Table 7-3 – The circumstances of homicide.
(Chicago, 1967)

	Percent
Altercations	82
General domestic	17
Money	9
Liquor	7
Sex.................................	2
Triangle............................	6
Racial.............................	1
Children	2
Other	38
Robbery................................	12
Strong arm	3
Armed	9
Teen gang disputes.......................	3
Others	3
Total	100
Number of cases	551

Source: Chicago Police Department.

Table 7-3 shows that four out of five homicides occur as a result of altercations over such matters as love, money, and domestic problems.

The relationship in homicides between victim and attacker is also significant.

Table 7-4 – Relationship between victim and attacker in homicide.
(Chicago, 1967)

Relationship	Percent
Friends or acquaintances	41
Spouse or lover	20
Other family	7
Neighbors	3
Business...............................	3
No relationship	22
Undetermined	4
Total	100
Number of cases	554

Source: Chicago Police Department.

Table 7-4 shows that 71 percent of the Chicago killings involved acquaintances, neighbors, lovers, and family members—people likely to have acted spontaneously in a moment of rage and not necessarily with a single determination to kill.

The circumstances under which most homicides are committed also suggest that the homicides are committed in a moment of rage and are not the result of a single-minded intent to kill. Planned murders involving a single-minded intent, such as gangland killings, seem to be the spectacular but infrequent exception.

The nature of homicide was succinctly described by the chief of the Homicide Section of the Chicago Police Department when interviewed on television after Chicago's 600th homicide of 1968 had occurred: "There was a domestic fight. A gun was there. And then somebody was dead. If you have described one, you have described them all."[9]

Not only do the circumstances of homicide and the relationship of victim and attacker show that most homicides do not involve a single-minded determination to kill, but also the choice of a gun does not seem to indicate such intent. Table 7-5 shows the similar circumstances of firearms and knife homicides.

Table 7-5—Circumstances of homicide, by weapon.
(Chicago, 1967)

	Gun (percent)	Knife (percent)
Altercations:		
General domestic	21	25
Money	6	7
Liquor.	2	8
Sex	1	3
Gambling	2	1
Triangle	5	5
Theft (alleged)	—	—
Children	2	1
Other	41	30
Armed robbery	9	9
Perversion and assault on female . . .	2	7
Gangland	1	—
Other.	2	—
Undetermined	6	4
Total	100	100
Number of cases[1]	265	152

[1]Another 93 homicides were committed with other weapons.
Source: Chicago Police Department.

---

[9]Comdr. Francis Flanagan, Dec. 12, 1968.

The similarity of circumstances in which knives and guns are used in homicide suggests that the motive for an attack does not determine the weapon used.

There is further evidence that those who use a gun are no more intent on killing than those who use a knife. The Chicago study showed that a greater percentage of the knife attacks than gun attacks resulted in wounds to vital areas of the body—such as the head, neck, chest, abdomen, and back—where wounds are likely to be fatal. Also, many more knife attacks than gun attacks resulted in multiple wounds, suggesting that those who use the knife in these attacks have no great desire to spare the victim's life.

In spite of the foregoing, it might be contended that if gun murderers were deprived of guns they would find a way to kill as often with knives. If this is so, knife attacks in cities where guns are widely used in homicide would show a low fatality rate, and knife attacks in cities where guns are not so widely used would show a higher fatality rate. Analyses of 11 cities for which the pertinent data were available revealed no such relationship.[10] There is no evidence to contradict that the gun and knife are interchangeable weapons. Since the fatility rate of the knife is about one-fifth that of the gun, a rough approximation would suggest that the use of knives instead of guns might cause four-fifths, or 80 percent, fewer fatalities.[11]

This rough approximation can be applied to cities with differing levels of gun availability, as measured by the percentages which gun attacks are of all attacks. Houston, Texas, and New York City are the extreme examples used in Table 7-6.

Table 7-6 —Gun and knife attacks in Houston and New York, 1967.

	Houston		New York	
	Number	Percent	Number	Percent
Frequency of—				
Knife attacks	1,040	58	10,330	76
Gun attacks	750	42	3,270	24
Total attacks	1,790	100	13,600	100
Percent of deaths:				
Gun attacks	....	19.7	....	8.9
Knife attacks	....	3.7	....	2.7
All attacks (irrespective of weapon) ..	....	11.7	....	4.2

Source: Data supplied by FBI from supplemental information filed by police departments.

[10]San Diego, Los Angeles, San Francisco, Dallas, Houston, St. Louis, Detroit, Pittsburgh, Boston, New York, and Philadelphia. (See App. D.)
[11]The figure may vary from city to city, but nationally reported firearms attacks are 4.75 times as deadly as knife attacks.

If the level of gun attacks in Houston were reduced from 42 percent to New York's level of 24 percent, 322 gun attacks would have been knife attacks (18 percent of 1,790). At present, these 322 gun attacks result in 63 fatalities (19.7 percent of 322). If they were knife attacks, roughly 12 fatalities would result (3.7 percent of 322)—a reduction from 20 deaths per hundred attacks to 4 per hundred.

The foregoing material on homicide permits the simple conclusion that when an attacker uses a gun, the victim is more likely to die than when an attacker uses a knife. It is therefore not a coincidence that as the number of firearms homicides has increased in recent years, the number of all homicides has also increased. Indeed, the increase in the number of homicides results at least in part from the increased use of firearms, as shown in Figure 7-2.

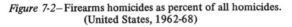

Figure 7-2—Firearms homicides as percent of all homicides.
(United States, 1962-68)

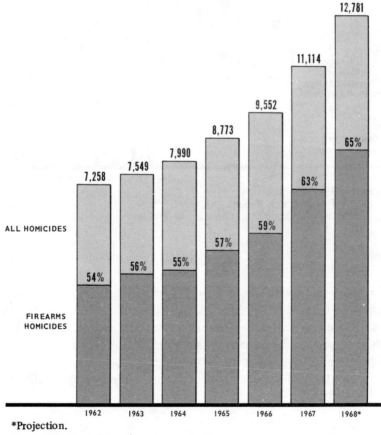

*Projection.
Source: Uniform Crime Reports.

Aggravated Assault

Aggravated assault is an attack intended to inflict severe bodily harm. It is usually committed with a weapon that can cause death. Since aggravated assault differs from homicide only insofar as the attacked victim survives, the analysis of homicide in the preceding pages applies to aggravated assault.

As with homicide, the use of firearms in aggravated assaults has risen in recent years more than the increase in the rate of such attacks; this is set forth in Figure 7-3.

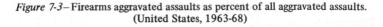
Figure 7-3–Firearms aggravated assaults as percent of all aggravated assaults. (United States, 1963-68)

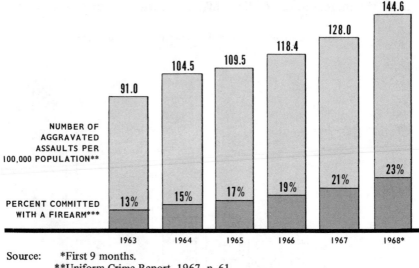

Source: *First 9 months.
            **Uniform Crime Report, 1967, p. 61.
            ***Uniform Crime Report for the year involved.

Robbery

Robbery is the one major property crime that is also a crime against the person. In 1967, 63 percent of all armed robbers used guns. When compared to all robberies (armed as well as other), guns were used in 36 percent of such crimes.[12]

The use of firearms is considerably higher in the much more dangerous and lucrative indoor robbery than in the outdoor robbery, as shown in Table 7-7.

---

[12]1967 Uniform Crime Report, pp. 13, 15.

Table 7-7– Use of firearms in indoor and outdoor robberies.
(Dallas and Philadelphia, 1968)

	Indoor	Outdoor
Robberies with firearms (percent)	80	31
Number of robberies	518	652

Source: A serial sample by Task Force from the 1968 offense reports provided by
Dallas and Philadelphia Police Departments.

Interviews with robbers by a psychiatric investigator confirm
that the gun often is an essential ingredient in robbery:

Robbery appears to be a crime made infinitely more possible
by having a gun. To rob without one requires a degree of
strength, size and confidence which was lacking in many of
the men with whom I spoke. . . . For the most part the men
involved in robbery were not very large and not very strong.
Some were not very aggressive. Some of these men could not
possibly carry out a robbery without a gun. In short, there
was a clear reality element in the need for a gun once a man
made the decision to rob. . . . [A]lthough the men needed a
gun to rob, the converse was also true: they needed to rob
in order to use a gun . . . it was the gun which provided the
power and the opportunity for mastery.[13]

Because the attack on the person is usually incidental to the
main goal of the robber, the overall fatality rate resulting from robberies is relatively small. Nevertheless, the fatality rate is considerably higher for firearms robberies than for robberies with other
weapons, as shown in Table 7-8.

Table 7-8– Fatality rate in robberies.
(New York City, 1965-68)
[per 1,000 robberies]

Firearms robberies	Other robberies
5.5	1.5

Source: Police Department, City of New York.

The fatality rate from firearms robberies is almost four times as
great as the rate from other armed robberies.

---

[13]Dr. Donald E. Newman, Director, Psychiatric Services, Peninsula Hospital and Medical
Center, Burlingame, Calif. Portions of Dr. Newman's complete report are attached as
App. E.

Summary

Homicide is seldom the result of a single-minded intent to kill. Most often it is an attack growing out of an altercation and committed in a rage that leads to fatal injuries. Firearms were used in 65 percent of homicides in this country in 1968. When a gun is used, the chances of death are about five times as great as when a knife is used. In the last 5 years the number of firearms homicides has increased by almost 50 percent.

Aggravated assault differs from homicide only in its outcome— the victim survives. Although the knife is still the No. 1 weapon used in aggravated assault, the share of gun attacks is increasing, and in 1968 nearly one in four aggravated assaults involved firearms.

One third of all robberies are committed with guns. The chances of the victim's being killed increase substantially if the robber uses a gun.

Chapter 8

THE FIREARMS USED IN CRIME

With some 90 million firearms distributed among half of the households of the United States, the firearms used in crime are but a small fraction of the total. For the criminal, however, firearms are an important matter.

As noted in the preceding chapter,[1] firearms in 1967 were used in the United States in 63 percent of the homicides, 37 percent of the robberies, and 21 percent of the aggravated assaults. And the use of firearms in homicide and aggravated assaults is increasing. For the first 9 months of 1968, firearms were used in 65 percent of all homicides and 23 percent of all aggravated assaults.[2]

Although only about 27 percent of the firearms in this country are handguns,[3] they are the predominant firearm used in crime. Figure 8-1 shows the predominance of the handgun in each of the three major types of crimes involving firearms.

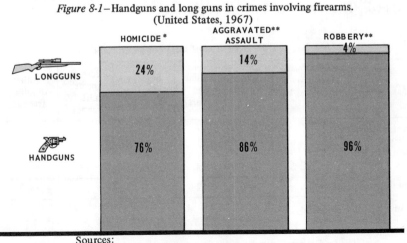

Figure 8-1–Handguns and long guns in crimes involving firearms.
(United States, 1967)

Sources:
*1967 Uniform Crime Report.
**Police departments of 10 large cities.

[1]Ch. 7, Fig. 7-1.
[2]Uniform Crime Reports for the first 9 months of 1968.
[3]Ch. 1, *supra*.

Nationwide, the handgun is the dominant firearm used in homicide. When firearms are involved in aggravated assault and robbery in large cities, the handgun is almost invariably the weapon used.

A study of firearms confiscated in the District of Columbia, 95 percent of which were handguns, revealed that nearly half of the confiscated handguns had been imported.

Table 8-1—Origin of confiscated handguns.
(Washington, D.C., 1967-68)

	Percent
Foreign...	48
Domestic	52
	100
Number of guns	1,085*

*The origin of another 56 guns could not be determined
Source: District of Columbia Police Department.

In order to determine the age of handguns used in criminal activity, lists containing a subsample of domestically produced handguns confiscated by police in Washington, D. C., Chicago, New York City, and the State of West Virginia were sent to domestic manufacturers with requests for information on the date of manufacture of each weapon and the place to which it was shipped. The results of this study are set forth in Table 8-2.

Table 8-2—Age and origin of confiscated domestic handguns.

	Range in age (years)	Median age (years)	Percent older than 50 years	Percent former military weapons	Number of guns traced
Washington, D.C.	2 to 69	4	4	13	23
Chicago	2 to 88	11	18	11	74
West Virginia	2 to 65	13	30	9	23
New York City.........	2 to 91	13	25	15	68
Total sample average	2-91	12	23	12	188

Source: Task Force study.

The confiscated domestic handguns ranged in age from 2 to 91 years; 23 percent were older than 50 years; their median age was 12 years. These figures corroborate the longevity of firearms discussed in Chapter 1. They also confirm the legacy of existing weapons that prior American firearms policies have passed down, a legacy that can be expected to haunt future attempts at firearms control.

The study also found that 12 percent of the confiscated firearms originally had been sold to the military.[4]

Table 8-3 gives the results of an analysis of a sample of confiscated handguns of foreign origin.

Table 8-3.—Age and origin of confiscated foreign handguns

	Range in age (years)	Median age (years)	Percent older than 50 years	Percent former military weapons	Number of guns traced
Chicago	1 to 51	2	3	0	34
Washington, D.C.	1 to 46	4	0	15	45
Total sample average	1 to 51	3	1	9	79

Source: Task Force study.

These foreign weapons are, on the average, somewhat newer, and fewer of them are former military weapons.

In an attempt to determine how guns used in crime were acquired, samples of handguns confiscated in crime in Detroit and Los Angeles were studied. Both cities require an application to purchase a handgun, but in both cities relatively few of these applications are denied and thus possession of firearms is not significantly restricted.

In Detroit, a sample of 113 handguns confiscated by police during shootings in the city of Detroit during 1968 showed that only 25 percent of the confiscated weapons had been recorded previously in connection with a gun permit application. In Los Angeles, a sample of 50 handguns involved in homicides, 100 handguns involved in aggravated assaults, and 100 handguns involved in robberies was analyzed at the request of the Task Force. Figure 8-2 shows the proportion of firearms for which there was a record of an application. Three fourths of the handguns used in homicide and about one half of the handguns used in the other two crimes had been recorded.

---

[4]The FBI has advised the Task Force that 22.5 percent of the stolen firearms on its records (totaling 184,711 in November 1968) were military type weapons. The volume of military handguns which have been brought back to this country by returning servicemen is discussed in ch. 1. Over 165,000 military handguns have been sold by the Army to civilians in the United States. (See App. H.)

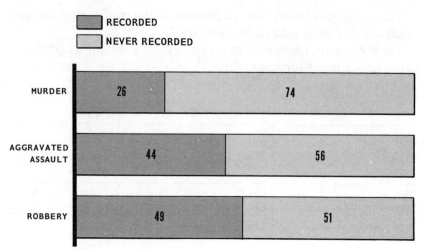

Figure 8-2—Handguns used in crime: recorded—unrecorded.
(Los Angeles, 1968)

Sources: Los Angeles Police Department; Task Force study.

Figure 8-3, based on a subsample of 20 of the confiscated hand-guns that were once registered in each category of crime in Los Angeles, compares the name of the last recorded owner with the name of the suspect in the crime committed with the handgun.

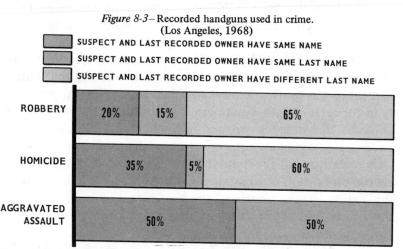

Figure 8-3—Recorded handguns used in crime.
(Los Angeles, 1968)

Sources: Los Angeles Police Department; Task Force study.

In crimes in which the handguns used were recorded, the suspect was the last recorded owner in 35 percent of the homicides, 50 percent of the aggravated assaults, and 20 percent of the robberies. In addition, in 5 percent of the homicides and 15 percent of the robberies, the handguns were recorded under the same family name as that of the suspect, suggesting that when a gun is in the household another member of the family may misuse it. Most of the recorded guns used in crime (60 percent for homicide, 50 percent for aggravated assault, and 65 percent for robbery) were apparently used by persons other than the last recorded owners. Since only 6 percent of these weapons had been reported as stolen,[5] sales of secondhand firearms seem to be a major source of firearms used in crime.

Summary

The criminal's primary firearm is the handgun. Although only about one quarter of all firearms in this country are handguns, they are used in three quarters of the homicides involving firearms. Of the handguns used in crime in the District of Columbia, nearly half are imported. Samples of crime firearms made in this country reveal that one in five is more than 50 years old and one in six is a military weapon. Most of the firearms used in crime are acquired by criminals in unrecorded purchases or burglaries.

---

[5]Guns are probably stolen at a rate higher than the 6 percent figure suggests. Many thefts may go unreported because the owner has never recorded his ownership or does not know the weapon's make or serial number.

Chapter 9

FIREARMS AND COLLECTIVE VIOLENCE

Another task force of this Commission is investigating mass demonstrations, riots, and civil disorders. The focus of this Task Force is solely on one aspect of the problem—the role firearms have played in recent collective violence and the role they may play in collective violence of the future.

Firearms and Recent Collective Violence

The National Advisory Commission on Civil Disorders studied disorders in 23 cities[1] throughout the country. Although it found that sniping occurred in at least 15 of these disorders[2] and that theft of firearms and ammunition was a substantial problem, the Commission did not specifically study the role played by firearms. It did, however, engage the Stanford Research Institute (SRI) to conduct such an inquiry. The SRI report, published in July 1968,[3] reported:

- In the Watts riot of 1965, more than 700 guns were stolen, 115 persons (78 of whom had previous criminal records) were arrested with firearms, and 118 persons were injured by gunfire.
- During the riots of April 1968, following the assassination of Dr. Martin Luther King, Jr., 25 of 39 persons killed died of

---

[1]Atlanta, Ga.; Cambridge, Md.; Cincinnati and Dayton, Ohio; Detroit and Grand Rapids, Mich.; Houston, Tex.; Jackson, Miss.; Milwaukee, Wis.; Nashville, Tenn.; Phoenix and Tucson, Ariz.; Rockford, Ill.; Tampa, Fla.; New Haven, Conn.; Bridgeton, Elizabeth, Englewood, Jersey City, Newark, New Brunswick, Paterson, and Plainfield, N. J.

[2]The report of the Kerner Commission stated: "Of 23 cities surveyed by the Commission, there had been reports of sniping in at least 15. . . . What is certain is that the amount of sniping attributed to rioters—by law enforcement officials as well as the press—was highly exaggerated. . . . According to the best information available to the Commission, most reported sniping incidents were demonstrated to be gunfire by either police or National Guardsmen." (Report, p. 180.)

[3]Arnold Kotz, "Firearms, Violence, and Civil Disorders," Stanford Research Institute, July 1968, pp. 23-40.

55

gunshot wounds, 11 by police and 14 by private citizens or unknown persons. In Washington, D.C., alone, 32 persons were
treated for gunshot wounds, and 88 were arrested for carrying
a dangerous weapon.

• The July 1967 riot in Newark, N.J., was examined in detail.
Of 23 persons killed as a direct result of this riot, all died from
gunshot wounds. Ten of the 23 were killed by law officers, 1 by
a sniper, and 2 by unknown persons. Either law officers or snipers
could have been responsible for 9 of the remaining 10. Sixty-five
of 587 civilian injuries reported were gunshot wounds; and 9 of
129 injuries to police and other officials were gunshot wounds.
Of 250 sniping incidents reported to police, 79 were subsequently
verified, although no snipers were apprehended. Of 66 persons
arrested for firearms violations, 40 had previous criminal records
and 7 had previous records for illegal possession of weapons; 28
rifles and shotguns, 36 pistols and revolvers, 1 zip gun, and 1 submachine gun were seized.

• The July 1967 riot in Detroit was also examined in detail.
Thirty-eight of the 43 persons killed died from gunfire, including
three public safety officials. Twenty-eight civilians were killed
by police gunfire, and 7 by gunfire from civilians or unknown
persons. Ten of these civilians were innocent bystanders. Twenty-
four of 290 injuries to public safety officials were gunshot
wounds, including 5 by accidental discharge, while 36 of 109
injuries to other persons were from gunfire. Two hundred thirty-
eight arrests were made for carrying concealed weapons, at least
118 of which were firearms, while 178 rifles and shotguns and
195 pistols and revolvers were seized. Although more than 100
sniping incidents were reported, this number appears to have
been exaggerated.

The riots in Chicago in April 1968 were investigated by a commission appointed by Mayor Daley. This commission found that
sniper fire occurred in one area of the city, wounding two police
officers and seriously hampering firemen. Seven of nine deaths
and 48 wounds were caused by gunfire.[4]

Another task force of this Commission investigated the disorders
in the Glenville area of Cleveland from July 23 to 28, 1968. Before
the disorders, Cleveland police had information that a group called
the Black Nationalists of New Libya had gone to Detroit and Pittsburgh to acquire semi-automatic weapons. Some members of the

---

[4]"Report of the Chicago Riot Study Committee to the Honorable Richard J. Daley,"
dated Aug. 1, 1968.

group were also seen examining deer rifles with telescopic sights at a Cleveland department store. The disorders apparently began when the Black Nationalists opened fire on two uniformed city employees, presumably mistaken for police officers, attempting to tow away an illegally parked car. About the same time, other Black Nationalists began firing at police cars stationed in the area to watch over the group's headquarters. When additional police arrived, rifle fire from surrounding apartment buildings increased and was returned by the police, first with handguns and later with rifles and shotguns. Before order was restored in the 4 block area, 3 police officers, 3 Black Nationalists, and a civilian passerby were killed, and over 20 others were wounded. (The body of one of the Black Nationalists thought to have been killed has never been found.) Police and National Guard troops called in during the ensuing fires and looting confiscated 25 weapons in the immediate area: 3 semi-automatic military rifles (M1 carbines); 2 bolt-action military rifles; 10 .22 caliber civilian rifles (4 with telescopic sights); 2 shotguns; 2 .30 caliber civilian rifles; 5 .38 caliber revolvers; and 1 .32 caliber revolver.

Some Cleveland police officers stated this was the first time they had faced semi-automatic weapons and were critical that they were not authorized to carry similar arms in patrol cars. Others insisted the snipers had machineguns and submachineguns. Although no such weapons were found, one of the suspects was charged with illegal possession of a machinegun.

Considering the magnitude of the recent civil disorders and the extensive property damage caused, firearms so far have not played a major role in urban riots. In many cases reports of sniping activity have subsequently proved to be false or exaggerated and most of the gunfire casualties were shot by police or troops. Yet the civil disorders have stimulated gun buying and the growth of black and white extremist groups, leaving this country with a dangerous legacy: the highly explosive combination of fear and firearms.

Firearms and Future Collective Violence

Organized extremist groups of widely differing persuasions currently advocate stockpiling of firearms as a matter of organization policy, in anticipation of either some form of domestic guerrilla warfare or increasingly restrictive firearms control, or both.[5]

Different groups envision different types of conflict. Those on the far right, notably the Minutemen, originally viewed themselves

---

[5]Excerpts from the speeches and literature of extremist groups are collected in App. F.

as a prospective resistance movement in the event of a Communist takeover of the United States by foreign military attack. Today most rightwing groups no longer consider a Communist military invasion imminent or even very likely, but they see evidence of internal Communist subversion in civil disorders and the rise of extreme leftist and Black Nationalist groups, who they believe are promoting violence and social unrest. In this context, rightwing extremists view themselves less as future "freedom fighters" than as vigilantes or counter-revolutionaries who may one day have to use their weapons against traitors and insurgents to preserve law, order, and national security.

With the change in the enemy's color from red to black, rightwing extremism is apparent not only in paramilitary groups, such as the Minutemen, but also in the proliferation of neighborhood protective associations. Now arms are stockpiled "in the home" as well as "in the hills."

Black extremist groups likewise urge members to stockpile firearms, usually for neighborhood and home defense, but sometimes for guerrilla and terrorist activities. Ironically, both black and white extremist groups are remarkably similar in their firearms policies and their opposition to strict firearms control. This opposition has proved embarrassing to those who oppose certain gun laws on the ground that they are not effective or not enforceable.

To date, no extremist organization, white or black, has caused large scale violence. Rightists have staged abortive attacks on "Communist" encampments; racists (presumably Klansmen) have murdered civil rights workers; and Black Nationalists have attacked police and engaged in sniping during civil disorders. Such acts of violence and inflammatory statements of extremist leaders have further stimulated the arms buildup and increased the capacity of such groups to engage in more extensive and costly collective violence in the future.

Although the violence of extremist groups may be more potential than actual, the violence involving juvenile gangs (including some motorcycle gangs) has occurred in several large cities over a period of many years. Such gangs range from loosely knit neighborhood, ethnic, or social groups to well-organized groups with strong leadership and an obedient membership, though the latter appear to be rare.

Firearms substantially increase the potential seriousness of violence by juvenile gangs. The possession of firearms by one gang provides incentive for rival gangs to arm themselves, and any violence that may result will be more likely to involve death or serious injury.

Juvenile gangs generally are not "paramilitary" in organization or operation, but stockpiling of weapons is not uncommon. Fighting gangs, in particular, often gather weapons in anticipation of actual or potential threats from rival gangs. Extensive caches of gang weapons are sometimes discovered, and many gangs often discuss real or imagined arsenals of firearms. However, large numbers of guns have not, in the past, been involved in specific episodes involving gangs. Typically, incidents in which guns are present involve a single weapon which often is passed among various members of a group before it is used. Studies suggest that the use of guns by members of juvenile gangs is often related to interaction within the gang or with other gangs.[6]

Although juvenile gangs in the past have been essentially apolitical in character, it is possible that some will be attracted to extremist causes and adopt extremist firearms policies. These is evidence that some juvenile gangs have already become involved in the political arena.

Unorganized group violence, or mob violence, tends to relate to particular events and specific targets such as storming a jail, looting a store, or attacking another group. Like juvenile gang violence, it probably will occur whether or not the participants are armed. Possession of firearms by civil authorities or another organized group may even mitigate or deter mob violence on a particular occasion. However, once a conflict has occurred, fear of future disorders frequently leads to an arms buildup and to a higher degree of organization among all groups in the affected area.

Sources of firearms vary among different groups. Extremist organizations tend to be equipment conscious, favoring high powered military weapons and firearms specifically designed for combat purposes. Most such firearms are acquired through legitimate channels, though buyers often use false names or otherwise attempt to conceal the fact of ownership. Juvenile gangs appear to arm themselves through the most convenient and least costly channels: pawnshops, "street" sellers, theft, and home manufacture ("zip guns," sawed-off weapons). Unorganized groups—rioters and street mobs—generally use firearms already possessed by some of their members and supplement these with whatever other firearms can be looted.

---

[6]See, for example, cases described and interpreted in James F. Short, Jr., and Fred L. Strodtbeck, *Group Process and Gang Delinquency* (Chicago: University of Chicago Press, 1965), pp. 191, 200-207, 251 ff.

Summary

The availability of firearms at relatively low cost makes it easy for extremist groups and individuals to obtain such weapons; the possession of firearms by some groups encourages opposition groups and individuals similarly to arm themselves; and possession of firearms by any group invites quicker and deadlier response on the part of rival armed groups and law enforcement agencies.

Chapter 10

FIREARMS AND SELF-DEFENSE

Preceding chapters examined the role of firearms in crime. This chapter attempts to evaluate the utility of firearms as weapons of defense against crime.

Many Americans keep loaded firearms in homes, businesses, and on their persons for the purpose of protection. Evidence of this practice is found in a 1966 poll[1] in which about 66 percent of householders with guns list "protection" as one reason for having them and in a 1968 poll[2] which revealed that guns were kept for protection in 26 percent of retail business establishments. Times and dangers have changed from frontier days when a gun was often necessary for survival. The extent to which guns are actually useful for defensive purposes must be reappraised.

Statistics show that handguns are more closely associated with self-defense than with sporting purposes. A national sample of shooters was asked in 1964 to give "good reasons" for owning different types of firearms; the responses are shown in Figure 10-1. Ninety-five percent of the shooters mentioned hunting as a good reason for owning a rifle or shotgun, but only 16 percent gave hunting as a good reason for owning a handgun. On the other hand, 71 percent mentioned self-defense as a good reason for owning a handgun, while rifles and shotguns were mentioned as self-defense weapons by only 41 percent of the shooters.

The defensive value of firearms must be examined in terms of the different types of crime commonly committed against persons and property and where these crimes occur.

---

[1] The poll, conducted by the National Opinion Research Center for the Crime Commission, asked: "Is there a gun, pistol, rifle or shotgun in the house that is for the protection of the household, even though it is also used for sport or something else?" Thirty-seven percent of all households polled answered in the affirmative. Since, as shown in ch. 2, a 1966 Gallup poll showed 59 percent of all households reported firearms ownership, and there are 60.4 million households, about 66 percent of households with guns have them for self-defense.
[2] "Crime Against Small Business," Small Business Administration (Jan. 1969), Table 21 at p. 118.

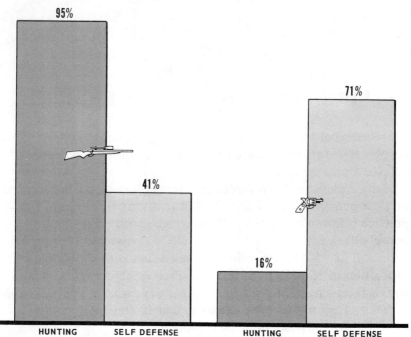

Figure 10-1–"Good reasons" for owning long guns and handguns.
(United States, 1964)

Source: Manufacturer's Market Research, 1964 (See App. D).

Defense of the Home

The three principal crimes involving an invasion of the home are
burglary, robbery, and sexual attack.

Burglary is the most common type of intrusion of the home and
causes the greatest property loss, but it rarely threatens the homeowner's life. The burglar typically seeks to commit his crime without being discovered, if possible by entering a home that is not
occupied. Consequently, he is more likely to steal the home-defense
firearm than be driven off by it. For example, over 18,000 home
burglaries in the Detroit Metropolitan Area in 1967 resulted in the
killing of only one burglary victim in the City of Detroit.[3] In New
York City, over 150,000 burglaries were reported in 1967,[4] yet only
20 victims of burglary were killed in the decade from 1958 to 1967.[5]

---

[3]The burglary data are those submitted to the FBI by all reporting agencies in the
Detroit Standard Metropolitan Area. The City of Detroit is the major portion of the
SMSA total.
[4]Uniform Crime Reports, 1967, p. 77.
[5]Data provided by the New York City Police Department.

The risk to the burglar, though somewhat greater than to the homeowner, is still extremely small. In Detroit, from January 1964 through September 1968, seven residential burglars were shot and killed by their intended victims—an average of just under two a year. If the ratio of fatal to nonfatal deadly assaults with firearms is used as the measure of the nonfatal injuries inflicted on home burglars,[6] between 12 and 20 additional home burglars were probably shot but not killed each year in Detroit. When measured against the burglary rate, no more than two in a thousand burglaries in Detroit are foiled by shooting the burglar.

In addition, of course, householders with firearms may foil burglaries by interrupting or frightening the burglar. There are no available statistics on the frequency of such events.

Home robbery differs from home burglary in that the robber confronts his victim and uses force. Home robberies occur far less frequently than home burglaries. While killings by home robbers are a small portion of all homicides (between 2 and 3 percent in Los Angeles and Detroit), home robbery, when it occurs, is far more dangerous than home burglary. For example, from January 1964 through September 1968 in Detroit, 17 victims died as a result of home robberies, compared to three deaths of home burglary victims.

Firearms are of limited utility in defending against home robbers because the robber is usually able to surprise and overwhelm his victim. Detroit reported three cases of the victim killing a home robber in 5 years. In Los Angeles, where about a thousand home robberies were reported in 1967, 8 home robbers were shot and killed from January 1967 to October 1968. No information is available on the number of robbers wounded, but if the ratio of fatal to nonfatal shootings is used, another 20 to 30 robbers were probably wounded by homeowners' firearms.[7] Compared to the overall rate of home robbery, perhaps 2 percent of home robberies appear to result in the firearms death or injury of the robber.

Examination of the circumstances surrounding the killing of victims by home robbers confirms that the element of surprise substantially limits the effectiveness of a firearm kept for purposes of defense against a home robber. In 11 of the 13 Detroit cases where data were available, the victim opened the door or the robber entered through an unlocked door. In two cases there was evidence

---

[6]See ch. 7, Table 7-2.
[7]This estimate of woundings of robbers, based on information from ch. 7, may be somewhat high. Robbers are more likely to be armed than either victims of criminal shootings or burglars, and when a homeowner engages a robber in a gunfight the incident may more often result in homicide.

of forced entry. In Los Angeles it appears that the victim was completely surprised in 6 of the 11 cases where data were available, and the circumstances are inconclusive in three of the other five cases. In the two remaining cases, the victims had some notice of the impending attack.

The low death rate of homeowners at the hands of home robbers and burglars and the limited opportunity homeowners have to defend themselves against such intruders suggest that having loaded firearms in the home does not now, nor is it likely to, result in substantial saving of life in the home. On the contrary, during 1967 more lives were lost in home firearms accidents in Detroit (25) than were lost in home robbery and burglary in 4½ years (23).

Home intrusions that result in sexual attacks are rare but serious events. Yet firearms would appear to be an even less effective method of self-defense than in robbery, since women generally are less capable of self-defense and less knowledgeable about firearms.

Further indication of the limited effectiveness of the use of firearms to defend against home intruders comes from the "Armed Citizen" columns published in *The American Rifleman.* Assuming the accounts are basically accurate, an analysis of 203 incidents printed between January 1966 and October 1968 disclosed that 69 percent of the incidents involved the use of firearms to protect businesses, while only 17 percent involved defense of the home,[8] even though many times more self-defense weapons are kept in the home.[9]

The available data provide no reason to doubt that the loaded gun is a relatively ineffective defense against a violent intruder in the home.

If keeping a gun does not materially protect the life and property of the homeowner by enabling him to shoot criminals, it nevertheless can be argued that firearms in the home deter criminals and thus save lives and property. The small number of burglars and robbers actually shot suggests shooting is practically no threat to the burglar but might be somewhat of a threat to the robber. It is an open ques-

---

[8]Of the 34 incidents of self-protection in the home, 12 appeared to be home robberies where the offender sought to confront the victim, and 22 seemed to be burglaries where the victim confronted the offender. A confirmatory check of 29 clippings submitted to the magazine for a recent issue and made available to the Task Force showed one of 29 incidents appeared to be home robbery.

[9]The results of the National Opinion Research Center poll in 1966, footnote 1, *supra*, can be projected to a total of 22.5 million households in the United States with self-protection firearms. The Small Business Administration study, footnote 2, *supra*, indicates about 535,000 retail businesses in the United States have self-protection firearms.

tion, however, whether home self-defense firearms provide an extra measure of deterrence.

The trend in crimes against the home during recent years has been sharply upward in spite of the fact that the number of home self-defense firearms has also been rapidly increasing. Yet increases in the crime rate occur for reasons unrelated to home firearms possession, and it is certainly possible that the crime rate would be still higher were it not for firearms. The increase in the crime rate may indeed be a cause of the increase in firearms ownership. As a result, comparisons over time of the incidence of crime and the ownership of firearms cannot provide reliable information about whether guns in the home deter crime.[10] It is possible, however, that in a given community a rising robbery or burglary rate might be reversed, at least temporarily, by a sudden and locally publicized increase in householders' gun buying or gun training. The long-term consequences of such arms buildups or programs may, however, outweigh the short-term benefits. (See ch. 11, *infra*.)

Crimes Against Business

Burglary and robbery also threaten places of business. Table 10-1 shows the number of business robberies and burglaries and the value of property lost in each category in Detroit during January 1968.

Table 10-1 — Robberies and burglaries of businesses in Detroit, January 1968.

	Number	Value of property lost
Robberies[1]	164	$ 88,661
Burglaries[2]	2,808	$819,163

[1]All robberies except "residential" and "highway."
[2]All but "residential" burglaries.
Source: Detroit Police Department.

In Detroit, burglars strike businesses 17 times more often than robbers and cause 9 times as much property loss.

---

[10]A method of investigating whether firearms in the home deter criminal intrusions would be to compare actual and potential crime rates in areas having high firearms ownership with similar areas having low firearms ownership. Such an evaluation scheme is difficult to carry out because there is little information on self-defense firearms ownership by area and because it is difficult to determine what areas are similar. An approximation of the ideal evaluation was attempted by using the rate per 100,000 population at which civilians killed criminals in the act of committing a crime as a measure of self-defense firearms ownership and using robbery rates per 100,000 as a measure of the potential crime rate. These computations are discussed in App. D.

A Small Business Administration report confirms that for the Nation as a whole, burglaries are the more frequent crime against business.[11] Because burglary usually occurs when the premises of a business are unoccupied, firearms are not an effective method of defending against burglary unless armed nightwatchmen are employed. But firearms may help the businessman to defend against robbery, a crime where the criminal and the businessman meet face to face.

Although financial loss from robbery may be relatively small compared to losses from other crimes such as shoplifting and burglary, business robbery is a substantial national problem. Business robbery appears to be concentrated in certain areas,[12] such as slums, and among certain businessmen, such as taxi drivers, operators of liquor stores, markets, and gas stations.

Of all crimes against business, robbery is also the primary threat to life. In Detroit in the last 5 years, 50 persons were killed during robberies of businesses, compared to six who died from business burglaries, three of which were attributed to looting during civil disorders.

Keeping a firearm is one of the many business countermeasures against robbery. Twenty-six percent of a sample of retail businessmen reported keeping firearms.[13] Businesses also have alarm systems, armed guards, dogs, and cameras. The limitations of firearms as a countermeasure against business robberies are highlighted in the recent Small Business Administration study:

> Because of the sudden, almost violent action of robbery, the victims are often taken by surprise and off their guard. The typical robbery occurs in a very short period of time, less than a minute.
>
> Almost invariably, police departments counsel against the victim of the robbery taking any action which might antagonize the robber. Instead he is cautioned to cooperate fully with the robber's wishes . . . . The typical businessman is neither adequately trained nor prepared mentally to face up to the robber.[14]

Although firearms training might assist businessmen in resisting robbers, the surprise and danger from robbers are inherent limita-

---

[11]"Crime Against Small Business," footnote 2, *supra*, Table 27, p. 127, and Table 29, p. 131.

[12]"Crime Against Small Business," footnote 2, *supra*, p. 3.

[13]*Id.*, Table 21, p. 118.

[14]Statement of Vern Bunn reprinted in "Crime Against Small Business," footnote 2, *supra*, p. 242.

tions on the effectiveness of firearms in the prevention of robbery. The Small Business Administration study, for instance, found that 3 percent of retail businesses with firearms reported being the victim of a robbery during the previous year. The same percent of retail businesses without firearms reported being victimized by robbery in the same period.[15]

However, stores that make a practice of having firearms for protection may be unusually vulnerable to robbery, because the stores with firearms are more apt to be in high crime areas and experience more burglary than non-firearms stores.[16] Thus, firearms could be reducing robbery rates in high crime areas. Also, the *known* possession of firearms may well deter robbers. For instance, if many businesses of a particular kind—such as bars—are known to have firearms, some deterrent effect may result.[17] And certainly, the conspicuous posting of armed guards can be expected to deter many potential robbers.

Thus, while there are obvious limitations on the businessman's use of firearms as protection against robbery, it is not known whether, when, or how much guns protect businessmen. It does appear, however, the possession of firearms by businessmen entails less risk of accidents, homicides, and suicides than firearms in the home.

Defense Against Street Crimes

States or cities generally prohibit the carrying of concealed weapons except by certain authorized persons or under certain circumstances. However, in some parts of the country many persons still carry guns in pockets or in cars—either within loosely framed laws or in violation of the law.

Such gun carrying usually is rationalized on the ground of self-defense. While no data exist which would establish the value of firearms as a defense against attack on the street, there is evidence that the ready accessibility of guns contributes significantly to the number of unpremeditated homicides and to the seriousness of many assaults. As with robbery of a place of business, the victim

---

[15]"Crime Against Small Business," footnote 2, *supra*, Table 29, p. 131.

[16]*Id.*, Table 28, p. 129, and Table 21, p. 118. This report also shows that 41 percent of retail business in ghetto areas have guns compared with the 26 percent national average.

[17]In Dallas, for instance, bars commonly have firearms. Other reasons, however, such as the low amount of cash held by Dallas bars, could explain why they are not frequently victimized in robberies. Small stores that stay open late in Dallas are victimized relatively more than in other cities.

of street robbery seldom recognizes his predicament until it is too late to defend himself except by engaging in a gun battle at great risk to his life.

Carrying guns entails the further risk of "overreaction" in ambiguous situations. An armed person may resort to deadly force mistakenly or unnecessarily or out of momentary rage.

Summary

Owning a gun for self-defense and protection of homes and businesses is deeply rooted in American tradition. Guns may be of some utility in defending businesses but, householders may seriously overrate the effectiveness of guns in protection of their homes.

In our urbanized society, the gun is rarely an effective means of protecting the home against either the burglar or the robber; the former avoids confrontation, the latter confronts too swiftly. Possession of a gun undoubtedly provides a measure of comfort to a great many Americans. But the data suggest that this comfort is largely an illusion bought at the high price of increased accidents, homicides, and more widespread illegal use of guns.

Chapter 11

MORE FIREARMS–MORE FIREARMS VIOLENCE

Previous chapters have indicated that in recent years this country has experienced a substantial increase in crime and in sales of firearms, particularly handguns. This chapter explores the consequences of this arms buildup in three different ways. The first is a case history of Detroit,[1] a city that has experienced a firearms buildup in recent years. The second is a comparison of gun ownership and gun use in crime in different regions of the country. The third is a study of armed crime in eight major American cities from which the Task Force, with the help of local police departments, has assembled data. All approaches provide evidence that the arms buildup, if it is partly a response to increased violence, also has contributed to it.

Detroit

Chapter 4 discussed the growth of gun sales in Detroit after civil disorders. In this chapter, the focus shifts from documenting the arms buildup to a study of its consequences.

Because Michigan law requires anyone who wants to buy a handgun to apply for a permit from the local police, the general trend of lawful handgun acquisitions can be determined from the number of permits issued. Figure 11-1 shows the annual rate of handgun permits issued in Detroit from 1965 through 1968.

---

[1] A research organization studied the role of firearms in civil disorders in two areas that experienced extensive riots in 1967—Detroit, Mich., and Newark, N.J. A dramatic increase in handgun purchases occurred following each disorder. (Kotz, "Firearms, Violence and Civil Disorders," Stanford Research Institute, July 1968.) Because the Detroit area has the larger population and because Michigan has recorded handgun purchases for a much longer time than New Jersey, the Task Force elected to study the urban arms buildup in Detroit.

Figure 11-1 — Number of new handgun permits issued in Detroit.
(1965-68)

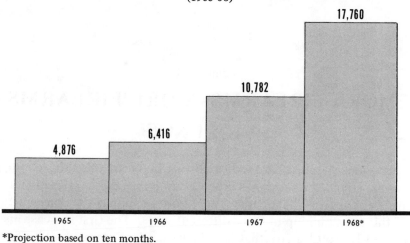

17,760

10,782

6,416

4,876

| 1965 | 1966 | 1967 | 1968* |

*Projection based on ten months.

Source: Detroit Police Department.

New permits for handguns rose sharply during each of the last 4 years, reaching a 1968 level almost four times the 1965 level.

Since Michigan law does not require a permit for shotguns or rifles, these figures apply only to handguns. These figures do not reflect out-of-state purchases or illegal acquisitions of handguns.[2]

Firearms Accidents

Firearms accident rates increased markedly during this period of surging urban armament. With the collaboration of the Wayne County Medical Examiner,[3] the Task Force made a study of firearms accident fatalities in Wayne County from 1964 through 1968, as shown in Figure 11-2. Wayne County accidental deaths from firearms tripled from 1966 to 1967,[4] although the level of such deaths had been stable over the prior 3 years. If the 1968 rate persists, more lives will have been lost by the end of 1969 as the result of increased firearms accidents in Wayne County than were lost in the 1967 Detroit civil disorders.

---

[2]"In the meantime, the illegal acquisition of firearms followed similar trends. . . . The number of guns stolen in the 5 months following the July 1967 riot was approximately 70 percent greater than the number of thefts reported in the 5 months preceding the riot. In the month of September 1967, more guns were reported stolen than in the previous two Septembers combined." (Kotz, *op. cit., supra*, footnote 1, pp. 44-45.)

[3]Wayne County covers Detroit and 10 other communities of 25,000 or more.

[4]Ten persons died in the first 6 months of 1967 compared to 20 during the last 6 months.

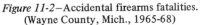

Figure 11-2–Accidental firearms fatalities.
(Wayne County, Mich., 1965-68)

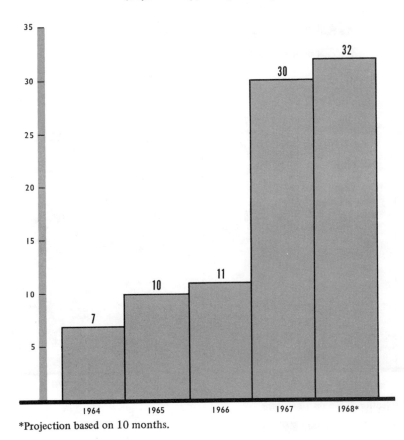

*Projection based on 10 months.

Firearms Suicides

The increase in handgun sales is also reflected in trends in firearms suicides as shown in Figure 11-3. Total suicides did not increase, but firearms suicides increased to some degree.

Figure 11-3–Suicides and firearms suicides in Wayne County, Michigan.
(1965-68)

FIREARMS

OTHER

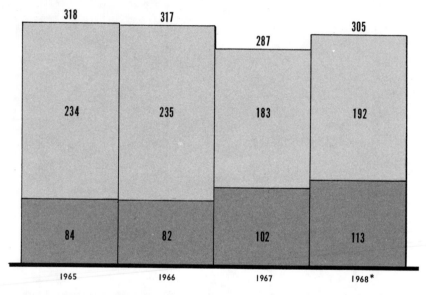

*Projection based on 10 months.

Source: Wayne County Medical Examiner.

Crime

The most significant aftermath of the arms buildup in Detroit is its impact on crime. Figure 11-4 shows trends in the use of firearms in violent attacks (homicides and nonfatal aggravated assaults) known to the police in Detroit from 1965 through 1968. Because the proportion of crimes involving firearms varies with the type of crime, this figure and Figure 11-5 use 1965 as a base year to show the later increases as a percentage of the 1965 level. During this period, attacks not involving firearms rose somewhat, while firearms attacks nearly doubled.

Figure 11-5 shows the trend of the use of firearms in robberies during the same period. Firearms robberies increased about twice as fast as robberies committed without firearms.

Figure 11-4—Trend in violent attacks,* with and without firearms.
(Detroit, 1965-68)
[1965 = 100]

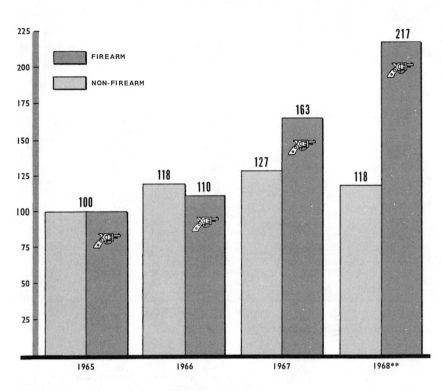

*Homicide and aggravated assault.
**Projection.

Source: Detroit Police Department.

Finally, Figure 11-6 shows the trend in homicides during the same period. Homicides committed with weapons other than firearms increased 30 percent over the 4 year period, while homicides with firearms increased 400 percent. Of 140 homicides in 1965, 55, or 39 percent, involved firearms. By 1968, 279 of 389 homicides, or about 72 percent, involved firearms.

The Detroit data show that the increase in handgun sales (Fig. 11-1) has been accompanied by parallel increases in firearms accidents (Fig. 11-2), suicides by firearms (Fig. 11-3), violent attacks with firearms (Fig. 11-4), robberies with firearms (Fig. 11-5), and firearms homicides (Fig. 11-6).

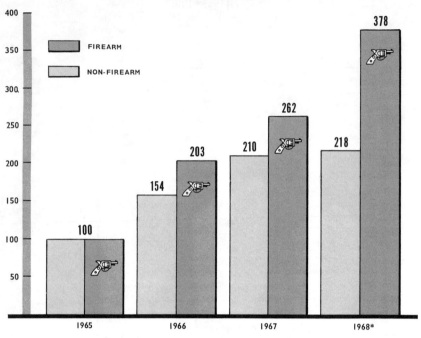

Figure 11-5–Trend in robberies, with and without firearms.
(Detroit, 1965-68)

*Projection based on 10 months.

Figure 11-6–Trend in criminal homicides, with and without firearms.
(Detroit, 1965-68)

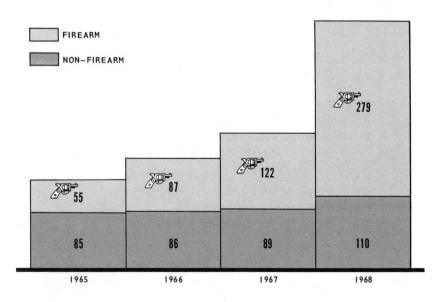

Regional Comparisons

The relationship between firearms possession and firearms violence can also be examined by comparing different regions of the United States. Figure 11-7 shows the frequency of reported gun ownership[5] in the four basic regions of the country and the percentage of homicides and aggravated assaults in these regions that are committed with firearms.

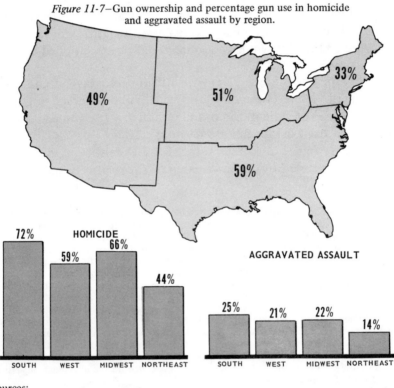

Figure 11-7—Gun ownership and percentage gun use in homicide and aggravated assault by region.

Sources:
  1967 Uniform Crime Report.
  1968 Harris poll (See App. D).

The percentage of homicides and aggravated assaults involving firearms parallels firearms ownership, except in the South, which lags behind the West and Midwest in reported handgun ownership[6] although it leads in total reported gun ownership. The Northeast, with the lowest firearms ownership, also shows the lowest rate of firearms crime.

---

[5]See ch. 2, Fig. 2-1.
[6]*Ibid.*

City Comparisons

More precise exploration of the relationship between firearms ownership and firearms crime would be possible if reliable gun ownership figures were available on a city-by-city basis. Although there is no direct method of determining gun ownership in our cities, the rough regional estimates and available city crime statistics provide some evidence that the use of guns in violent crime is related to total gun ownership. Figure 11-8 shows the percentage of gun use in homicide, robbery, and aggravated assault in eight major U.S. cities.[7] The homicide and aggravated assault statistics are those reported to the FBI, while the robbery data were supplied to the Task Force.[8]

As Figure 11-8 shows, cities with a high percentage of gun use in one type of violent crime tend to have a high percentage of gun use in other types of violent crime, and cities with low gun use in one crime tend to have low gun use in other crimes.[9]

Similarity in the rate of gun usage for different types of crime might be explained by gun ownership of the relatively small seg-

---

[7]The Task Force sought crime data from 14 major cities. In Dallas and Baltimore, data on the use of guns in robbery were not available. In Philadelphia, the data were not in a form that could be used in comparisons. In Detroit, Cleveland, and New Orleans, the crime statistics provided the Task Force differed substantially from the data reported to the FBI by these cities and the Task Force was unable to correct this discrepancy. For instance, in Detroit, 4,635 aggravated assaults were reported to the FBI for 1967, 1,267 of which were committed with guns. About the same number of gun assaults were reported to the Task Force—1,271, but almost twice as many total aggravated assaults—8,400. In Cleveland, about the same number of aggravated assaults were reported to the FBI and to the Task Force (1,290), but the FBI data showed about twice as many with guns (628) as the data provided to the Task Force (320). In New Orleans, 69 of 123 homicides in 1967 were reported to the FBI as committed with guns; the data supplied to the Task Force, however, indicated 203 instead of 123 total homicides. A description of the data supplied the FBI and the Task Force for the nine remaining cities is set forth in App. D.

[8]The figures reported to the FBI and to the Task Force are set forth in App. D.

[9]The rank order correlations obtained from this comparison are:

	Robbery	Aggravated assault
Homicide	.91	.83
Robbery	. . . . .	.83

Including the three cities removed because of major inconsistencies, the correlations are:

	Robbery	Aggravated assault
Homicide	.76	.77
Robbery	. . . . .	.63

Ranks are shown in App. D.

Figure 11-8—Percentage use of firearms in crime, eight U.S. cities, 1967.

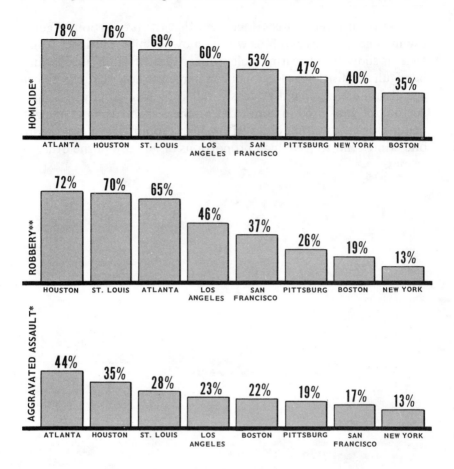

ment of the population that commits violent crime. Yet only a small portion of those who commit homicide are known to also commit robbery.[10]   Further, Figure 11-8 shows that the cities with high rates of gun use in crime are in the South and West, the areas with the highest gun ownership rates.[11]   Cities located in areas with relatively low rates of gun ownership, such as New York and Boston, tend to have the lowest rates of gun use in crime.   It would seem that the use of guns in violent crime rises or falls in relation to gun ownership.

---

[10]In Chicago, for example, only about a quarter of all homicide offenders known to the police have prior arrests for any crimes against the person.   (Data provided by the Chicago Police Department.)

[11]See Fig. 11-7, *supra.*

Summary

    Data from three sources document that the proportion of gun use in violence rises and falls with gun ownership. Statistics from Detroit show that firearms violence increased after an increase in handgun acquisitions. Regional comparisons show that the percentage of gun use in violent attacks parallels rates of gun ownership. A study of guns used in homicides, robberies, and assaults in eight major cities shows that cities with a high proportion of gun use in one crime tend to have high proportions of gun use in the other crimes.

PART III

SYSTEMS OF FIREARMS CONTROL

Part I dealt with patterns of firearms ownership and use in the United States. Part II focused on the relationship between firearms misuse and various forms of violence. This part shifts the focus from the problem to possible solutions.

Chapter 12 describes different strategies of firearms control; Chapters 13 and 14 discuss state, local, and federal firearms laws; Chapter 15 relates to firearms control and certain provisions of the federal Constitution; Chapter 16 discusses the firearms control policies of other nations; Chapter 17 discusses the controversy over the extent to which systems of firearms control can reduce firearms violence; Chapter 18 estimates the cost of various systems of firearms control; and Chapter 19 discusses ways in which advances in technology might assist firearms control.

Chapter 12

STRATEGIES OF
FIREARMS CONTROL

The goal of all firearms control is separation of the legitimate from the illegitimate use of guns. The ideal solution would be to leave legitimate gun uses undisturbed and prevent all illegitimate uses. This solution is obviously unattainable, but it provides a reference point for appraising the various strategies of firearms control in search of a control system that will prevent as much illegitimate gun use as possible while interfering minimally with legitimate uses.

One way to try to separate illegitimate from legitimate gun use is to regulate the place and manner in which firearms may be used through such laws as those prohibiting the carrying of firearms within city limits, the carrying of firearms in a motor vehicle, the carrying of concealed weapons on one's person, and the discharge of a firearm in populated areas. Such laws attempt to reduce firearms violence by police intervention before violence or crime actually occur. There are obvious limits to the ability of the police to discover persons who violate place and manner laws and to prevent firearms violence. These laws thus have limited capacity to deter violence.[1]

Laws that provide extra punishment for crimes when guns are used are a special form of place and manner laws. These laws are intended to affect the behavior of persons who are not deterred by ordinary criminal sanctions, on the theory that they might be persuaded not to use guns in order to avoid extra punishment. There

---

[1]Most firearms violence occurs outside the reach of normal police activity—in private dwellings, where police are not aware of it, and on the street, where concealed weapons are difficult to identify. Police officers must have a search warrant to search a home and reasonable grounds to search a suspect before they can intervene and prevent the potentially dangerous use of firearms. The deterrent effect of place and manner laws is diminished not only because of the difficulties of enforcement but also because such laws attempt to deter from illegal use of firearms the least reliable segment of our population. Even if more police were available to enforce these laws, firearms violence would be prevented only in a limited number of cases.

are little available data on whether such laws do in fact provide this extra measure of deterrence.

A second method of firearms control is to separate the legitimate from the illegitimate use of guns by limiting the possession of firearms to the more reliable segments of the population. The theory behind this approach is to keep guns away from irresponsible people rather than to try to influence behavior of persons who already have guns. Generally these "possession" laws attempt to single out relatively small definable groups who are thought to be a threat to society and to prohibit them from acquiring guns. Typically, these groups are persons with criminal records, drug addicts, the insane, the young, and alcoholics. Anyone who does not fall within these prohibited groups is generally permitted to own guns without restriction.

Attributing gun violence to such bad risk groups goes too far and, at the same time, not far enough. It goes too far because many of the people in the prohibited classes do not misuse firearms. It does not go far enough because many persons who misuse firearms are not members of the prohibited classes. Nevertheless, if the members of the prohibited classes are more apt to misuse guns than are average gun owners, such controls can reduce the illegitimate use of guns, provided the system does in fact prevent the bad risk groups from getting guns.

But keeping guns from bad risk groups is, under the best conditions, extremely difficult. A law which merely forbids people in certain categories from owning guns without establishing procedures which make it difficult for such persons to obtain guns is certainly not likely to keep guns from many members of the prohibited group. If nothing but a law on the books stands in their way, few are likely to refrain from buying guns.[2.]

Because laws regulating firearms possession are not self-executing, many systems back up the prohibition against gun ownership by bad risk groups with procedures to make it physically more difficult for such persons to obtain firearms. Systems of screening potential firearms owners are the most common. Because all persons who seek to own firearms must be screened in order to find the small number of ineligible persons, such systems affect the ways in which legitimate as well as illegitimate firearms owners can acquire guns.

---

[2]Firearms statutes prohibiting possession of guns by prescribed groups have one advantage over place and manner statutes in that such laws seek to affect conduct before firearms are obtained. It is certainly more realistic to try to prevent a person from obtaining a firearm than it is to control his use of the firearm once he has it.

The basic method of screening is to require *licensing* of individuals before they can obtain firearms.[3] Under a licensing system, an individual must prove himself eligible to own a particular firearm before he may purchase the firearm.

Licensing laws that allow all but the prohibited categories of persons to acquire guns can be called permissive, since most people are able to meet licensing requirements. Before an applicant can be denied a license or a firearm owner's identification card, the administering agency must show that the applicant is a member of one of the prohibited groups. Permissive licensing no doubt prevents many unauthorized persons from obtaining firearms through legitimate sources, such as retail dealers and individual citizens who are conscientious about the disposition of their secondhand firearms. It does little, however, to curtail the total number of firearms in circulation. Since the number of firearms in this country is substantial, even with permissive licensing firearms will be transferred from legitimate to illegitimate owners through hand-to-hand transactions and theft. Also, the more permissive the system, the more likely it is that firearms will be acquired by persons who may misuse them.

Another approach to firearms control is restrictive licensing. Under such a system a person seeking to buy a firearm, typically a handgun, must provide the licensing authority with evidence of good character and have a valid reason why he needs the firearm. In restrictive licensing, the presumption used in permissive systems is reversed: the applicant must give a sufficient reason for allowing him to have a gun rather than the licensing authority being required to show a reason for denying the request. Instead of saying "all but . . ." members of the prohibited classes may possess firearms, the restrictive system provides that "nobody but . . ." those who are specifically approved may possess the firearms covered by the system.

Restrictive licensing attempts to reduce firearms violence by substantially reducing the number of firearms in circulation. With fewer handguns outstanding, for example, the number of hand-to-hand transfers from legitimate to illegitimate users, the number of handgun thefts, and the number of situations in which legitimate users turn to handguns in moments of rage and frustration are all reduced. This inevitably reduces the legitimate uses of firearms as well.

---

[3] Such systems require either a permit or a license before one can obtain a firearm.

There are other controls designed to assist a licensing system in reducing illegitimate gun use. One such addition to a licensing system is the use of waiting periods. A waiting period between the time an individual wants to acquire a firearm and the date he can acquire that firearm attempts to reduce impulsive violence or compel the use of less dangerous weapons.

Another adjunct to licensing is registration. It identifies a particular firearm as the property of a particular licensed person and is an attempt to back up licensing by keeping track of the guns owned by legitimate gun users. A license to have a gun is similar to a license to drive, and registration of the gun is similar to the registration of automobiles. Gun registration systems require a gun owner to provide information about the guns he owns when the system goes into effect and to supplement this information whenever he disposes of a gun or acquires another gun. Because the registered guns can be traced back to him, it is hoped that the legitimate gun user will tend to be more responsible in the handling and storage of his firearms and more hesitant to transfer them to individuals not eligible to possess them. Such a system, of course, has no bearing on guns whose owners do not register or that are lost from the registration system because of theft or loss.

Firearms registration can be strengthened by a system of audits to determine whether individuals listed as owning particular firearms are still in possession of such guns.[4] Auditing would encourage individuals to report loss, theft, or other transfers of their firearms and, at the same time, deter licensed firearms owners from transferring weapons to ineligible owners.

An alternative to registration would be to require notification by gun dealers or owners whenever a gun is transferred by sale or gift or lost or stolen. Any dealer or private individual who transfers or loses a firearm would have to supply to a firearms control agency information on the manufacturer, model and serial number of the firearm, the name and address and license number of the transferor and, except in cases of theft or loss, of the transferee.

A transfer notice system would generate about one-tenth as much information in its first year as registration[5] and would thus put a lesser burden on gun owners. Over a period of years, how-

---

[4]Like income tax audits, firearms audits could be conducted on a sampling basis with a random number of registrations audited each year.

[5]Of the approximately 90 million firearms in this country, about 9 million changed hands in 1968—about 5 million new guns were imported or domestically manufactured and approximately another 4 million used guns were sold in the secondhand market. See ch. 3 and App. C.

ever, a transfer notice system might provide essentially the same results as registration for less expense and inconvenience.[6]

Registration and transfer notice are similar in that both depend on compliance by law-abiding citizens.[7] They are also similar in that enforcement of either system might be substantially strengthened by imposing, in addition to criminal penalties, civil liability for the consequences of any subsequent firearms misuse on all persons who lose or transfer guns without giving the required notice.[8]

But the two systems are also different. In a registration system, the owner who has previously registered his guns is encouraged to report any subsequent transfer or loss because he is on record as the owner of the guns. This encouragement for giving notice of any later transfer or loss does not exist under a transfer notice system. However, the simplicity of the transfer notice system might lead to its being followed even if there is no incentive to do so as a result of existing records on gun owners.

Another difference is that, even when certain legal safeguards are adopted, registration may lead to more enforcement difficulties under the fifth amendment than transfer notice. This is discussed in detail in Chapter 15.

Summary

Different strategies of firearms control—regulation of the place and manner in which firearms can be used, regulation of who may possess firearms, permissive and restrictive licensing, registration and transfer notice—can be combined in a variety of ways to produce a comprehensive system of control. Because handguns and long guns do not contribute equally to firearms misuse, it may be appropriate to use different strategies for different types of firearms.

---

[6]Whether a registration or a transfer notice system were adopted, illegitimate firearms users could not be expected to abide by either system.

[7]As discussed in detail in ch. 15, *infra*, making a registration or transfer notice system applicable to illegitimate gun users might raise constitutional questions which could jeopardize efforts to prosecute such persons under other firearms laws.

[8]Civil liability is now imposed for ultra-hazardous activities such as keeping wild animals and blasting.

Chapter 13

STATE AND LOCAL
FIREARMS LAWS

Firearms control, like other aspects of law enforcement in the United States, has traditionally been a matter of state and local responsibility. This local emphasis has over the years led to a situation where it is safe to assert that the United States has more firearms legislation than any other country in the world.[1]

These laws present an astonishing diversity of rules and regulations, ranging from almost total lack of control to attempts at restrictive licensing. Between these extremes lies a great variety of approaches and degrees of strictness.

Almost all states have *some* firearms control legislation.[2] The earliest and most numerous state and local laws relate to the carrying or use of firearms. In the 1600's, Massachusetts prohibited the carrying of defensive firearms in public places.[3] Kentucky in 1813, Indiana in 1819, Arkansas and Georgia in 1837 passed laws prohibiting the carrying of concealed weapons.[4] Many states and most cities today have laws attempting to regulate what has been called the place and manner in which firearms may be carried or used. Even when there is a will to carefully draft and painstakingly enforce these laws, however, their effect is questionable. An Arkansas statute, enacted in 1881, for instance, makes it a crime to

---

[1]Congressman John D. Dingell of Michigan testified before the Senate Juvenile Delinquency Subcommittee that there are "over 20,000 laws governing the sale, distribution and use of firearms." Hearings, 89th Cong., 1st sess., p. 376 (1965). The basis of this estimate is not provided, but it presumably includes many local laws prohibiting the discharge of firearms within town or city limits.

[2]The principal provisions of state firearms laws are summarized in App. G.

[3]Crim. Code of Province of Mass. C. 18 §6. This statute was re-enacted after the Revolution. 2 Mass. Laws 1780-1800, §653. See 98 U. Pa. L. Rev. 906, n. 4 (1950).

[4]The Kentucky law was subsequently ruled unconstitutional because of a state constitutional provision allowing citizens to have arms. *Bliss* v. *Commonwealth*, 2 Litt. 90 (Ky. 1822). After a constitutional amendment, a new firearms law was ruled valid. *Hopkins* v. *Commonwealth*, 3 Bush. 480 (Ky. 1968). Indiana Laws 1819, c. 23. Ark. Rev. Stat. c. 44, div. 8, art. I, §13. Georgia Laws 1837, p. 90.

"wear or carry in any manner whatsoever as a weapon, any . . . pistol." In addition to the problems of determining what is meant by carrying a pistol "as a weapon,"[5] the law provides further: "Nothing . . . shall be so construed as to prohibit any person from carrying such pistols as are used in the army or navy . . . when carried uncovered in the hand."[6] It is difficult to determine what effect, if any, the Arkansas law has on firearms used in that state. Texas provides another example. For years it has been unlawful for anyone "to carry on or about his person, saddle, or in his saddle bags, or in his portfolio or purse any pistol . . ."[7] This does not apply, however, to "travellers," and the Texas courts have attempted for decades to determine who is exempt as a "traveller."[8] As noted in Appendix A,[9] Jack Ruby was probably not violating Texas law by routinely carrying in the trunk of his car the pistol used to kill Lee Harvey Oswald so long as he was en route between his residence and his business. When he varied from this route, however, and took the pistol from the trunk of his car to carry it on his person, Ruby probably violated Texas law.

In addition to laws relating to the place and manner in which firearms can be used, all but five states[10] prohibit certain categories of individuals from possessing handguns. The persons excluded from possession include minors, felons, aliens, fugitives, persons of unsound mind, narcotics violators, and drunkards.[11] Seldom does one state prohibit all or nearly all of these categories from having handguns.[12]

---

[5]Carrying a pistol to kill hogs is not carrying it "as a weapon." See annotation to Ark. Stats. Ann., Title 41, sec. 4501. A similar statute in Tennessee prohibits carrying a pistol "with intent to go armed." The Supreme Court of Tennessee has interpreted this to mean that "the intent with which it [the pistol] is carried must be that of going armed, or being armed, or wearing it for the purpose of being armed." *Liming* v. *State*, 417 S.W. 2d 769, 773 (1967).

[6]Ark. Stats. Ann., Title 41, sec. 4501.

[7]Texas Penal Code Ann., Art. 483.

[8]A person going 18 miles is not exempt as a traveler, but one going 60 miles is exempt (*Creswell* v. *State*, 39 S.W. 372 (1897); *Impson* v. *State*, 19 S.W. 677 (1892)). Yet going 40 miles to a neighboring city and back in broad daylight is not exempt (*George* v. *State*, 234 S.W. 87 (1921)).

[9]See App. A.

[10]Arkansas, Indiana, Iowa, Mississippi, and Tennessee.

[11]Many states exclude only one category of persons from owning firearms. For instance, in Idaho, only Indians cannot have handguns; in Minnesota, Utah, and West Virginia, only aliens are excluded; in Georgia, Virginia, Vermont, and Kentucky, only minors are excluded; in New Mexico, only prisoners are denied guns; in Ohio, minors under 18 and tramps are excluded.

[12]One of the more comprehensive laws is New Jersey's, where all firearms are denied to felons, fugitives, persons afflicted with mental disorder, persons convicted of crime, narcotics violators or addicts, and habitual drunkards.

Most of the states that restrict the possession of firearms have done so by simply passing a law against possession, without attempting to screen ineligible individuals through the use of applications, licenses, or permits.

Only 20 states[13] and the District of Columbia attempt to screen ineligible individuals by requiring, *before* a handgun (or a firearm) can be purchased, that the purchaser either fill out an application to be submitted to the dealer, obtain a permit or license from a local law enforcement agency, or obtain a firearms owner's identification card from a state agency. Even in these 21 jurisdictions which attempt to screen gun purchasers, the systems vary. Only a few systems require the dealer to hold up the sale until the local law enforcement agency approves the application submitted to the dealer.[14] Other states allow the handgun to be delivered within a prescribed time even if no response from the local law enforcement agency has been received.[15] Of the 31 states with no procedure whatsoever to screen persons from buying guns, a few require firearms dealers to notify local police *after* a gun has been sold.[16]

All but two of the state screening systems are permissive in that they exclude individuals from owning guns only if the state can give a reason, such as a criminal record or mental incompetency, why permission should be denied. Thus in 48 states and the District of Columbia most people can own firearms without having to give a reason.

New York and Massachusetts are the two exceptions. Both have enacted statutes that empower the police to issue a handgun permit only when the individual establishes that he is of good character and gives a good reason why he should have a handgun. New York's Sullivan law, passed in 1911, is the most famous example of this approach. Under the law, a license is issued to authorize possession of a handgun in the home; a different license is issued to authorize possession in a place of business; still another license is required to carry a handgun concealed on the person. Anyone possessing or carrying a concealable firearm without the proper license commits an offense.

New York conducts an extensive investigation of the applicant before granting a license. A license issued in New York City is

---

[13]Alabama, California, Connecticut, Delaware, Hawaii, Illinois, Indiana, Maryland, Massachusetts, Michigan, Missouri, New Jersey, New York, North Carolina, North Dakota, Pennsylvania, Rhode Island, South Dakota, Tennessee, and Virginia.
[14]See, e.g., Iowa, Oregon, and Washington.
[15]See, e.g., Massachusetts, New York, and the District of Columbia.
[16]See, e.g., Maryland and Rhode Island.

valid throughout that state, but a license issued elsewhere in the state is not valid in New York City. The license has the owner's photograph and shows the serial number of the licensed firearm.

Most state screening systems create a waiting period between the time a prospective owner wants to acquire a firearm and the earliest date on which he can take possession. This period ranges from 48 hours in Alabama, the District of Columbia, Pennsylvania, and South Dakota to a period of 5 days in California, 7 days in Maryland and Connecticut, 15 days in Tennessee, and a matter of months in some cases in New York.[17]

Registration has never been a popular approach to state firearms control. Only Mississippi has enacted what appears to be registration independent of any licensing or permit system.[18] Some states with handgun licensing systems require either the dealer or the owner to register guns after they have been acquired. Although a few states maintain a central state file of such information,[19] such records are generally maintained only at the local or county level and there is no statewide collection of the information.[20] Thus, of the estimated 24 million handguns in the United States, the records maintained by the states with statewide data cover only about 3 to 5 million.[21] One reason for this is that only the District of Columbia appears to have supplemented its licensing law by requiring, when the law became effective, that all firearms already in circulation be registered.

In addition to state laws, some cities have passed firearms control laws stricter than those that would be applicable to their citizens under state laws. Philadelphia in 1965, for example, passed a restrictive handgun licensing system much stricter than the permis-

---

[17]Alan S. Krug, "Does Firearms Registration Work," National Shooting Sports Foundation (July 1968).
[18]The status of the Mississippi registration law is unclear since it was apparently repealed in 1946 and then amended in 1950. See editors' notes to Mississippi Code Ann. Title 31, sec. 8621.
[19]See, e.g., California, New York, and Maryland.
[20]See, e.g., Connecticut, Hawaii, North Carolina, Mississippi, and Missouri.
[21]Information supplied the Task Force from state records indicates handgun licenses have been issued as follows. (It is possible that more than one license has been issued for some handguns.)

Michigan	1,134,869	Massachusetts .	176,000*
New York . . .	812,484	West Virginia. .	105,000*
New Jersey . . .	257,000*	Maryland	60,142

*Estimate

Data from California would probably increase the total to close to 5 million handgun licenses.

sive Pennsylvania handgun licensing law. In 1968, New York City and Chicago both passed registration laws.[22]

Table 13-1 is an attempt to summarize the varying degrees of control reflected in existing state firearms laws. The two columns on the left show that all but five states prohibit at least one category of persons from owning handguns, but that only a few states extend these restrictions to rifles and shotguns. The two middle columns show that less than half of the states supplement prohibitions against possession by screening the persons who purchase or possess handguns.[23] Only a handful of these states also screen the purchase or possession of rifles and shotguns. The two columns on the right show that only two states have restrictive licensing of handguns and that no state has such a system for rifles and shotguns.

The emphasis on local control and the great range in the type and strictness of controls presently on the books have created a number of substantial problems. Until the end of 1968, it was perfectly legal to sell or ship weapons from a state which had little or no firearms control to a state with a stricter system. The diversity of state firearms control systems led to a situation where one state's loose laws posed a threat to efforts by other states to impose tighter controls because of the difficulty of keeping firearms from flowing from jurisdictions where they are readily available into jurisdictions with tighter controls. State and local firearms control systems have for years been frustrated by the interstate movement of firearms. In Massachusetts, a 10-year study showed that 87 percent of the guns used in crime came from other states.[24] In New York City, 65 percent of a sample of domestic handguns confiscated by police came from outside the state and another 18 percent were of foreign or military origin.[25] Similarly, in Detroit 75 percent of firearms used in a sample of shootings in 1968 analyzed by the Detroit Police Department were never registered in Michigan and were therefore probably not sold by any Michigan

---

[22]In Chicago (with a population in 1960 of 3.5 million), 194,687 handguns have been registered from the time registration became effective in 1968 until April 1969. Handgun registration has been required since 1965 in Las Vegas and Clark County, Nev. (with a population in 1960 of 303,000), and approximately 120,000 handguns have been registered.

[23]As noted earlier, there is wide variety in the scope and effectiveness of state screening systems.

[24]Richard Caples, Commissioner of Public Safety, Boston, Mass., Hearings before Senate Subcommittee To Investigate Juvenile Delinquency, 89th Cong., 1st session, p. 346 (1965).

[25]See ch. 8.

Table 13-1–Summary of state firearms control laws

	Some persons prohibited from owning		Screening of purchase or possession through applications, licenses, or permits		Restrictive licensing	
	Handguns and concealable weapons	Rifles and shotguns	Handguns and concealable weapons	Rifles and shotguns	Handguns and concealable weapons	Rifles and shotguns
Alabama	X		X			
Alaska	X					
Arizona	X					
Arkansas						
California	X		X			
Colorado	X					
Connecticut	X		X			
Delaware	X	X	X	X		
District of Columbia	X	X	X	X		
Florida	X	X				
Georgia	X					
Hawaii	X	X	X	X		
Idaho	X					
Illinois	X	X	X	X		
Indiana	X		X			
Iowa						
Kansas	X					
Kentucky	X					
Louisiana	X					
Maine	X					
Maryland	X	X	X	X		
Massachusetts	X	X	X	X		
Michigan	X		X	X	X	
Minnesota	X					
Mississippi	X		X			
Missouri	X					
Montana	X					
Nebraska	X					
Nevada	X					
New Hampshire	X					
New Jersey	X	X	X	X		
New Mexico	X		X			

Table 13-1–Summary of state firearms control laws—Continued

	Some persons prohibited from owning		Screening of purchase or possession through applications, licenses, or permits		Restrictive licensing	
	Handguns and concealable weapons	Rifles and shotguns	Handguns and concealable weapons	Rifles and shotguns	Handguns and concealable weapons	Rifles and shotguns
New York	X	X	X	X	X	
North Carolina . .	X	X	X			
North Dakota . .	X		X			
Ohio	X					
Oklahoma . . .	X					
Oregon	X					
Pennsylvania . .	X		X			
Rhode Island . .	X		X			
South Carolina .	X					
South Dakota . .	X		X			
Tennessee . . .			X			
Texas	X					
Utah	X					
Vermont . . .	X					
Virginia	X		X			
Washington . . .	X					
West Virginia . .	X	X				
Wisconsin . . .	X					
Wyoming	X	X				

dealer. Many were probably brought in from Toledo, Ohio, where a 1968 survey showed that, of 13,000 handguns sold by one dealer alone, 5,448 went to Michigan residents.[26]

The Federal Gun Control Act of 1968, discussed in the next chapter, attempts to curtail the interstate flow of firearms and restore effectiveness to state and local firearms controls. It is too early to determine the impact of this Act.

The handicap placed on even the most stringent state and local firearms laws by the uncontrolled interstate movement of firearms has led to continuing efforts to coordinate firearms policies in the United States through uniform or model state laws. In 1923, the United States Revolver Association promulgated a model firearms law, applicable only to handguns, that was adopted in a few states. Later rewritten as the Uniform Firearms Act, it had been enacted in 10 states and the District of Columbia[27] by 1936, but often with modifications. A more restrictive act requiring a permit to purchase handguns was drafted in 1940 as the Uniform Pistol Act, but was passed by only two states.[28]

In 1968, three new uniform laws were proposed—one by the National Association of Attorneys General,[29] one by the National Council of State Governments,[30] and one, the "Model Firearms Owners Identification Bill," was sponsored by the firearms manufacturers.[31]

If the past is prologue, coordinated uniformity of state firearms control laws is not on the horizon. Proponents of a national firearms policy have accordingly turned their attention to proposals for a federal system of firearms control.

Summary

State and local firearms regulation in the United States is a patchwork quilt of more than 20,000 laws, many of them obso-

---

[26]Testimony of Sheldon S. Cohen, Commissioner of Internal Revenue, Commission Hearings, Oct. 9, 1968, Tr. 1076.

[27]New Hampshire and North Dakota (1923); Indiana (1925); Hawaii and Rhode Island (1927); Pennsylvania (1931); California and the District of Columbia (1932); South Dakota and Washington (1935); Alabama (1936).

[28]South Dakota and New Hampshire (without the licensing provisions).

[29]This proposal would require all firearms owners to have either a permit (for handguns) or a firearms owner's identification card (for long guns) issued by a state agency.

[30]This proposal would require a permit to own a handgun and registration of all long guns.

[31]This proposal would establish a permissive system whereby all but felons, addicts, drunkards, and persons afflicted with mental disease would be entitled to have a firearms owner's identification card and to own as many firearms as they chose.

lete, unenforced, or unenforceable. Serious efforts at state and local regulation have consistently been frustrated by the flow of firearms from one state to another. Attempts to establish uniform state and local firearms laws have failed.

Chapter 14

FEDERAL FIREARMS LAWS

During its first 150 years as a federal union, the United States had no national firearms legislation.[1] The first federal firearms possession law was passed in 1934 as a tax to discourage the use of machineguns and sawed-off shotguns and rifles. Although a number of additional laws were proposed in the 1930's and one was passed in 1938, no additional federal firearms laws were seriously considered until the 1960's when a series of proposals were made, including laws for the licensing of firearms owners and registration of firearms. These efforts culminated in the Gun Control Act of 1968 that attempted to curtail mail-order sales and regulate the interstate movement of firearms.

This chapter reviews the history of proposals for federal firearms control and discusses the major provisions of existing firearms laws.

During prohibition the rise of organized, interstate crime led Americans for the first time to view crime as a national rather than a local problem. But even then federal laws to control crime were not proposed as a solution. A national commission which conducted the first federally sponsored study of crime in the United States,[2] for instance, concluded in 1931 that crime was nationwide in scope and organized in nature but proposed only the mildest federal cooperation—a national fingerprint file and a crime statistics agency.

---

[1]Federal laws relating indirectly to firearms were passed at the beginning of this century when the Secretary of the Army was directed to support private shooting clubs and to sell firearms and ammunition at cost to members of the National Rifle Association. Such programs escalated from the appropriation of $2,500 for trophies in 1903 to the appropriation of almost $5 million for various activities in the 1960's. These laws are discussed in detail in App. H.

An excise tax on firearms was considered by Congress as early as 1911 and was subsequently enacted. The proceeds of this federal tax are today returned to the states for use in wildlife conservation.

Finally, Congress in 1927 closed the mails to handguns. See 18 U.S.C. §1715.
[2]The National Commission on Law Observance and Enforcement, popularly known as the Wickersham Commission.

Instead of federal anticrime measures, the commission proposed uniform state laws.[3]

The administration of Franklin D. Roosevelt, however, viewed crime and violence as a national problem requiring a federal solution.[4] President Roosevelt proposed a series of virtually unprecedented federal anticrime bills,[5] including a bill which would have regulated the sale and ownership of machineguns and concealable weapons. These bills encountered substantial opposition from hunting and shooting interests and from those who felt the federal government should not assume jurisdiction of traditionally state and local matters. However, a series of sensational kidnapings and machinegun battles between federal agents and public enemies in 1933 and 1934 increased the demands for federal action.[6] The firearms bill remained stalled in Congress, however, until April 1934, when John Dillinger broke jail, robbed several banks, and engaged federal agents in machinegun battles. Dillinger's exploits caused a national furor, and the firearms bill and several other anticrime measures were quickly passed.

Before the proposed firearms bill was passed, however, all provisions applying to handguns were removed. The National Firearms Act of 1934 accordingly applied only to machineguns, short barreled rifles and shotguns, silencers, and unconventional concealable firearms, such as caneguns. It was basically a tax measure, imposing a heavy tax on the transfer of any of the covered weapons and a similar occupational tax on manufacturers, importers, and dealers. Anyone owning such a firearm, including manufacturers, importers, and dealers, was required to register the gun as were all persons who might subsequently acquire such a weapon unless they had in effect registered it by submitting a form and paying the transfer tax.[7]

---

[3]Until the 1930's the control of crime was generally deemed the complete responsibility of state and local police. See, e.g., Arthur C. Millspaugh, *Crime Control by the National Government,* ch. 3 (Washington, D.C.: Brookings Institution, 1937). See also Max Lowenthal, *The Federal Bureau of Investigation* (New York: William Sloane Associates, 1950); Don Whitehead, *The FBI Story* (New York: Random House, 1956).

[4]See "Crime: Cummings on Warpath. . .," *Newsweek,* Dec. 22, 1934, p. 5. See also Carl Brent Swisher, *Selected Papers of Homer Cummings, Attorney General of the United States, 1933-1939* (New York: C. Scribner's Sons, 1939); William Seagle, "The American National Police," *Harper's* Nov. 1934.

[5]These bills proposed to enlarge the power of the FBI and make it a federal crime to assault federal officers, rob national banks, and flee across state lines to avoid prosecution.

[6]The "Kansas City Massacre" involving "Pretty Boy" Floyd; the kidnaping of wealthy St. Paul brewer William Hamm, Jr., by the Barker-Karpis gang; and the kidnaping of Oklahoma City oilman Charles Urschel by Machine Gun Kelly.

[7]See 68A Stat. 721, 72 Stat. 1428.

In 1937,[8] and again in 1939,[9] the Supreme Court upheld this act as a valid exercise of the taxing power. In 1968, however, the Supreme Court ruled that the fifth amendment privilege against self-incrimination invalidated prosecution for failure to register or for possession of an unregistered weapon, on the ground that the act's registration provisions compelled one to incriminate oneself by admitting unlawful possession.[10] In an effort to overcome this problem, the act was amended in October 1968 to provide that information submitted in registering could not be used in any prosecution against the registrant.[11] The National Firearms Act appears to have succeeded in taking machineguns out of general circulation and reducing their use by criminals, although sawed-off shotguns are still used on occasion in armed robbery, and there has been evidence in recent years that extremist groups are acquiring submachineguns and other fully automatic weapons.[12]

In 1935, the Roosevelt administration again sought comprehensive control of firearms by proposing to extend the 1934 act to require that all firearms be registered.[13] Although subsequently trimmed to cover only handguns, the bill lay dormant in Congress, along with another bill which would have outlawed the interstate sale of handguns.

These bills had the backing of the American Bar Association, the International Association of Chiefs of Police,[14] and, according to a Gallup poll, 79 percent of the Nation's population.[15] They were strongly opposed by sporting and firearms interests, however. The National Rifle Association advocated as an alternative a bill that

---

8*Sonzinsky* v. *United States,* 300 U.S. 506 (1937).

9*United States* v. *Miller,* 307 U.S. 174 (1939).

10*Haynes* v. *United States, 390 U.S. 85* (1968). The fifth amendment problems raised by Haynes and other cases are discussed in ch. 15 and App. K.

1182 Stat. 1227, Public Law 90-618 (Oct. 22, 1968). The act was also amended to require registration by all owners of such firearms, not just by illegal possessors.

12See ch. 9, *infra.*

13Attorney General Cummings vowed a "fight to the finish" for a federal law requiring the registration of all firearms: "Show me the man who doesn't want his gun registered, and I will show you a man who shouldn't have a gun." Address by U.S. Attorney General Homer Cummings before the annual convention of the International Association of Chiefs of Police, Oct. 5, 1937, as quoted in Carl Bakal, *The Right to Bear Arms* 176 (New York: McGraw-Hill, 1966).

14See Bakal, *op. cit. supra,* footnote 13, at 197.

15On May 1, 1938, Gallup reported that 84 percent of adults favored a law requiring owners of pistols and revolvers to register with the government. Nearly 30 years later, in a May 1967 survey, 85 percent of adults said they would back such a law. *Gallup Opinion Index: Gallup Political Scoreboard,* pp. 6-7 (July 1968).

only provided for licensing of manufacturers, importers, and dealers at modest fees, but did not require registration of all firearms.[16] It was this bill that was ultimately enacted by Congress as the Federal Firearms Act of 1938. The other bills died.

The Federal Firearms Act of 1938 covered all firearms and most handgun ammunition. Before shipping in interstate commerce, the law required firearms manufacturers, importers, and dealers to obtain a federal license, at an annual fee of $25 for manufacturers and importers and $1 for dealers. Dealers and manufacturers were prohibited from shipping a firearm in interstate commerce to a felon, fugitive from justice, person under indictment, or anyone not having a license to purchase, if such a license was required by local law. The prohibited class (felons, etc.) was also forbidden to ship or receive firearms which were or had been in interstate commerce. The act also prohibited knowingly shipping or receiving in interstate commerce stolen firearms or firearms with altered serial numbers. Finally, dealers were required to maintain permanent records of firearms received and sold.[17]

Just as the courts had upheld the National Firearms Act of 1934, the Federal Firearms Act of 1938 was declared a constitutional exercise of the commerce power.[18] Yet, the Federal Firearms Act did not succeed in curtailing the flow of firearms into undesirable hands. Few states coordinated their laws with the federal law by requiring individuals to have a license before they could buy firearms.[19] Even if states had done so, any person who paid $1 for a federal dealer's license could be shipped a firearm without regard to such a state law.[20]

Moreover, the act was ambiguous in prescribing standards for becoming a firearms dealer. Aside from excluding felons, there

---

[16]See, e.g., *The American Rifleman,* May 1938. The previous month the NRA had observed in the same publication: "The Attorney General's previous efforts to secure drastic federal firearms laws have been killed by the active and audible objections of the sportsmen of America."

[17]See 52 Stat. 1250 (1938). Repealed, 82 Stat. 234 (June 19, 1968).

[18]*Cases* v. *United States,* 131 F. 2d 916 (1st Cir. 1942), *cert. denied sub nom. Velazquez* v. *United States, 319 U.S. 770 (1943); United States* v. *Tot,* 131 F. 2d 261 (2d Cir. 1942), *rev'd on other grounds,* 319 U.S. 463 (1943).

[19]Sheldon S. Cohen, Commissioner of Internal Revenue, Hearings before the Senate Subcommittee To Investigate Juvenile Delinquency, 90th Cong., 1st sess., pp. 45-46 (1967). South Carolina, for instance, prohibited entirely the sale of handguns, but since it was not a "license-to-purchase" state, handguns could be shipped into South Carolina without violating the Federal Firearms Act.

[20]*Ibid,* p. 50.

were no explicit disqualifications.[21] Since "dealer" was defined
as "any person engaged in the business of selling firearms," it could
be argued that a license application by anyone not engaged in the
business of trading in firearms could be denied.[22] The Treasury
Department, however, felt it could not deny such applications and
in practice did not even make an investigation of applicants, partly
because the $1 fee was too small to defray costs.[23] As a result, the
Treasury estimated that of the 104,087 persons holding federal
licenses in 1964, 25 percent were not actually engaged in the firearms business.[24]

The prohibition against sales to felons and fugitives was also defi-
cient. The act prohibited only "knowing" sale to such persons—a
difficult charge to prove, especially if the dealer took the simple
precaution of requiring the purchaser to sign a form stating he was
not such a person.[25] Juveniles were not effectively deterred in any
way from ordering or receiving weapons, nor were insane persons,
alcoholics, or narcotic addicts.

Some of the ineffectiveness of that act may have been due to its
administration. The Secretary of the Treasury designated the Internal Revenue Service to enforce the act, since it already administered
the National Firearms Act. The Commissioner of Internal Revenue
duly promulgated regulations but in so doing did not exercise all
the authority given him by the act.[26] In a belated attempt to correct this deficiency, the Service in 1957 proposed changes in these
regulations. One change would have required all manufacturers
and importers to imprint a serial number on each firearm. Another
would have required each purchaser of a rifle or shotgun to sign for
the weapon. Still another would have required manufacturers and
dealers to maintain records of ammunition sales and to retain all

[21]Sheldon S. Cohen, Commissioner of Internal Revenue, Hearings before the Senate
Subcommittee To Investigate Juvenile Delinquency, 89th Cong., 1st sess., pp. 70-71
(1965).

[22]Sheldon S. Cohen, Commissioner of Internal Revenue, Hearings before the House
Committee on Ways and Means, 89th Cong., 1st sess., pp. 151-152 (1965).

[23]*Ibid;* Sheldon S. Cohen, Commissioner of Internal Revenue, Hearing before the
Senate Subcommittee To Investigate Juvenile Delinquency, 90th Cong., 1st sess.,
p. 57 (1967).

[24]Joseph W. Barr, Under Secretary of the Treasury, Hearings before the Senate Subcommittee To Investigate Juvenile Delinquency, 90th Cong., 1st sess., p. 40 (1967).

[25]Sheldon S. Cohen, Commissioner of Internal Revenue, Hearings before the House
Committee on Ways and Means, 89th Cong., 1st sess., pp. 153-161 (1965). An
example of such form was recommended by the National Rifle Association in the
American Rifleman, Oct. 1968, p. 130.

[26]Sheldon S. Cohen, Commissioner of Internal Revenue, Hearings before the Senate
Subcommittee To Investigate Juvenile Delinquency, 90th Cong., 2d sess., p. 127
(1968).

sales records permanently rather than for 6 years. But even then
the Service did not propose that dealer licenses be issued only to
persons actually in business or that purchasers be required to produce identification.[27]

The proposed changes were opposed by the National Rifle Association, firearms manufacturers and dealers, and many outdoor
writers.[28]

In response to this opposition,[29] the Service retreated from its
proposed regulations, dropping the dealer's record keeping requirement for ammunition sales and the requirement that firearms buyers
sign for guns. Serial numbering of handguns and high-powered
rifles, but not of .22 caliber rifles, was adopted, and dealers were
required to retain sales records for 10 years, not permanently.[30]

Three years earlier, in 1954, the Mutual Security Act had empowered the President to regulate the flow of firearms and ammunition exports and imports "in furtherance of world peace and the
security and foreign policy of the United States." [31] The President
vested this power in the Office of Munitions Control of the State
Department. Under State Department regulations, persons engaged
in importing, exporting, or manufacturing "munitions" are required
to register, pay a $75 annual fee, and keep records of firearms ac-
quisitions and disposals for 6 years. Prior approval is required for
every export and import shipment. However, customs regulations
have permitted individuals to bring into the country three firearms
and 1,000 rounds of ammunition without prior approval.[32]

The State Department construes the Mutual Security Act to allow
it to control firearms imports only to the extent of determining
whether they are consigned to authorized dealers or individuals. In
approving or disapproving imports, the Department applies foreign
policy considerations—banning, for instance, importation of firearms manufactured in Communist countries. But the Department

---

[27]See 22 F.R. 3153 (May 3, 1957); 22 F.R. 4851 (July 10, 1957).
[28]Sheldon S. Cohen, Commissioner of Internal Revenue, Hearings before the Senate
Subcommittee To Investigate Juvenile Delinquency, 90th Cong., 2d sess., pp. 126-
127 (1968).
[29]The arguments used by the opposition, which even urged repeal of all federal firearms
laws, were essentially the same arguments used in the 1930's. Indeed, the timelessness
of some of these arguments can be seen from a debate handbook by Lamar T. Beman,
Outlawing the Pistol (New York: H. W. Wilson, 1926), an excerpt from which is attached as App. I.
[30]23 F.R. 343 (Jan. 18, 1958).
[31]22 U.S.C. 1934 (1967).
[32]22 C.F.R. 121-25.

contends the act gives it no "authority to deny importation of fire-arms for which there is a legitimate commercial market merely because some of these guns at some point get in the hands of juve-niles or incompetents." [33]

In the 1950's, sales of firearms by domestic manufacturers de-creased substantially as a result of competition from imported for-eign military weapons. Some of these foreign weapons were left over from World War II, and others were rendered surplus when NATO adopted a common cartridge about 1953. Domestic manu-facturers appealed to the State Department for relief under the Mutual Security Act, contending that their diminishing sales had forced the layoff of skilled gunsmiths and the scrapping of modern-ization projects, to the "imperilment of national security." [34]

The State Department apparently did not agree that national security was endangered by the rising tide of imports and refused to change its import policies. Thereupon, on April 28, 1958, then Senator John F. Kennedy of Massachusetts, a firearms producing state,[35] introduced a bill to "prohibit the importation of firearms originally manufactured for military purposes." [36] But the bill failed to pass. Instead, a substitute was enacted, which only pro-hibited the importation of military weapons which the United States had sent abroad under its foreign assistance program.

Early in 1957, the U.S. Senate Subcommittee on Juvenile Delin-quency began an inquiry into the relationship between weapons, particularly firearms, and juvenile delinquency. Answers to ques-tionnaires sent to police chiefs and criminologists led the sub-committee to launch a full-scale study of firearms in the early 1960's.[37] Following public hearings in 1963, Senator Thomas J. Dodd, subcommittee chairman, introduced a bill requiring any mail-order buyer of handguns to furnish the seller a notarized statement that he was over 18, not a convicted felon or under

[33]John W. Sipes, Director of the Office of Munitions Control, Department of State, Senate Subcommittee To Investigate Juvenile Delinquency, 90th Cong., 1st sess., pp. 192-193, 238 (1967).

[34]See Petition of 6 American Sporting Arms Manufacturers to the Office of Civil and Defense Mobilization, June 29, 1959.

[35]See James E. Serven, "Massachusetts: Cradle of American Gunmaking," *American Rifleman,* No. 26 (Mar. 1968).

[36]S. 3714, 104 Cong. Rec. 7442 (Apr. 28, 1958). Ironically, the Kennedy bill would have barred from this country the gun which was used to kill its sponsor 5 years later.

[37]See S. Rept. 1903, Committee on the Judiciary, 87th Cong., 2d sess. (Aug. 21, 1962); S. Rept. 1429, Committee on the Judiciary, 85th Cong., 2d sess., pp. 7-8 (Mar. 27, 1958).

indictment for a felony, and that shipment of the gun would not violate any local law. The bill also required the seller to notify the carrier whenever he dispatched a package containing a handgun and forbade the carrier from delivering to anyone it had reason to believe was under 18.[38]

Four days after President Kennedy was assassinated, the Dodd bill was amended to cover rifles and shotguns. The amended bill would have required each buyer of a mail-order gun to list the name and address of the chief law enforcement officer in his area, and required the seller, before shipment, to notify that officer by registered mail.[39]

But even the new Dodd bill fell short of the strict firearms controls for which a Gallup poll found wide popular support. In December 1963, this poll showed that 79 percent of the population expressed the view that no one should be permitted to own a gun without a police permit.[40]

As hearings continued, mail, which had run eight to one in favor of the bill shortly after the assassination, began instead to reflect substantial opposition. In a 2-week period the Commerce Committee received 20,000 letters, postcards, and telegrams in opposition to the bill and only two in support.[41] The Dodd bill died in committee, along with other firearms bills introduced in Congress in 1963 and 1964.

Senator Dodd reintroduced the bill in the next Congress and added a new bill to restrict the importation of military surplus weapons. On March 8, 1965, President Johnson proposed gun control legislation to "assist local authorities in coping with an undeniable menace to law and order." Senator Dodd introduced

---

[38]See S. Rept. 1608, Committee on the Judiciary, 88th Cong., 2d sess., pp. 6-7 (Oct. 2, 1964).

[39]Ibid.

[40]In 1938 a Gallup poll asked: "Do you think all owners of pistols and revolvers should be required to register with the government?" Seventy-nine percent of the sample replied in the affirmative. In Jan. 1940 the same question produced a 73 percent affirmative response. In July 1959, Gallup asked: "Would you favor or oppose a law which would require a police permit for the purchase of guns, shells, or ammunition?" Fifty-four percent favored such a law. In December 1963, just after President Kennedy's assassination, 79 percent of the people favored requiring a police permit to buy a gun. The same question elicited a 73 percent favorable response in Jan. 1965, 71 percent in Sept. 1965, 68 percent in Aug. 1966, and 73 percent in Aug. 1967. (Information supplied by Ithiel deSola Pool, Massachusetts Institute of Technology.)

[41]Richard Harris, "Annals of Legislation: If You Love Your Guns," New Yorker, Apr. 20, 1968.

the administration proposal in the Senate, and an identical bill was introduced in the House.[42] These bills would have—

(1) Prohibited the interstate mail-order sale of firearms to individuals;

(2) Prohibited over-the-counter sales of handguns to persons from out of state;

(3) Prohibited importation of firearms not usable for "sporting purposes";

(4) Set 18 as the minimum age for the purchase of rifles and shotguns and 21 as the minimum age for the purchase of handguns; and

(5) Provided new standards and increased fees for becoming a licensed firearms dealer.[43]

Extensive hearings were held in both the Senate and the House on these and other firearms bills, but no bill was reported out of committee in 1965.

In March 1966, the Juvenile Delinquency Subcommittee sent a slightly amended firearms bill to the Senate Judiciary Committee, where it remained for a number of months. Then, on August 1, Charles J. Whitman killed or wounded some 44 persons by rifle fire from the tower of the University of Texas. The next day the President renewed his call for gun legislation, and the Judiciary Committee agreed to discuss the latest Dodd bill at its next meeting. However, there was no quorum at that meeting and no action was taken until late September, when the committee rejected the administration bill in favor of a bill that did little more than limit interstate shipment of handguns.[44] This bill was not reported out of committee until 3 days before the 89th Congress adjourned—too late for any action to be taken.[45]

In 1967, President Johnson again urged gun control measures, and Senator Dodd again introduced the administration proposal, substantially identical to the original administration proposal in the previous Congress.[46] About this time, the President's Commission on Law Enforcement and the Administration of Justice issued its report recommending far stricter firearms legislation than the

---

[42]Senator Thomas J. Dodd, Hearings before the Senate Subcommittee To Investigate Juvenile Delinquency, 89th Cong., 1st sess., pp. 1-19 (1965).

[43]*Ibid.*

[44]S. Rept. 1866, Committee on the Judiciary, 89th Cong., 2d sess. (Oct. 19, 1966).

[45]See *Congressional Quarterly,* pp. 812-13 (Apr. 12, 1968).

[46]Senator Thomas J. Dodd, Hearings before the Senate Subcommittee To Investigate Juvenile Delinquency, 90th Cong., 1st sess., pp. 1-26 (1967).

administration had suggested—including state laws requiring a license to possess a handgun and federal registration of all guns within 5 years for all states failing to establish their own registration systems.[47]

Firearms legislation never reached the floor of either Chamber of Congress in 1967, although subcommittees of the House and Senate Judiciary Committees approved the administration bill—the first time in years that a firearms control bill was approved by a House committee.[48]

In his 1968 State of the Union address, President Johnson urged Congress to enact a law prohibiting the mail-order sale of firearms. Congress had not acted on April 4, 1968, when Dr. Martin Luther King, Jr., was fatally shot in Memphis, Tenn. In the wake of subsequent riots, the Congress did not outlaw mail-order sales of firearms, but it did include in the Civil Rights Act of 1968 an amendment subjecting to federal penalties anyone who manufactures or transports a firearm in interstate commerce intending that it be used in a civil disorder, or who instructs another person in the use of firearms with the knowledge, reason to know, or intent that the person use the firearm in a civil disorder.[49]

On April 29, 1968, the Senate Judiciary Committee reported favorably on a bill providing for federal grants to state law enforcement agencies which the House had passed in 1967. The new Senate bill added among other things provisions relating to the control of handguns. During the Senate debate in May, Senator Edward M. Kennedy offered an amendment incorporating the administration proposals restricting mail-order sale of all firearms, but the amendment was defeated by a 53-29 vote.[50] The bill was passed in the Senate, but the House did not consent to the Senate changes.

On June 5, 1968, Senator Robert F. Kennedy, after winning the California presidential primary, was mortally wounded by an assailant armed with a .22 caliber revolver.[51] After the Senator's death, President Johnson urged Congress and the 50 states to adopt comprehensive gun controls. Of the bill then pending in the House, he stated: "This halfway measure is not enough. It covers adequately only transactions involving handguns. It leaves the deadly commerce in lethal shotguns and rifles without effective control. . . ."

---

[47]"The Challenge of Crime in a Free Society," *Report*, President's Committee on Law Enforcement and the Administration of Justice 242-243 (1967). See App. A.
[48]See *Congressional Quarterly*, p. 813 (Apr. 12, 1968).
[49]82 Stat. 90, Public Law 90-284.
[50]*New York Times*, June 9, 1968, p. 2E.
[51]*New York Times*, June 6, 1968, p. 1; *New York Times*, June 5, 1968, p. 1.

He called on the Congress to ban mail-order sales of long guns as well as handguns and to ban sales to youngsters and nonresidents. He also asked the Governors of the 50 states to review and amend their firearms laws. The House, however, passed the pending Senate bill and sent it to the President for his signature.[52] In spite of his disapproval of certain of its provisions, the President on June 19, 1968, signed the Omnibus Crime Control and Safe Streets Act of 1968.[53]

Two of the 10 titles in this act relate to firearms. Title IV is the administration's firearms control bill. In this title, Congress declared: "[T]he ease with which any person can acquire firearms other than a rifle or shotgun. . . is a significant factor in the prevalence of lawlessness and violent crime in the United States."[54] Title IV repealed the Federal Firearms Act of 1938, effective December 19, 1968, and replaced it with other restrictions, particularly on handguns.[55]

In Title VII of this act, Congress declared:

that the receipt, possession or transportation of a firearm by felons, veterans who are other than honorably discharged, mental incompetents, aliens who are illegally in the country, and former citizens who have renounced their citizenship, constitutes—

(1) a burden on commerce or threat affecting the free flow of commerce,

(2) a threat to the safety of the President of the United States and Vice President of the United States,

(3) an impediment or a threat to the exercise of free speech and the free exercise of religion guaranteed by the first amendment to the Constitution of the United States, and

(4) a threat to the continued and effective operation of the Government of the United States and of the government of each state guaranteed by Article IV of the Constitution.[56]

The operative provisions of Title VII make illegal the receipt, possession, or transportation in commerce of firearms by the per-

---

[52]*New York Times,* June 7, 1968, p. 1.
[53]82 Stat. 197, Public Law 90-351 (June 19, 1968).
[54]82 Stat. 225, Public Law 90-351 (June 19, 1968).
[55]82 Stat. 225-235, Public Law 90-351 (June 19, 1968).
[56]82 Stat. 236-237, Public Law 90-351 (June 19, 1968).

sons described, or their employees in the course of employment, and establish a maximum penalty of 2 years' imprisonment and a $10,000 fine.[57]

Even while President Johnson was signing the Omnibus Crime Bill, committees in the House and Senate were laboring over bills to extend its provisions to include rifles and shotguns.[58] When the President, 6 days later, called again for federal registration of all firearms, the congressional committees were not receptive to the proposal and delayed acting on any of the new firearms bills.[59] After 3 months, however, the Gun Control Act of 1968 was passed and signed.[60]

Under the Gun Control Act of 1968, which revises Title IV of the Omnibus Crime Bill—

(1) no one except licensed manufacturers, dealers, and importers may "engage in the business" of importing, manufacturing, or dealing in firearms or ammunition or "in the course of such business" ship, transport, or receive any firearm or ammunition in interstate commerce;

(2) standards for obtaining firearms licenses are considerably tightened and fees raised;

(3) licensees may not ship firearms or ammunition interstate to nonlicensees;

(4) licensees may not furnish firearms or ammunition to anyone they know or have reason to believe is a fugitive from justice, a convicted felon or under indictment for a felony, an unlawful drug user or addict, or an adjudicated mental defective or one who has been committed to any mental institution;

(5) licensees may not sell rifles or shotguns or ammunition therefor to anyone they know or have reason to believe is under 18 or handguns or ammunition therefor to anyone under 21;

(6) licensees may not sell firearms or ammunition to anyone who is prohibited from possessing or purchasing by state or local law applicable at the place of sale or delivery, unless there is reason to believe the purchase or possession is not illegal;

(7) licensees may not sell firearms to persons who do not appear personally, unless the purchaser submits a sworn statement that his purchase is legal, a copy of which the licensee must forward to the

---

[57]*Ibid.*

[58]See H. Rept. 1577, Committee on the Judiciary, 90th Cong., 2d sess., pp. 6-7 (June 21, 1968).

[59]*New York Times,* June 30, 1968, p. 1E.

[60]82 Stat. 1213, Public Law 90-618 (Oct. 22, 1968).

chief law enforcement officer in the purchaser's locality 7 days before shipment;

(8) licensees must note in their records the names, ages, and places of residence of firearms and ammunition purchasers;

(9) licensed importers and manufacturers are required to put serial numbers on all firearms;

(10) fugitives from justice, convicted felons or persons under indictment for a felony, unlawful users of certain drugs, adjudicated mental defectives, and persons once committed to a mental institution may not receive, ship, or transport any firearm or ammunition in interstate or foreign commerce or receive any firearm or ammunition which has been so shipped or transported;

(11) no one may provide a firearm to anyone who he knows or has reason to believe is a nonresident of the state;

(12) no one except licensees may transport into or receive in their state of residence firearms acquired elsewhere;

(13) no one may deliver a firearm or ammunition to any carrier without written notice;

(14) carriers may not transport or deliver firearms or ammunition in interstate commerce with knowledge or reasonable cause to believe the shipment, transportation, or receipt would violate the act;

(15) no one may make a false statement intended to or likely to deceive a licensee with respect to the lawfulness of his acquisition of a firearm or ammunition;

(16) no one may import a firearm unless he satisfies the Secretary of the Treasury that it is "particularly suitable for or readily adaptable to sporting purposes" and is not a surplus military firearm;

(17) nonlicensees may not transport, ship, or receive in interstate commerce and licensees may not sell or deliver to anyone any "destructive device" (explosive, incendiary, poison gas, grenade, mine, rocket, missile, or weapon with a bore of one-half inch or more), machine gun, short-barreled rifle, or short-barreled shotgun, except as specifically authorized by the Secretary of the Treasury consistent with "public safety and necessity."

The maximum penalty for violation of any of the above provisions is a 5-year prison term and a $5,000 fine. Additionally, shipment, transportation, or receipt of a firearm with intent to commit an offense punishable by imprisonment for more than 1 year, or with knowledge or reasonable cause to believe that such an offense is to be committed with the firearm, is punishable by a fine up to $10,000 and imprisonment up to 10 years. Anyone who uses or carries a firearm in the commission of a federal felony is liable for imprisonment from 1 to 10 years for the first offense, and from 5 years to life for the second. A second offender may not be given a suspended or probationary sentence.

Certain of the above provisions have minor exceptions, some of which are important enough to note. First, a licensee may sell a firearm to a resident of a contiguous state "if the purchaser's state of residence permits such sale or delivery by law,"[61] and if an affidavit of legality is furnished by the purchaser. The dealer must send notice of the sale to the chief law enforcement officer of the out-of-state locality where the nonresident says he lives; 7 days after receiving a return receipt of such notice, the dealer may turn the firearm over to the contiguous state resident. Second, a licensee may loan or rent a firearm to a nonresident for temporary use for lawful sporting purposes.[62] Third, the act does not apply to the loan or sale of firearms or ammunition through the National Board for the Promotion of Rifle Practice.

The act also provides for the issuance of licenses to "collectors" of firearms who deal in firearms "curios and relics." The statute deliberately leaves open the definition of what firearms are "curios and relics." Finally, members of the armed forces are permitted to have certain "war souvenirs."

The Gun Control Act also amended Title VII of the Omnibus Crime Bill to provide that only "dishonorably" (rather than "other than honorably") discharged veterans may not possess firearms.[63]

The provisions of the Gun Control Act of 1968 have been reviewed in detail[64] to demonstrate the underlying federal firearms policy of using federal power to curtail interstate commerce in fire-

---

[61]As of this writing, the IRS interprets this to require enabling legislation by the contiguous states before interstate shipments can be made. This interpretation has been criticized by shooting and hunting clubs.

[62]It is possible that this provision could be used to evade the law by allowing firearms to change hands as rentals with high security deposits.

[63]Usually only one or two persons per year receive dishonorable discharges. Information provided by Col. David Martin, Action Officer, Separation Branch, Promotions and Separations Division, U.S. Army, on Nov. 13, 1968, to Research Associates, Inc., and printed in "A Preliminary Cost Analysis of Firearms Control Programs," Dec. 20, 1968, p. 46.

[64]Some other more specialized federal laws and regulations pertaining to firearms might be mentioned. The Federal Aviation Act of 1958 (49 U.S.C. § 1472), for instance, prohibits persons without special authorization from carrying a firearm on or about their person while aboard a carrier aircraft, although unloaded firearms in baggage not accessible to the passenger are permitted (FAA Regulation No. SR-448A). Hunting and the use of firearms in national parks and monuments are also prohibited (36 C.F.R. §31). Further, there are many regulations governing the transportation of explosives.

arms and leaving each of the states free to adopt the degree of control it sees fit. This policy may be a desirable balance between federal and state power. On the other hand, even if the interstate flow of firearms is successfully restricted, the policy may not provide sufficient protection from the misuse of firearms if too many states refuse to adequately regulate the sale and ownership of firearms.

Whatever the effectiveness of the current federal firearms policy, the prospect for developing a more effective policy is not encouraging. In spite of continuous public support for more stringent control of firearms since the 1930's, federal firearms laws have been enacted in this country only after sensational acts of violence have shocked the nation. Moreover, public debate on the problems of firearms misuse too often involves little more than repeating hackneyed arguments that only harden already firmly held views. Further research on the long range effect of current firearms policy and upon the relationship of firearms to violence will, hopefully, improve the quality of future debates on firearms policy in the United States.

Summary

Public opinion in this country has favored regulation of firearms since the 1930's. Yet, from the enactment of the first federal firearms possession law in 1934, federal gun laws have been enacted in this country only after sensational episodes of gun violence. The Gun Control Act of 1968, which followed the assassinations of Dr. Martin Luther King, Jr., and Senator Robert F. Kennedy, commits the federal government to support state and city gun control laws by reducing the interstate flow of firearms which has long frustrated local control efforts. Proposals for a federal system of screening firearms owners have not been enacted.

Chapter 15

FIREARMS CONTROL AND
THE CONSTITUTION

In the United States, the powers granted to federal and state legislatures are limited by the federal Constitution. Two provisions in the first 10 amendments to the Constitution are of significance to firearms control—the right to bear arms mentioned in the second amendment and the fifth amendment privilege against self-incrimination.[1]

The Second Amendment

The amendment is sometimes quoted in a way that would cast doubt on the constitutionality of all firearms control laws—"the right of the people to keep and bear Arms shall not be infringed." But this is only the second half of the sentence which reads in full: "A well regulated Militia, being necessary to the security of a free State, the right of the people to keep and bear Arms shall not be infringed."

The U.S. Supreme Court and lower courts have consistently interpreted the second amendment as a prohibition against federal interference with the state militia and not as a guarantee of an individual's right to bear arms. The courts thus read the amendment as relating solely to collective military preparedness and conclude that the federal government may regulate firearms as it wishes, so long as it does not thereby interfere with state military personnel in the performance of their official duties with the state militia. Nor does the amendment restrict the power of the states to regulate firearms. Each state may control firearms as it wishes, consistent with its own constitution, so long as it does not interfere with the exercise of federal powers, such as the power to equip the army.[2]

---

[1]The broad power of the federal government to regulate interstate commerce would seem a sufficient basis to support most federal firearms laws.
[2]For a more elaborate discussion of these principles, see App. J.

The Fifth Amendment

The fifth amendment privilege against self-incrimination confers a much discussed[3] individual right to refuse to help the government secure one's own conviction. This privilege applies not only to criminal cases but also to civil and administrative proceedings if there is a likelihood of later criminal prosecution. Therefore, it was not entirely unexpected when, in January 1968, the Supreme Court of the United States handed down three cases that created a fifth amendment problem for firearms control laws.[4]

As discussed in detail in Appendix K, the most prudent way to view these cases is to assume that fifth amendment objections to firearms control statutes will be sustained when those statutes require a person to reveal that he is in violation of some federal, state, or local law. Suppose, for instance, a felon possesses a firearm in violation of some law.[5] By registering the fact of his possession, he clearly would incriminate himself.

There are a number of ways of dealing with this registration problem. The first is to ignore it. The felon thus has two courses of action: he may simply not register and still be able to defeat any prosecution for his failure to register by claiming the fifth amendment privilege. He will, however, still be liable for illegal possession of a firearm. On the other hand, the felon might register. Since that registration would have been required by law, he would be able to defeat any criminal prosecution for possession of a firearm if that prosecution is based on information obtained from his registration. Therefore, in order to prosecute successfully for illegal firearms possession, the authorities would have to establish that their evidence was in no way obtained from the registration

---

[3]See, e.g., Mansfield, *The Albertson Case: Conflict Between the Privilege Against Self-Incrimination and the Government's Need for Information,* 1966 Sup. Ct. Rev. 103; McKay, *Self-Incrimination and the New Privacy,* 1967 Sup. Ct. Rev. 193; Note, *Required Information and the Privilege against Self-Incrimination,* 65 Colum. L. Rev. 681 (1965). One observer has concluded that "the law and lawyers have never made up their minds just what [the privilege] . . . is supposed to protect." Kalvan, *Invoking the Fifth Amendment: Some Legal and Impractical Considerations, 9 Bull. Atom. Sci.,* pp. 181, 182-83 (1953).

[4]*Haynes* v. *United States,* 390 U.S. 85 (1968); *Grosso* v. *United States,* 390 U.S. 62 (1968); *Marchetti* v. *United States,* 390 U.S. 39 (1968). For a discussion of these cases, see App. K.

[5]The Omnibus Crime Control and Safe Streets Act of 1968, 82 Stat. 197, 236-37 (June 19, 1968), prohibits felons from possessing firearms.

system.[6] Such proof might be difficult, and state authorities are not pleased at the prospect.[7]

A second possible approach is to incorporate a "restrictive use" provision into the registration statute. Recent amendments to the National Firearms Act, for example, require every person owning a firearm covered by the act to register, whether his possession is legal or not. But none of the registration information may "be used directly or indirectly, as evidence against that person in a criminal proceeding with respect to a violation of law occurring prior to or concurrently with registration."[8]

Under this approach, a person who illegally possesses a firearm can be prosecuted if he fails to register. Of course, he could have been prosecuted for illegal possession anyway, so this merely creates two offenses where only one formerly existed. Perhaps such a system would encourage illegal possessors to register out of fear of a possible additional criminal charge. But this seems unlikely. A

---

[6]This was recognized by the Supreme Court in *Marchetti* v. *United States,* 390 U.S. 39 (1968), which overturned a federal wagering tax statute. The government had argued, and Chief Justice Warren in dissent took the view, that the wagering tax statute should be upheld but that further criminal use of any information obtained under the statute should be prohibited. The Court refused to adopt this approach:

> [T]he imposition of such restrictions would necessarily oblige state prosecuting authorities to establish in each case that their evidence was untainted by any connection with information obtained as a consequence of the wagering taxes; the federal requirements would thus be protected only at the cost of hampering, perhaps seriously, enforcement of state prohibitions against gambling. 390 U.S. at 59-60.

[7]". . . I would oppose the enactment of federal legislation [requiring] . . . the registration of weapons. . . . [I]f this were a federal requirement, it could create grave constitutional problems with respect to the enforcement of state law prohibiting possession of the registered weapon. . . . [T]he Supreme Court . . . in the recent *Haynes* decision [ruled that compliance with the] . . . federal requirement for registration of sawed-off shotguns and rifles . . . would violate the privilege against self-incrimination of an individual who had failed to register such a weapon. This means in effect . . . that if an individual had registered the weapon under federal law, and then were brought before a state court for violation of the state law as applied to the same weapon, he might very well assert that the state prosecution was tainted by the unconstitutional disclosure under the federal law. . . . . . [T]his would. . .mean that the state authorities had to assume the burden of proving that the facts upon which they proceeded did not depend upon the disclosure made under the federal law." Testimony of Elliot L. Richardson, Attorney General, Commonwealth of Massachusetts, Commission Hearings, Oct. 10, 1968, Tr. 1272-1273. See also testimony of Luis M. Neco, Deputy Police Commissioner of the Police Department of the City of New York, Commission Hearings, Oct. 10, 1968, Tr. 1241-1242.

The Commissioner of Internal Revenue, on the other hand, believes a federal registration law would create no substantial problem. By restricting access to registration records, and requiring all who use the records to sign for the material used, he asserts, the federal government could readily prove that a given prosecution was not the product of information from its files. See testimony of Sheldon S. Cohen, Commissioner of Internal Revenue, Commission Hearings, Oct. 9, 1968, Tr. 1091-1095.

[8]82 Stat. 1232, Public Law 90-618 (Oct. 22, 1968).

person already taking a risk by illegally possessing a firearm is not likely to be greatly deterred by the prospect of an additional penalty for not registering. Additionally, it has been federal practice not to prosecute under the National Firearms Act when a state prosecutes for some other offense. If followed generally, this practice would undercut any possible deterrence arising out of a second penalty.

Under this approach also, in any prosecution for illegal possession, the authorities would have to establish that their evidence was untainted by the defendant's registration. Further, there are problems in drafting such a restrictive use provision, for it must be "coextensive" with the protection offered by the fifth amendment.[9] The Supreme Court has ruled that the fifth amendment covers future or "prospective," as well as past, criminal acts, although it has observed that "prospective acts will doubtless ordinarily involve only speculative and insubstantial risks of incrimination."[10]

A third possible approach is that adopted by the gun registration ordinance of the City of Chicago. This ordinance provides that any person who possesses a firearm in violation of any Chicago, state, or federal law is *not* required to register and that any attempted purported registration is null and void.[11] The hypothetical felon thus need not register in Chicago. He will still be liable for illegal possession, however, and the authorities who prosecute him for this offense will not have to establish that their evidence is untainted by information from the registration files. If the felon does register, his doing so clearly was not "compelled" and he has no claim under the fifth amendment.

By requiring legitimate users to register their firearms and exempting illegitimate users, the Chicago approach creates an apparent paradox. Registration, however, is only one aspect of a total system of firearms control. Provisions making it illegal for ineligible persons to possess a firearm are all that is needed to send the illegal possessor to jail when he is discovered. Registration contributes to firearms control not by pointing the finger at illegal possessors but by reducing the flow of guns from legitimate to illegitimate users. Given this limited function, making registration ap-

---

9See, e.g., *Counselman* v. *Hitchcock*, 142 U.S. 547, 585 (1892).
10*Marchetti* v. *United States*, 390 U.S. 39, 45 (1968). The meaning of "speculative and insubstantial" is not clear. Does the intent by a person, whose possession of a firearm is legal, to use that gun in a future holdup create a "substantial" risk that registration will serve to incriminate him? Probably not, but only a future court case can resolve the issue.
11Chicago Municipal Code, ch. 11.1 (1968).

plicable only to all legitimate gun owners is not paradoxical but is a consistent part of a larger system of firearms control.

There is still another way of minimizing fifth amendment objections. Requiring an owner to register the gun he possesses in violation of some law may raise a fifth amendment objection. Requiring firearms dealers to supply information about persons who obtain firearms from the dealers would seem to present fewer difficulties under the fifth amendment because the person supplying the information is no longer incriminating himself. In addition, the dealers could be granted immunity from any prosecution for the illegal sale of firearms and then be obliged to supply information which might incriminate illegal gun buyers. Similarly, whenever a gun is sold or given away by a private individual, the former owner can be given immunity and required to submit information on the gun and its new owner. As discussed in Chapter 12, a notice similar to the warranty card now in use with many products might readily be adapted to this purpose and probably would not create fifth amendment difficulties.

Fifth amendment problems may still linger on the fringe of firearms control. For instance, fifth amendment objections might be raised about firearms licensing laws. A firearms statute which simply prohibits possession of firearms by defined classes of persons—such as felons—cannot raise a fifth amendment problem. Yet license systems requiring persons to file an application by which authorities pass upon their qualifications and involving the maintenance of records on who owns what firearms might lead to self-incrimination when information obtained during the application process leads authorities to uncover a crime in which the applicant has been involved.

An application that requires one to list all firearms presently owned might also create a fifth amendment question when a license is denied by the authorities who suspect from the filing of the application that the applicant may still possess a firearm. Even if this process is found to be incrimination, it might be "prospective," and it is difficult to anticipate whether the Supreme Court would rule that the fifth amendment has been violated.

Until these questions are resolved, all firearms licensing and registration statutes must be carefully drafted to minimize possible conflict with the fifth amendment.

Summary

The second amendment raises no legal barrier to federal or state firearms legislation. The fifth amendment, however, could be invoked against enforcement of such laws. Fifth amendment problems might be minimized by exempting from licensing, registration, or transfer notice requirements all persons in those categories prohibited by law from possessing firearms. This exemption of illegal possessors would not decrease the effectiveness of firearms control because other parts of the control system could allow prosecution of such persons without requiring them to incriminate themselves.

Chapter 16

FOREIGN FIREARMS LAWS

Firearms control systems that appear to work well in other countries with cultures and traditions different from the United States would not necessarily help to lessen the American problem of firearms misuse. Yet it would be unwise to ignore what other nations have accomplished in controlling firearms violence.

Our sources in this chapter are collections of foreign firearms statutes and rough estimates of handgun ownership rates supplied by representatives of foreign governments. The text of a firearms law is, of course, an insufficient basis for evaluating the quality of any country's firearms control system since the laws on the books may not be enforced. Yet such laws do illustrate the variety of ways in which other countries attempt to control the misuse of firearms.

During 1968, two surveys of foreign firearms laws were made. The State Department asked 102 of its diplomatic posts for information on local firearms laws, and the Library of Congress analyzed firearms laws of 30 countries, predominantly in Europe.[1] The 29 European countries reviewed[2] require either a license to carry a firearm or registration of the ownership or sale of each privately owned firearm, or both.

At least five European countries totally prohibit the private possession of handguns.[3] In regard to other types of firearms, the Soviet Union allows anyone with a hunting license to possess smooth-bore hunting arms. Shotguns were not stringently controlled in England until 1968, when a form of shotgun licensing was established.

---

[1]Albania, Austria, Belgium, Bulgaria, Canada, Ceylon, Czechoslovakia, Denmark, France, East Germany, West Germany, Great Britain, Greece, Hungary, Israel, Italy, Japan, the Netherlands, Norway, Peru, Poland, Rumania, the Soviet Union, Spain, Sweden, Switzerland, Turkey, Uganda, Venezuela, and Yugoslavia.
[2]Albania, Austria, Belgium, Bulgaria, Cyprus, Czechoslovakia, Denmark, England, Finland, France, East Germany, West Germany, Greece, Hungary, Iceland, Ireland, Italy, Luxembourg, Malta, the Netherlands, Norway, Poland, Portugal, Rumania, Spain, Sweden, Switzerland, the Soviet Union, and Yugoslavia.
[3]Albania, Cyprus, Greece, Ireland, and the Soviet Union.

In North and South America, 15 of the 19 canvassed countries[4] require a license to possess or to carry a firearm or registration of all firearms, or all of these. Paraguay has no controls whatsoever. Mexico has only local controls; El Salvador imposes no restrictions except in urban areas; and Nicaragua has no restrictions on ownership but does limit carrying of firearms.

In Asia and Australia, 21 countries[5] were canvassed and all require either a license to possess or carry or registration of firearms, or both. The only exceptions are Australia and New Zealand, which impose no restrictions on shotguns, although they have severe restrictions on handguns, and Afghanistan, which imposes no restrictions on sporting weapons, although it, like Japan, completely outlaws possession of handguns.

In Africa, 25 of the 33 nations[6] canvassed require registration of the ownership or sale of firearms. The remaining eight have licensing systems relating to ownership or carrying. Three[7] entirely prohibit the possession of handguns, four prohibit possession of military weapons,[8] and one (Algeria) allows sporting firearms to be possessed only by sporting clubs.

While these surveys may conceal substantial gaps between law and practice, they disclose that foreign countries, with few exceptions, have comprehensive national systems of firearms control. Although national firearms control may not be as appropriate for the federal system in this country, it must be noted that such large and diverse countries as Canada and Brazil have both adopted national programs of firearms control.

These surveys also show that while many foreign countries regulate all firearms without distinguishing between different types, other countries treat handguns and long guns differently, prohibiting or regulating handguns while imposing fewer restrictions on rifles or shotguns. In many countries, the distinction between long guns and handguns is an accepted part of firearms control and

---

[4]Barbados, Bolivia, Brazil, Canada, Chile, Colombia, Costa Rica, Dominican Republic, Ecuador, El Salvador, Guatemala, Jamaica, Mexico, Nicaragua, Panama, Paraguay, Peru, Trinidad and Tobago, Venezuela.
[5]Afghanistan, Australia, Ceylon, India, Indonesia, Israel, Japan, Jordan, Kuwait, Laos, Malaysia, Nepal, New Zealand, Pakistan, Philippines, Saudi Arabia, Singapore, South Vietnam, Thailand, Turkey, Upper Volta.
[6]Algeria, Botswana, Burundi, Cameroon, Central African Republic, Chad, Dahomey, Ethiopia, Ghana, Guinea, Guyana, Kenya, Lesotho, Liberia, Libya, Malagasy Republic, Malawi, Mali, Mauritius, Morocco, Niger, Nigeria, Rhodesia, Rwanda, Senegal, Sierra Leone, Somalia, U. of S. Africa, Tanzania, Togo, Tunisia, Uganda, and Zambia.
[7]Guinea, Morocco, and Tanzania.
[8]Algeria, Chad, Malagasy Republic, and Senegal.

not a way-station toward extending handgun regulation to long
guns as well.

In order to provide some insight into firearms ownership in foreign countries, representatives of 20 foreign governments were
asked to provide estimates of handgun ownership per 100,000
population. Responses were received from 10 countries and reflect
a significant contrast to handgun ownership in the United States.
Table 16-1 shows the estimates of handgun ownership for five
European countries with significant rural populations—Ireland,
Greece, Finland, Yugoslavia, and Austria; two densely populated
European countries—the Netherlands and Great Britain; two nations with widespread military training—Switzerland and Israel; and
finally Canada and the United States.

Table 16-1—Estimated handgun ownership per 100,000 population.

Ireland	Under 500
Finland	Under 500
Netherlands	Under 500
Greece	Under 500
Great Britain	Under 500
Switzerland	(*)
Yugoslavia	500-1,000
Israel	1,000
Austria	3,000
Canada	3,000
United States	13,500**

*"Insignificant."
**See ch. 1.

Source: Consulates of countries involved.

A few of the handgun estimates in Table 16-1 deserve special
mention. Israel, close to a state of war, still has relatively few private handguns. The Swiss response reflects a distinction between
long guns and handguns:

It is generally felt that the number of handguns in possession
of civilians is rather insignificant as there seems to be no special need for self-protection. On the other hand every Swiss
male of military age keeps his uniform and with it the assault
rifle with 48 bullets at home.

Canada, with a frontier tradition and a great expanse of sparsely populated territory, owns handguns at a rate about a fourth of the U.S. rate.[9]

The European countries for which data were obtained combine stringent handgun controls with relatively low rates of handgun ownership. Some of these countries might have low handgun ownership even if handgun regulations were not so stringent for the simple reason that their citizens do not care to own handguns. But even in Canada, with a long tradition of firearms use and a permissive licensing system for handguns, the handgun ownership ratio is much lower than the United States.

Summary

Most countries have passed national firearms control laws. The great majority of these laws appear to be more stringent than the laws of most states in the United States, although many of the foreign laws may not be effectively enforced. Many countries regulate handguns more stringently than long guns, and rough estimates of handgun ownership in 10 countries are all far below the rate of handgun ownership in the United States.

---

[9]The Canadian figure in Table 16-1 includes a police estimate of 75,000 to 100,000 illegally held handguns, many of which are reported by Montreal police to have come across the border from the United States. Those handguns owned in Canada are also concentrated among fewer individuals: the 543,000 handguns registered in Canada are owned by 175,000 people—an average of 3.1 per owner—while the Harris poll conducted for the Commission shows that for Americans owning handguns, the average is 1.4 per owner. Thus, while the United States has about four times as many handguns per 100,000 as Canada, it may have up to eight times as many handgun owners.

Chapter 17

CAN WE REDUCE FIREARMS VIOLENCE?

One of the most controversial issues in the recent debates over firearms legislation is whether any system of screening owners could be effective in reducing gun violence. Both sides often take extreme positions. Proponents of firearms control sometimes seem to urge that even the mildest form of firearms legislation will eliminate gun misuse. Opponents of controls may argue that no gun laws can prevent criminals from having guns and that all efforts at control are accordingly futile. The statistical materials assembled to support these extreme positions often reveal more about the frailty of partisan research than about the potential effectiveness of different types of legislation.[1]

This chapter is a discussion of some of the evidence that has been produced in the gun control controversy. Data on the effectiveness of firearms control measures in the United States usually come from one of two comparisons, neither of which is completely satisfactory. The most frequent approach is to compare crime rates in the United States with those in foreign countries. This comparison generally shows that most industrially developed Western nations experience far lower rates of gun crime than the United States. This does not necessarily mean, however, that adopting the foreign firearms control systems in this country would reduce our firearms violence to the lower foreign levels. A multitude of other factors—such as traditions and cultural traits—contribute to the level of gun violence in any country. Moreover, no other nation in history has ever instituted firearms control with so many firearms already in circulation among persons accustomed to having them.

---

[1]Compare "Firearms Facts," U. S. Department of Justice (June 1968); testimony of Philip Burdette, Vice President and General Manager, Remington Arms Co., Inc., representing the firearms manufacturers, Commission Hearings, Oct. 11, 1968; Alan S. Krug, Assistant to the Director, The National Shooting Sports Foundation, Inc., "The True Facts on Firearms Legislation," 114 Cong. Rec. 1, 90th Cong., 2d sess. (Jan. 29, 1968); Zimring, "Games with Guns and Statistics," 1968 Wisconsin Law Review #4.

In spite of the many factors that contribute to the level of a country's gun violence, it is possible that foreign crime statistics might provide some insight into the potential results of instituting firearms controls in the United States. In England and Wales, for instance, licenses to possess handguns and rifles have for years been issued only after an extensive police investigation of the applicant. Licenses are usually granted only to supervised members of gun clubs or to farmers who need these firearms to control vermin.

Table 17-1 compares the rates of firearms and nonfirearms homicide and robbery in England and Wales with comparable rates in

Table 17-1—Homicide and robbery with and without guns,
England and Wales vs. United States, 1967

	England and Wales[1]	United States[2]
Homicide with guns.	1	38
Homicide without guns.	3	23
Total	4	61
Robbery with guns	6	372
Robbery without guns	91	648
Total	97	1,020

Sources:
[1]"The Use of Firearms in Crime in England and Wales," 1967, Home Office (unpublished).
[2]Uniform Crime Reports, 1967.

the United States. Using this comparison, the U.S. rate of gun homicides may be as much as 40 times higher than in England and Wales, and the U.S. gun robbery rate may be over 60 times higher.[2] Yet, this comparison does not prove that the different rates of gun crimes are caused by differences in gun control. The rates at which robbery and homicide with other weapons are committed in our country are also higher. This and other factors could explain why the rates of firearms crimes also differ. International comparisons using rates of gun crime can thus be quite misleading. In order to allow for national differences in the level of violence, Table 17-2 compares the United States with England and Wales to show only the percentage of all robberies and homicides in which guns are used.

---

[2]These comparisons cannot be exact because the English statistics are understated relative to U.S. statistics as a result of the English practice of deleting a crime from the statistics if subsequent court proceedings determine no crime was committed.

Table 17-2—Firearms homicides and robberies as percent of all homicides and robberies, England and Wales vs. United States, 1967

	England and Wales[1]	United States[2]
Homicides	18	64
Robberies.	6	36

Sources:
[1]"The Use of Firearms in Crime in England and Wales," 1967, Home Office (unpublished).
[2]Uniform Crime Reports, 1967.

Even when the greater incidence of homicide and robbery in the United States is eliminated from the comparison, Table 17-2 shows that, when robbery occurs in the United States, guns are used six times as often as in England and Wales. When homicide occurs, guns are used about three times as often in the United States. These statistics also show that, even under England's restrictive handgun licensing, some robberies and homicides are still committed with guns.

The lower rate of firearms usage in violent crime committed in England and Wales suggests that a firearms control system that makes it substantially more difficult to obtain guns may have something to do with reducing the use of firearms in criminal behavior.

Comparison of English crime statistics with our own also reveals that in England, where handguns are difficult to obtain legally, long guns are not used in crime much more often than in the United States. For instance, in England before stricter shotgun controls were put into effect in 1967, shotguns were used in 10 percent of all homicides compared to 9 percent in the United States.[3]

A second approach that is often used in an effort to measure the effectiveness of firearms controls is to compare crime statistics in an area of the United States which has gun control laws with an area which has no effective controls. These comparisons can be misleading because the areas compared may be quite different in history, tradition, social mobility, racial composition, and other factors that bear on the incidence of crime. Such comparisons may also be misleading because state and local firearms control systems have for years been frustrated by the interstate movement of firearms, and it is accordingly difficult to confirm that any difference in crime rates is attributable to the presence or absence of gun controls. It is known, for instance, that half or more of the guns used

---

[3]"The Use of Firearms in Crime in England and Wales," Home Office, 1967 (unpublished). Uniform Crime Reports, 1967, p. 7.

in crime in states which have strict firearms control laws flow in from other jurisdictions.[4]

In spite of the frustrating effects of interstate firearms movements on state and local gun control efforts, it appears that guns are used in a smaller proportion of violent crimes in areas of this country with the strictest handgun controls than in other areas.

Figure 17-1 compares the percentage use of guns in homicides and robberies in New York City and Boston[5] with the percentage use of guns in homicides throughout the country and the average percentage use of guns in eight major cities.[6]

Figure 17-1—Percentage of gun use in violent crime, 1967

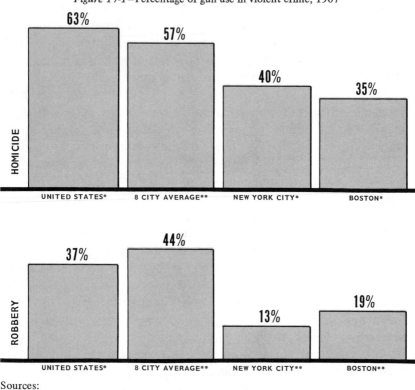

Sources:
  *Uniform Crime Reports, 1967.
  **Local Police Departments, see App. D.

---

[4]See ch. 13, *supra*.
[5]See ch. 11, Fig. 11-8.
[6]Atlanta, Boston, Houston, Los Angeles, New York City, Pittsburgh, St. Louis, and San Francisco. See ch. 11.

Figure 17-1 shows that gun use in New York City and Boston, both of which have restrictive handgun licensing, is lower than in other cities or in the nation as a whole, but higher than the rates reported in England and Wales. Although factors other than firearms control laws can affect gun use in different cities, it is plausible to conclude that firearms control systems that substantially reduce total gun ownership also reduce the use of guns in violence. This is a simple corollary of the proposition discussed in Chapter 11: fewer guns—less gun violence.

Since handguns constitute only one fourth of the guns in this country but are used in more than three fourths of gun crimes, a system of nationwide restrictive licensing for handguns which substantially reduces handgun ownership below present levels can be expected to also curtail firearms violence. Even though such a system would not reduce long gun ownership, it would not appear to risk a massive shift to the use of long guns in crime.

Restrictive handgun licensing is the only reasonable system that will substantially reduce handgun ownership. It is thus a far more certain method of reducing firearms violence than permissive licensing. Available data on states with permissive licensing systems in the United States suggest that the wide distribution of legally held firearms and the free interstate flow of firearms cause severe difficulties in any attempts to keep firearms from illegitimate users. On the basis of present evidence, it cannot be assumed that permissive licensing laws have proved effective in the past.[7]

A national system of permissive licensing that successfully keeps guns from the prohibited groups (felons, fugitives, addicts, drunkards, etc.) could be expected to reduce gun violence. The critical question is whether such a system, provided it is not frustrated by the interstate flow of firearms, can in fact keep guns from such groups while the total number of guns in circulation is not reduced. The danger of transfer of firearms from legitimate to illegitimate users might be somewhat abated by a registration or transfer notice system. But panic buying, thefts, and hand-to-hand transfers of firearms to illegitimate users would continue to cause misuse of guns, even if a permissive screening system were vigorously enforced. Gun misuse would also continue to come from persons with no criminal record or history of mental instability who turn to handguns in moments of rage or frustration.

---

[7]See App. D.

It is our conclusion that, on balance, a national system of permissive screening might reduce, to some degree, the role of firearms in violence. Restrictive screening of handguns, on the other hand, promises more certain and more substantial reductions in firearms violence.

Summary

The gun control controversy has often involved comparing crime statistics from states with firearms control laws with statistics from states with no such laws, and similar comparisons of the United States with foreign countries. These comparisons are never wholly satisfactory, but when care is exercised to focus not upon the number of crimes committed but solely upon the proportion of crimes involving guns, the inference can be drawn that control systems that substantially reduce the number of guns are effective in reducing the level of gun violence. Since handguns are the major problem, a nationwide restrictive licensing system for handguns promises a more certain and more substantial reduction of gun violence in this country than a permissive system.

Chapter 18

THE COSTS OF
FIREARMS CONTROL

This chapter discusses some of the costs of different forms of firearms control. Any system of screening firearms owners will involve monetary costs of administration and may involve such nonmonetary costs as inconvenience to gun owners and limitations on the use and ownership of firearms. The monetary costs can be assessed against the community as a whole through the use of public funds from general taxes, or against firearms owners in the form of special fees, or through a mixture of both approaches.

Costs of Administration

The dollar cost of any system of screening persons who seek to own a firearm depends upon the number of applications processed and the unit cost of processing.

The number of applications processed varies substantially between permissive and restrictive systems. The unit cost of processing varies with the thoroughness of the screening process and the efficiency with which it is conducted. Both permissive and restrictive screening systems normally involve: (1) an application for permission to possess a firearm, (2) investigation of the applicant, and (3) a decision whether the license should be issued. If the license is denied, this decision is normally subject to appeal.

Investigation of the applicant's background is the most costly portion of the screening process.[1] A check of FBI records to determine whether the applicant has a criminal record costs $2.43.[2] A check to determine whether the applicant has a history of mental disorder costs about 50 cents in Maryland with a system of centralized mental health records. A check of the records of the Federal

---

[1]See "A Preliminary Cost Analysis of Firearms Control Programs" submitted to the Commission by Research Associates, Inc., Dec. 20, 1968, Table 1, p. 16.
[2]*Id.*, p. 14, n. 3.

Bureau of Narcotics to determine any history of drug use costs another 50 cents.[3] A more detailed background investigation can cost more than 10 times as much as the foregoing checks of federal and state agencies.[4]

Exhaustive investigation of applicants under a permissive licensing system is clearly the most expensive system of firearms control because of the high unit cost of the investigation and the large number of applicants processed. Such an exhaustive investigation is, however, inconsistent with the fact that under permissive licensing all but a few persons will be allowed to have firearms. A simple records check would seem to be sufficient to determine whether the applicant is a member of any of the categories of persons who are prohibited from having a firearm. Confining the investigation of applicants to a records check would also keep total costs relatively moderate even though there are a large number of applicants. Assuming renewals at 3- to 5-year intervals, a permissive licensing system can be operated for about $1 per gun owner per year, or a correspondingly smaller cost per citizen.[5]

Restrictive licensing assumes that relatively few individuals should be allowed to own the firearms covered by the system (normally handguns). It requires more detailed investigation of each applicant. The investigation seeks to verify the reasons given for wanting a firearm and may also cover the applicant's character and reputation. Also, since restrictive licensing requires the applicant to meet rigorous standards of need, persons denied a license may seek judicial review of the decision of administrative agencies more frequently than with a permissive system.

The higher cost per application under restrictive licensing may be offset by the smaller number of applications generated. After an initial flurry of applications when the system is first introduced, it is likely that the number of applicants would soon stabilize, particularly as the standards for granting applications become generally known.

New York City, for example, has had restrictive handgun licensing since 1911.[6] One study of the New York City system found the average cost per application of the approximately 20,000[7] original and renewal applications processed during 1968 was about

---

[3]*Id.*, p. 14, n. 4.
[4]*Id.*, Table 1, p. 16.
[5]See, e.g., the cost of the Illinois firearms owner identification card program, *id.*, pp. 27-28.
[6]See ch. 13.
[7]"A Preliminary Cost Analysis of Firearms Control Programs," *supra*, footnote 1, p. 26.

$72.[8] Yet even this unusually high unit cost amounts to only
about 19 cents per citizen.[9]

Maintaining an existing restrictive licensing system is, of course,
less costly than the initial introduction of such a system. When a
restrictive licensing system begins, many persons must give up
previously lawful firearms. A schedule of compensation for firearms surrendered by owners who can no longer possess them lawfully must accordingly be established at the outset of restrictive
licensing. If an average of $20 were paid for 22 million of the 24
million handguns in this country, such payments throughout the
nation would cost $440 million. This expense would not recur,
however, and in evaluating the costs of a restrictive system it should
be spread over a period of years.

If a system of full registration or transfer notice is added to a
permissive licensing system, the supplemental administrative costs
of recording ownership would be minimal, particularly if the process
were similar to systems now used by private industry. One estimate, for instance, puts the annual cost of a national firearms registration system at $22.5 million, or 25 cents per firearm.[10] Requir-
ing gun owners to report losses or transfers personally to local
officials would cost more than reporting by mail, but the cost per
firearm would still be low.

In order to assure that a recording or transfer notice system is
being observed, owners should be audited from time to time to
insure that the registered owners still possess their firearms. Auditing can be done by mail, in person, or preferably by a combination
of both. The cost of an auditing system would depend primarily
on the size of the sample of firearms owners audited each year.

Who Should Pay

The proportion of the costs of a firearms system that should be
passed on to applicants in the form of fees and the proportion that
should be paid from general funds is essentially a political question.
Yet, the decision may have a marked effect on the operation of
the system. A basic principle of any firearms control system should
be that assessment of fees not be used as a method of reducing the
number of persons licensed to possess firearms. If the costs passed

---

[8]*Id.*

[9]Based on a total cost of $1.5 million in 1968 (*id.*, p. 26) and an estimated New York
   City population of 8 million.

[10]*Id.*, Table 4, p. 32. The cost of preparing and processing a warranty card has been
   estimated by a camera manufacturer to be 4.5 cents per camera. (Information supplied to Research Associates, Inc., by Eastman Kodak Co.)

on to applicants become too high, ability to pay rather than need for the firearm would become a criterion for determining firearms ownership. Such economic discrimination is inconsistent with the theory of either restrictive or permissive licensing. Both systems are intended to benefit the community as a whole by reducing gun violence, and it would seem only fair that non-gun owners should pay for part of the system, particularly when costs per application are high.

A second basic principle should be that no fee or only a minimal fee should be charged for registration or a notice of transfer or loss, even when such costs are passed on to gun owners. The cost of an efficiently designed registration or transfer notice adjunct is low, and basing fees on the number of firearms owned would be more of a tax on guns than assessment of fees to support the system.

The unit cost of a permissive licensing system is relatively low, and even if most of the costs were passed on to firearms owners, the economic burden on applicants would not be great. With restrictive licensing, however, the high cost per application might cause economic discrimination if too large a share of the cost is passed on to the relatively small number of applicants. Fairness would suggest a limitation on the share of the cost of a restrictive licensing system that should be passed on to applicants.

Nonmonetary Costs

Any system of firearms control involves some inconvenience to firearms owners. A permissive system would cause the least inconvenience, particularly if licenses are issued for terms of 3 to 5 years and processing procedures are streamlined. Only a small segment of the population would not have the opportunity to possess and use guns.

Because it places a greater burden on applicants and substantially reduces the number of firearms in use, restrictive licensing would result in diminished opportunities to own and use firearms. Restrictive licensing of long guns would adversely affect hunting, skeet shooting, and other phases of outdoor recreation.[11] Such activities might have to be confined to gun clubs or hunting preserves, where sporting firearms could be stored.

If restrictive licensing were applied to handguns only, hunting and other shooting activities would not be significantly curtailed.

---

[11] An indirect result of any reduction in hunting and sport shooting would be the reduction of tax revenues from gun and ammunition sales and reduced hunting fees which now are used in promotion of conservation programs.

It would, however, reduce the number of handguns in this country and thus affect existing handgun owners. Target shooters might be permitted to store and use their handguns only at public or private arsenals or ranges, and collectors might be required to render their handguns incapable of firing. Most persons would not be issued licenses to keep handguns in their automobiles, homes, or on their persons. This elimination of widespread handgun possession is the essential difference between restrictive and permissive licensing of handguns. Restrictive licensing for handguns would replace freedom of choice with a legal standard that would allow only a limited number of persons to have handguns. The removal of so many handguns from homes can properly be viewed as an added cost of a restrictive licensing system, for many handgun owners will consider it a hardship to give up their guns.

The balance between permissive and restrictive licensing of handguns lies in the choice that must be made between the benefits to society of limiting the number of persons with handguns and the value placed on widespread possession of handguns.

Summary

The costs of any firearms control system include both the funds needed to administer the system and the effect on opportunities for legitimate firearms use. The monetary cost of an efficiently administered permissive or restrictive licensing system would not be excessive. Restrictive licensing, however, would significantly reduce the legitimate use of the controlled firearms.

Chapter 19

TECHNOLOGY AND
FIREARMS CONTROL

Advancements in technology could contribute substantially to
the effectiveness of firearms control laws. This chapter discusses
three developments that might help reduce firearms violence:
(*a*) devices to trace firearms, (*b*) devices to detect the presence
of firearms, and (*c*) nonlethal weapons.

Tracing Firearms

Proponents of firearms control measures often suggest that all
guns should be "fingerprinted" by conducting a ballistics test in
the hope that the firearm and its owner can be identified if the
gun is subsequently misused. Unfortunately, the storage of nearly
100 million bullets and the development of a system of classifying
test bullets so that bullets used in crime can be traced to a particular firearm are problems of great magnitude. Moreover, no method
of adequately preserving the rifling marks on a test bullet has yet
been devised. As a result, the marks on a test bullet would change
over the years. At the same time, as firearms are used, rifling and
other distinctive marks imparted to bullets change to the extent
that bullets fired from the same firearm at different times have
quite different markings. Also, the "fingerprints" left by a gun
will change if barrels or other firearms parts are replaced.

The foregoing problems might be avoided by a system of giving
each gun a number and the development of some device to imprint
this number on each bullet fired from the gun. Another suggested
method of tracing firearms is to implant an identifying capsule
with a distinctive number in each bullet and require firearms
dealers who sell the ammunition to maintain records of the persons who buy all such numbered ammunition. Since over 4.4

billion bullets were manufactured in this country in 1967,[1] many
practical and technical problems must be overcome before any
such idea can be translated into a working system.

A practical system of tracing bullets from 90 million firearms
cannot be reasonably anticipated in the near future.

Detection Devices

More sophisticated methods of detecting people who carry firearms would help our police enforce firearms laws. Devices which
sound an alarm when a metal object passes near the sensing instrument, for instance, might be used to detect firearms in airports,
railroad stations, or other locations where a single checkpoint
could be established. A simple induction coil placed in a doorway
allows detection of any firearm which passes close enough to
disturb the magnetic field. Magnetic devices of this kind, however,
are subject to false alarms from keys, coins, or other metal objects.
X-ray devices would eliminate false alarms but cause health hazards.
A combination of magnetic and X-ray devices might be feasible if
persons passing the checkpoint were requested to remove coins
and keys before entering the magnetic field. If the magnetic de-
tector indicated the presence of a metal object, X-ray equipment
might be used to identify the object.

Detection of firearms in crowds is considerably more complex,
but might be accomplished through radar or ultrasonic devices.
Firearms might also be detected in crowds by chemically treating
(or tagging) gun metal or ammunition so that it has a detectable
scent which can be picked up by a sensitive "sniffing" device. If
radiation hazards can be overcome, newly manufactured firearms
or ammunition might also be "tagged" with a radioactive substance
detectable by a geiger counter.

Although adequate devices to detect firearms have not been
developed, such developments could be made in the near future.
Further research and development work should be pursued.

Nonlethal Weapons

The desirability of developing a firearm or other weapon that
would immediately incapacitate but not kill or seriously injure
has been discussed for many years. Such a weapon would be of

---

[1]The three major firearms manufacturers have advised the Task Force that in 1967,
4,391,504 bullets were manufactured for sale in the United States. Of these, nearly 1
billion were shotgun shells.

considerable benefit to police officers and homeowners or merchants using self-defense weapons. New types of disabling gases and chemical agents have been developed for effective use against crowds. The drawback to date in the use of such substances against individual attackers has been to devise a means of delivering the substances. Development of a "soft" chemical bullet or other disabling projectile of limited penetrating power would be a major breakthrough. Two years ago the National Commission on Law Enforcement and Administration of Justice[2] recommended research and development work on a nonlethal weapon. The need is greater now, and the extensive resources of the firearms industry, other segments of private industry, governmental agencies, and foundations involved in fostering scientific research should be joined to embark on a program for the development of nonlethal weapons.

Summary

Technological advancements in tracing firearms to owners, in detecting firearms in public places, and in development of nonlethal weapons or ammunition would help reduce firearms misuse by making firearms control systems more effective. Government and private industry must engage in a concerted program of scientific research and development to promote such technological advancements.

---

[2]See App. A.

PART IV

RECOMMENDATIONS

One out of every two hundred deaths in this country results from the criminal or accidental use of firearms. About the same number of deaths are the result of firearms suicides.[1] Thousands more are wounded each year, and untold others are threatened by someone holding a gun.

An overwhelming majority of the guns in this country are used responsibly. The handgun is the principal weapon of gun misuse, accounting for more than three fourths of all criminal gun violence. Although handguns constitute only about one fourth of all guns in civilian hands in the United States, the number of such guns is formidable—24 million. This amounts to an average of 40 handguns for every 100 households. And the rate is increasing because handgun sales have risen dramatically in the last decade.

It can surprise no one that high rates of gun violence are connected with high rates of handgun ownership. When the number of handguns increases, gun violence increases, and where there are fewer guns, there is less gun violence.

If there were fewer handguns in this country, the knife and other weapons might replace the gun as instruments of violence. Even so, deaths and injuries would be reduced because a gun attack is five times as deadly as an attack with another weapon.

---

[1] Of the 1,852,000 people who died in 1967 in the United States, approximately 18,900 died of gunshot wounds: about 9,000 suicides, 2,900 gun accidents, and 7,000 homicides.

139

The stockpile of handguns in this country is a legacy of traditional American attitudes toward firearms and decades of lax firearms control. Yet, the handgun in the house generally creates more danger than safety. The use of handguns for target shooting can be accommodated without such a stockpile of guns, and the handgun is unimportant as a hunting weapon. At the same time, civil disorder, racial tension, and fear of crime are turning our nation into an armed camp and have increased the role of firearms in violence. The vicious circle of Americans arming themselves to protect against other armed Americans must be broken. Finding effective and appropriate methods of reducing gun violence must be recognized as a national problem.

We have concluded that the only sure way to reduce gun violence is to reduce sharply the number of handguns in civilian hands in this country. We recognize this will be a massive and expensive task. But, the price is one that we should be prepared to pay.

Rifles and shotguns are a different story. These hunting and sport shooting weapons are an important part of the life of the nation. Their use in crime, by comparison with handguns, is limited.

Many countries distinguish between handguns and long guns in their firearms laws. Yet, no other country has ever attempted to control handguns with over 24 million such guns already in circulation. The success of any such undertaking must depend upon public understanding and support.

We submit the following recommendations with regard to public education, research, and legislation.

Public Education

Public education programs to inform Americans fully about the role of firearms in accidents, crime, and other forms of violence; a publicity campaign to reduce the number of loaded guns in American homes.

As symbols of our frontier tradition, toys for our children, and props for our movies and television, firearms are so commonplace to Americans that we seldom pause to reflect on their impact on our lives. Our casual attitude toward firearms may be shaken temporarily when tragedy strikes close to home or when the nation as a whole is aroused by a sensational act of gun violence. But Americans do not know the whole story of gun misuse in this country.

An information program is necessary to secure broad public support for meaningful firearms legislation and to encourage the safe and responsible use of firearms. Only after we know the risks to ourselves, our families, and our friends can we appreciate the need for legislation and for voluntary measures to eliminate the loaded gun from the home. If a citizen elects to own a firearm, he must understand the duties and responsibilities of such ownership and the safest methods of handling and storing firearms in his home or business. In addition to reappraising his own attitude toward keeping firearms in his home, each American must also appreciate how the security of our society is affected by millions of guns in millions of homes.

We urge in particular that the National Rifle Association and other private organizations devoted to hunting and sport shooting be enlisted with interested citizens and the media to assist in pointing out the dangers of loaded firearms in the home and the need for meaningful firearms legislation.

Research

Research to hasten the development of an effective nonlethal weapon and improved methods of firearms detection; further research on strategies to reduce firearms misuse.

Scientific and technical research is needed to develop an effective nonlethal weapon or ammunition that would incapacitate but not kill an attacker. Replacing existing police and home defense weapons with nonlethal weapons would not interfere with self-protection, but would eliminate many fatal firearms incidents. Private industry, the government, and foundations charged with allocating funds for scientific research should be encouraged to join forces in developing nonlethal weapons.

Scientific research is also needed to develop methods of tracing and detecting firearms so that law enforcement officers can obtain a higher degree of compliance with existing and future firearms laws. No effective means of tracing firearms or ammunition is on the horizon, but electromagnetic, X-ray, chemical, and sensing devices using radioactive materials might allow the development of feasible firearms detection devices.

Research on the relationship between firearms and violence, and on methods of reducing gun violence, is necessary and should receive continuing private and governmental support. At the same time, we cannot use the excuse of incomplete knowledge to postpone dealing with problems which demand immediate attention.

Legislation

Efforts to obtain uniform state firearms laws through voluntary action of the states have proven unsuccessful. We recommend a federal law establishing minimum federal standards for state firearms control systems. Within 3 years each state would enact a firearms control system meeting the federal standards or a federally administered system based on these standards will be established within that state. Federal guidelines to maximize consistency in interpreting the federal standards should be issued, although each state would be able to adjust its system to meet the federal standards in light of local conditions. Any state failing to enact a firearms law meeting federal standards would be subject to the establishment of a federal firearms control system within its borders.

Handguns: A federal standard of restrictive licensing to confine handguns to persons who need them and to substantially reduce the number of handguns now in civilian hands in this country.

We recommend a national standard of restrictive handgun licensing to reduce substantially the 24 million handguns now in civilian hands in this country and thereby reduce the toll of gun violence. This handgun licensing system should be national in scope because the problem is national, and because a nonexistent or ineffective control system in one state makes it difficult for neighboring states to control gun violence. Yet, different states have different cultural patterns and crime problems, and handgun laws must vary somewhat in accordance with these differences. We recommend, therefore, that federal legislation establish minimum standards for handguns and allow the states some flexibility in adapting these standards to local conditions.

Under state administered restrictive licensing systems, applicants would have to establish both their eligibility to possess and a particular need for a handgun and pass a test designed to determine whether they know how to use and safely store a handgun.

The objective of this state administered national system would be to reduce the number of privately owned handguns in this country to a necessary minimum. All those who are not issued licenses and who must give up their handguns would be duly compensated.

Federal law should prescribe the following minimum standards for state handgun laws:

(1) All handgun owners and purchasers of handgun ammunition must be licensed. Licenses may be issued only to those who establish a need for such a firearm. Although need would be determined separately by each state, federal guidelines can en-

courage consistency. For instance, police officers, security guards, and some retail merchants should qualify for handgun licenses. Normal household protection would not constitute sufficient need. Under such guidelines, the number of legally held handguns would be reduced to about 10 percent or less of the present 24 million.

(2) Handgun licenses will be denied to persons convicted of or under indictment for crimes of violence, fugitives, narcotics addicts, mental incompetents and defectives, and minors under 21.

(3) A safety test will be required before issuance of a license.

(4) Firearms dealers will be regulated to insure that they sell handguns or ammunition only to persons with licenses. Dealers and individuals intending to sell or transfer handguns will be required to submit reports on all such transactions and wait 20 days before delivering the gun to the transferee; during this period, the state will verify that it is the license holder who intends to acquire a handgun. No such report will be required for sales of ammunition. Pawnshops will be prohibited from dealing in handguns or ammunition.

(5) The license program will be administered by a state agency without discrimination as to race, sex, or religion.

(6) Licensed handgun owners will be required to supply information on each handgun they own and to notify police promptly if a handgun is stolen or lost. A system of periodic auditing of licensed handgun owners to insure that they still own the handguns licensed to them will be administered by a state agency.

(7) A federally financed program to purchase handguns from private citizens and to grant amnesty to persons who relinquish illegally owned handguns will be administered by a state agency.

> Long guns: A federal standard of permissive licensing to allow all persons except a small segment of prohibited persons legally to own and use long guns.

We recommend a federal law establishing as a minimum national standard a long gun owner's identification card system in each state similar to the systems now in effect in Illinois and New Jersey, and a system to record any sale or transfer of a long gun.

Identification card—Except for persons under indictment for or convicted of a crime of violence, fugitives, narcotics addicts, and mental incompetents and defectives, all persons would be eligible for a long gun identification card. Persons under 18 would be allowed to use long guns under adult supervision. The state administering agency will issue to each qualified applicant a card, similar to a military identification card, showing his name, address, description, photograph, fingerprint, and social security number.

Transfer notice—We do not recommend registration of all existing long guns. The principal value of a registration system would be to guard against the future flow of firearms from legitimate to illegitimate owners. This objective might be achieved, at lesser cost, by a system of transfer notice. Under such a system, every dealer and individual who transfers a firearm to another person would be required to fill out a form, printed on a computer punchcard, giving the date of the transfer, the type, serial number, and model of the gun, his and the transferee's name, address, and social security and identification card numbers. Blank copies of such forms could be obtained in banks, post offices, state and local governmental offices, and other locations. The transfer would be confirmed by a postcard notice requesting the new owner to verify his ownership. Owners who wish to register long guns could do so at any time by filling out a transfer notice card.

Federal law should prescribe the following minimum standards for state long gun laws:

(1) All long gun owners and purchasers of long gun ammunition must have an identification card. Cards will be issued to all applicants except those

prohibited from owning any firearm—persons under indictment for or convicted of a crime of violence, fugitives, mental incompetents and defectives, narcotics addicts, and minors under 18.

(2)   Serially numbered identification cards, similar to military identification cards, showing name, address, personal description, photograph, thumbprint, and social security number will be issued on filing of the proper application to all qualified persons regardless of need.

(3)   A written test that could be administered by mail, based upon a manufacturer's safety booklet attached to each gun sold, will be required.

(4)   Long gun owners and firearms dealers will be required to sell or transfer long guns or long gun ammunition only to persons with identification cards. Dealers and individuals intending a sale or transfer of a long gun will be required to submit a report of the transactions. No such report will be required for sales of ammunition. Pawnshops will be prohibited from dealing in long guns or ammunition.

(5)   The identification card program will be administered by a state agency without discrimination as to race, sex, or religion.

General provisions: A federal firearms agency; limit domestic manufacture to guns suited for sporting purposes; strict enforcement and amendment of the Gun Control Act of 1968; gun turn-in campaigns; shooting clubs for storage of sporting handguns; revision of FBI crime reports; customs declaration for all firearms.

In order to obtain the maximum benefits from the foregoing handgun and long gun proposals, we also recommend:

(1)   Establishment of a federal firearms agency to accumulate and store firearms information obtained by state and local firearms agencies and to act as a clearing house of firearms information for federal, state, and local law enforcement agencies. The director of this agency might also be empowered

to supervise state firearms system to insure fair administration that does not discriminate on the basis of race or other unlawful grounds. A federal review system could also be provided to allow aggrieved parties recourse through the federal courts, on either their own initiative or that of the U.S. Department of Justice.

(2) The Gun Control Act of 1968 bans imports of guns that are not suited for sporting purposes. This ban should be extended to firearms of domestic manufacture, excepting only the manufacture of handguns for use by law enforcement agencies and licensed owners.

(3) Federal firearms laws should be amended to eliminate the possibility of firearms dealers transferring to nonresidents by renting guns with a high security deposit that is subsequently forfeited. In addition, licensed federal firearms dealers should be strictly policed to eliminate all but legitimate dealers. Licensed dealers should be required to maintain security procedures to minimize theft of firearms, particularly during civil disorders.

(4) Public and private campaigns should be fostered in states and cities to encourage persons to turn in unwanted guns. Such turn-ins could be coordinated with occasional amnesty days when illegally owned handguns could be turned in without penalty.

(5) Public and private shooting clubs should be allowed to store handguns suitable for sporting purposes and to permit target shooters to use them on the premises.

(6) The FBI should revise its crime reporting system to obtain a statistical breakdown of crimes involving firearms by type of weapon—handgun, rifle, or shotgun.

(7)   Customs regulations should be amended to require written declaration of each firearm brought into this country from abroad and impounding of such firearms until legality of ownership is established.

APPENDICES

FIREARMS PROPOSALS OF PRIOR COMMISSIONS

Prior commissions have made observations and recommendations bearing on the use of firearms in our country. This appendix reviews the work of these earlier commissions and comments on the status of their recommendations.

The Commission on Law Enforcement and Administration of Justice

Established by President Johnson on July 23, 1965, this Commission reported in February 1967. In chapter 10 of its report, entitled "Control of Firearms," this Commission found:[1]

(1) During 1963, 4,760 persons were murdered by firearms. During 1965, 5,600 murders, 34,700 aggravated assaults, and the vast majority of the 68,400 armed robberies were committed by means of firearms. All but 10 of the 278 law enforcement officers murdered between 1960 and 1965 were killed by firearms. (p. 239)

(2) Although many of an estimated 50 million privately owned firearms belong to hunters, collectors, and sportsmen, 37 percent of the persons interviewed in a poll conducted by the National Opinion Research Center said that they kept firearms in their homes to protect themselves. (p. 239)

(3) Federal firearms statutes are ineffective in controlling mail-order sales of handguns, rifles, and shotguns. ". . . [P]ractically anyone—the convicted criminal, the mental incompetent, or the habitual drunkard—can purchase firearms simply by ordering them in those states that have few controls." (p. 240)

(4) State and local firearms laws are scattered and diverse. While some states, such as New York, have a strict control system for handguns, many other states have little or no control. The Commission found, for instance:

> Twenty-five States require a license to sell handguns at retail, 8 require a permit (or the equivalent) to purchase a handgun, 11 require a waiting period between purchase and delivery of a handgun, 1 requires a license to possess a handguns, 29 require a license to carry a handgun, 19 prohibit the carrying of a concealed handgun, 18 require a license to carry a handgun in a vehicle, 22 pro-

---

[1]All references are to the U.S. Government Printing Office edition printed in Feb. 1967.

hibit the carrying of a loaded firearm in a vehicle, and 4 States require the registration of firearms. (p. 240)

This patchwork system of firearms control led the Commission to conclude: "Strict controls by one State or city are nullified when a potential criminal can secure a firearm merely by going into a neighboring jurisdiction with lax controls, or none at all." (p. 240)

(5) Extremely low-priced surplus weapons are imported with ease into the United States from foreign countries. An estimated 1 million imported firearms are sold to U.S. citizens annually. Moreover, imported firearms constitute 80 percent of all crime connected firearms accumulated by police in Atlanta, Ga., although the figure was only 18 percent in Washington, D.C. (p. 241)

(6) In 1966 a Gallup poll disclosed that 67 percent of the persons interviewed favored "a law which would require a person to obtain a police permit before he or she could buy a gun." The same question put to firearms owners elicited a 56 percent response. In 1959, 59 percent of the persons interviewed by Gallup said that they would outlaw all handguns except for police use; 35 percent were opposed. (p. 241)

(7) The Senate Subcommittee on Juvenile Delinquency concluded that criminals generally purchase firearms through the mails or in retail stores, rather than stealing them. In many instances, homicides have occurred within minutes after a handgun is purchased by a person who would not have been granted a permit to purchase the weapon. As an example, the Commission observed: "During the first year's operation of a Philadelphia ordinance requiring a permit to obtain a firearm, 73 convicted persons were prohibited from purchasing firearms in the city." (p. 241)

Some recommendations made by the Crime Commission have been implemented and others have not. We discuss each of the major recommendations and make observations on what, if anything, has been done to implement them.

Recommendation

Federal and State Governments should enact legislation outlawing transportation and private possession of military-type firearms such as bazookas, machine guns, mortars, and antitank guns. (p. 242)

Status

The Gun Control Act of 1968, which became law on October 22, prohibits the transportation in interstate commerce of "destructive devices" except by licensed manufacturers, dealers, importers, or collectors, who must pay an annual license fee.[2] "Destructive devices" include bombs, grenades, rockets, missiles, mines, and other devices designed to expel a projectile more than 1/2 inch in diameter. The act also requires the registration of each destructive

---

[2]82 Stat. 1213, 1217, 1221-1222, Public Law 90-618 (Oct. 22, 1968).

device with the National Firearms Registration and Transfer Board and an application to the Secretary of the Treasury whenever any owner would like to sell his destructive device.[3] If the transfer is approved, a tax of $200 must be paid unless the transferee is a qualified manufacturer, importer, or dealer.[4]

It would seem that this system of Federal control of destructive devices established by the Gun Control Act of 1968 will allow the federal government to locate and keep track of destructive devices which exist in the United States; it clearly does not totally outlaw the transportation and private possession of destructive devices, as recommended by the Crime Commission.

The Crime Commission recommendation also asked the states to outlaw the transportation and possession of "destructive devices." Several states have for many years had statutes outlawing the possession of bombs and explosives.[5] Although "destructive devices" might well be encompassed by these earlier state statutes, four states[6] and the District of Columbia[7] have specifically enacted legislation to outlaw the possession of "destructive devices."

Recommendation

States should enact laws prohibiting certain categories of persons, such as habitual drunkards, drug addicts, mental incompetents, persons with a history of mental disturbance, and persons convicted of certain offenses, from buying, owning, or possessing firearms. (p. 242)

Status

Although not strictly within the Commission's recommendation, the federal government in the Gun Control Act of 1968 makes it unlawful for felons, persons under indictment, fugitives, unlawful users of marihuana or narcotics, adjudicated mental defectives, or persons committed to a mental institution to receive or transport any firearm in interstate commerce.[8] It is also unlawful for licensed firearms manufacturers, dealers, importers, or collectors to sell firearms to anyone within the prescribed group.[9] In addition, Title VII to the Omnibus Crime Control and Safe Streets Act of 1968, as amended by the Gun Control Act of 1968, makes unlawful the receipt, possession, or transporting in interstate commerce of any firearm by felons, dishonorably discharged veterans, adjudicated mental incompetents, aliens illegally in the

---

[3] 82 Stat. 1228-1229, Public Law 90-618 (Oct. 22, 1968).
[4] 82 Stat. 1228, 1233, Public Law 90-618 (Oct. 22, 1968).
[5] See, for instance, N.Y. Consol. Laws (McKinney's) Penal Law §§ 265.05 and 270.00; Kan. Stat. Ann. §§ 21.2444 to 21.2454; Ind. Stats. Ann. (Burns) 10-4713, Acts 1927; Mich. Comp. Laws 1948 §§ 750.204 to 750.211; Mo. V.A.M.S. §§ 564.570 and 564.580; R.I. Laws § 11-47-21; N.J. Stats. Ann. § A:151-41 (1966); Nev. Rev. Stats. Ann. 202.370 and 202.380; Tex. Penal Code Ann. (Vernon's), Art. 1723; Wisc. Stats. Ann. Title 16, § 164.20, and Title 45, § 943.06.
[6] West's Ann. Calif. Codes Penal, Ch. 25 §§ 12301 to 12307 (1967); Mass. Gen. Laws Ann. (to become effective in 1969); Ill. Ann. Stats. (Smith-Hurd), Ch. 38 § 24-1(7); Ga. Code Ann., Title 26 § 5503-5505.
[7] D.C. Code Art. 50 1(1) and 2(d).
[8] 82 Stat. 1220, Public Law 90-618 (Oct. 22, 1968).
[9] *Ibid.*

United States, and former U.S. citizens who have renounced their citizenship.[10]

Although the classes differ from state to state, many states have for years prohibited designated classes of persons from possessing firearms.[11] The most effective of these statutes would appear to be those of Massachusetts, New Jersey, and Illinois, which require identification cards or permits for all firearms owners and which deny cards or permits to such persons as felons, alcoholics, addicts, persons with mental afflictions, and others.

Although the firearms manufacturers advocate a model state law which would prohibit the sale of firearms to much the same classes or persons ineligible to possess firearms in Illinois and New Jersey, this act to date has not been passed in any state.

Recommendation

Each State should require the registration of all handguns, rifles, and shotguns. If, after 5 years, some States still have not enacted such laws, Congress should pass a Federal firearms registration act applicable to those States. (p. 243)

Status

Several states have had for several years systems whereby a permit is required to purchase a handgun.[12] As a result, these states generally have files showing the names and addresses of persons legally owning firearms and the model and serial number of the handguns owned. In essence, these states have all the information which could be obtained through a system of handgun registration.

We are unaware, however, of any state which has, since the Crime Commission recommendation, initiated a statewide registration system, although several cities, including New York City, Chicago, San Francisco, and Minneapolis, have done so.

Recommendation

Each State should require a person to obtain a permit before he can either possess or carry a handgun. Through licensing provisions, Federal law should prohibit mail-order and other interstate sales of handguns and should regulate such sales of rifles and shotguns.

Federal legislation . . . should prohibit the interstate shipment of handguns except between federally licensed importers, manufacturers, and dealers. A Federal licensee should also be prohibited from selling handguns to an individual not living in the State of

---

[10]82 Stat. 236-237, Public Law 90-351 (June 19, 1968).

[11]See Chapter 13, Table 13-1.

[12]See Haw. Rev. Code § 15307 (1933); Ill. Ann. Stats. (Smith-Hurd), Ch. 38 §§ 83-2.3 and 83.6; Mass. Gen. Laws Ann. Ch. 140 § 131 A (1926); Mich. Comp. Laws, 1948, § 750.232a; Mo. V.A.M.S. § 564.360 (1929, Amend. 1967); N.Y. Consol. Laws (McKinney's) Penal Laws § 400.00(12), (3) with photograph; N.C. Gen. Stats. Art. 53 §§ 14-402 and 14-404 (1919); N.J. Stats. Ann. § 2A:151-32(B), 1966.

the seller. The interstate shipment of shotguns and rifles should be delayed a sufficient time for law enforcement authorities in the buyer's home town to examine his sworn statement . . . and the consent of these authorities should be required before the weapon may be shipped. (p. 243)

Status

As noted in connection with the previous recommendation, several states have permit systems regulating the possession of handguns, although there would appear to be wide divergence in enforcement of such laws. The New York and Massachusetts systems appear to be strictly enforced, but this does not appear to be the case with other states, except perhaps New Jersey in recent years.

Regarding the remainder of this recommendation, the Gun Control Act of 1968 prohibits the mail order or interstate shipment of handguns, rifles, and shotguns, except from a federally licensed manufacturer, dealer, importer, or collector to another such manufacturer, dealer, importer, or collector. Shipments of rifles or shotguns (but not handguns) to contiguous states is allowed under the new federal law so long as the sale does not violate the law of either the seller's or buyer's residence and so long as the buyer executes an affidavit setting forth his name and address and swearing he is eligible to own the firearm. A copy of this affidavit must be sent to the chief law enforcement officer of the buyer's residence and 7 days must elapse before delivery can be made.

The Crime Commission also recommended a continuing effort to find nonlethal weapons to replace the handgun, so that victims of guns are merely incapacitated and not killed[13] (p. 256). This subject is discussed further in Chapter 19, *infra.*

The National Advisory Commission on Civil Disorders (the Kerner Commission)

This Commission was formed by President Johnson on July 29, 1967, to study the civil disorders which had occurred in various sections of the United States and to make recommendations to minimize their reoccurrence.

---

[13]The Task Force on Science and Technology elaborated in this way on the question of nonlethal weapons:

"A patrol officer, in meeting the diverse criminal situations he must face, has a limited range of weaponry—either the shortrange nightstick or the potentially lethal handgun . . . . If an officer feels that his life is threatened, he may shoot, with the attendant risk that suspects or bystanders may be killed . . . . If a suitable range of graduated alternatives were available, and if there is time for weapon selection, then officers could use the weapons most appropriate to the situation . . . . The qualities that must be sought in a general purpose nonlethal weapon are almost immediate incapacitation and little risk of permanent injury to the individual who is the target. It must also meet size, weight, and other operational standards. Survey of a wide range of possibilities leads to the conclusion that these requirements cannot be met by current technology. . . . *No lethal weapon is presently available that could serve as a replacement for the handgun, but a continuing effort to achieve such a weapon should be pursued."* (pp. 14-15, Task Force Report to the President's Commission on Law Enforcement and (Administration of Justice on Science and Technology, U.S. Government Printing Office edition, 1967)

The Kerner Commission apparently conducted no new studies on the role of firearms in the United States. It did, however, review the observations of the Crime Commission, stating:

(1) The Crime Commission studied the relationship between violent crime and the easy availability of firearms in the United States. (p. 289)[14]

(2) The Crime Commission surveyed existing Federal, state, and local gun control legislation and concluded: "Since laws, as they now stand, do not accomplish the purposes of firearms control, the Commission believes that all states and the Federal Government should act to strengthen them." The Commission recommended specific Federal and state legislation reasonably regulating the purchase, transportation, sale, and possession of firearms. (p.289)

(3) The fact that firearms can readily be acquired is an obviously dangerous factor in dealing with civil disorders. It makes it easier for a serious incident to spark a riot and may increase the level of violence during disorders. It increases the dangers faced by police and others seeking to control riots. (p. 289)

The Kerner Commission recommended—

(1) . . . that all state local governments should enact gun control legislation of the type recommended by the Crime Commission. (p. 289)

(2) . . . that Federal legislation is essential in order to make state and local laws fully effective, and to regulate areas beyond the reach of state government. *We therefore support* the President's call for control legislation and urge its prompt enactment. (p. 289)

The Kerner Commission also found that "certain recent disorders were accompanied by a drastic increase in the theft of firearms from stores and manufacturers." (p. 289) It recommended—

. . . that both state and local government should consider enactment of laws or ordinances controlling the storage of firearms and ammunition in order to diminish the possibilities of theft. Such laws could require, for example, that all firearms and ammunition be stored in heavily protected vaults or areas, or that essential parts of the firearms be so stored. (p. 289)

In this connection, the Kerner Commission recited the results of a survey of 26 police departments which unanimously agreed that "Closing stores selling firearms and ammunition was effective [in controlling civil disorders] ." (p. 290)

The Kerner Commission also made note of the firearms used by persons causing civil disorders and by the law enforcement forces attempting to curtail the disturbances. It said:

(1) Of 23 cities surveyed by the Commission, there had been reports of sniping in at least 15. What is probable, although the evi-

---

[14]All references are to the U.S. Government Printing Office edition dated Mar. 1, 1968.

dence is fragmentary, is that there was at least some sniping. What is certain is that the amount of sniping attributed to rioters—by law enforcement officials as well as the press—was highly exaggerated. (p. 180)

(2) According to the best information available to the Commission, most reported sniping incidents were demonstrated to be gunfire by either police or National Guardsmen. (p. 180)

In further discussing the firearms used by law enforcement officers, the Kerner Commission noted three serious problems which were involved in police use of firearms in civil disorders:

(1) the risk of killing or wounding innocent persons—bystanders or passersby who may in fact be hundreds of feet away when a shot is fired. (p. 176)

(2) [Whether there is any] justification for the use of deadly force against looting or vandalism. (p. 176)

(3) use of excessive force—even the inappropriate display of weapons—may be inflammatory and lead to even worse disorder. (p. 176)

In concluding, the Commission stated:

The Commission believes that equipping civil police with automatic rifles, machine guns, and other weapons of massive and indiscriminate destructive force is not warranted by the evidence. . . . We should not attempt to convert our police into combat troops equipped for urban warfare. (pp. 271-272)

The Commission further recommended:

The Federal Government should undertake an immediate program to test and evaluate available nonlethal weapons and related control equipment for use by police and control forces.

Federal support should be provided to establish criteria and standard specifications which would stimulate and facilitate the production of such items at a reasonably low cost.

. . . .

If these recommendations are adopted, the result will be better maintenance of law and order and better control of disorders and fewer risks to police and the public. Use should be made of the technology and resources of the Department of Defense and other appropriate Federal agencies. (p. 272)

The Commission also had some suggestions in regard to firearms used by National Guard and Army troops. It observed:

The rifle is the soldier's basic weapon. . . . This weapon has a psychological effect for a show of force that distinguishes military units from the police. Unfortunately, actual use of the rifle in riot control operations is generally inappropriate. It is a lethal weapon with ammunition designed to kill at great distances. Rifle bullets ricochet.

The may kill or maim innocent people blocks away from the actual
target. (p. 277)

The Commission recommended—

(1) that the Department of Defense immediately institute a research program that seeks to develop a new type of ammunition for
use in civil disorders. (p. 277)

(2) that the use of machine guns be prohibited for National
Guard forces assigned to riot control. Other mass destruction weapons of modern warfare—flame throwers, recoilless rifles, and artillery—
have no conceivable place in riot-control operations in densely populated American cities. (p. 278)

(3) that the Department of Defense make available to police departments various chemical agents for use in riot control so long as
advanced warning is given before they are used on a crowd. (p. 278)

As noted in our discussion of the status of the Crime Commission recommendations, the Gun Control Act of 1968 has implemented some (but by no
means all) of the Crime Commission recommendations reiterated in the Kerner
Commission report. As also noted above, a few states and municipalities have
enacted more stringent firearms controls consistent with the firearms proposals
made by the Crime Commission and the Kerner Commission. We are not
aware, however, that any state or local government has done anything to improve the security of stores selling firearms. Similarly, it would appear that
little real progress has been made in developing nonlethal weapons or ammunition to replace the handgun.[15]

Regarding the firearms used to control riots, the Department of Defense
has instituted a research program to develop ammunition suitable for use in
riot control; Army and National Guard forces have been ordered not to use
weapons of massive force in riot control duty; and procedures have been established whereby the federal government will make chemical agents useful
in riot control available to local law enforcement agencies.

The Commission on Crime in the District of Columbia

This Commission was appointed by President Johnson on July 16, 1965, to
investigate crime in the District of Columbia. The Commission's findings relating to firearms were:

(1) In the District of Columbia, handguns have become the
weapon of choice among people bent upon crime. The reasons for
this choice are clear: The handgun is readily obtained at a reasonable
price, it is easily concealed until needed, and it is an effective means
of threatening and applying force. (p. 619)[16]

(2) The use of handguns in crime in the District has constantly
increased since 1955. The report includes a table showing that 25
percent of the homicides committed in 1955 were done by handguns

---

[15]This is discussed further in ch. 19, *supra.*
[16]Report of the President's Commission on Crime in the District of Columbia, Dec. 15,
1966 (U.S. Government Printing Office edition, 1966).

and that this percentage had grown to 50 percent in 1966. In the same period, the number of assaults involving handguns rose from 5 percent to 22.7 percent, and handguns used in robberies increased from 13.3 percent in 1962 to 29.9 percent in 1966. (p. 620)

The Commission then analyzed the firearms laws regulating the sale of handguns in the District. It found in this regard:

(1) In effect, almost anyone who is willing to fill out a form and wait for 48 hours can buy a handgun. . . . During 1965 there were 2,486 handguns sold legally in the District of Columbia.
. . . Those who wish to obtain handguns without coming to the attention of law enforcement authorities can do so readily. The reservoir of unregistered weapons in the District of Columbia makes it possible to obtain guns without any waiting period or police clearance. . . . No estimate can reasonably be made as to the number of weapons which change hands each year in this manner. (pp. 620-621)

(2) A resident of the District of Columbia may go outside Washington and purchase a handgun under the laws of another jurisdiction, even if he is not legally entitled to purchase a weapon in the District . . . . District police officials reported . . . in 1965 that 58 percent of one Maryland gun dealer's sales were to District residents and that 40 percent of these buyers had police records. (p. 621)

(3) Possession of a handgun is legal in the District of Columbia for all but a few specified persons: Drug addicts, convicted felons, persons with prior weapons offense convictions, and certain misdemeanants. Anyone else may keep a handgun in his home or place of business without restriction, without regard to whether it was obtained legally or illegally, and without informing the police about the gun. (p. 621)

(4) No one may carry a handgun, openly or concealed, in the District unless he has been licensed to do so by the Metropolitan Police Department . . . . Licenses are granted sparingly; the police estimate that only about two dozen are extant. (p. 621)

(Law enforcement personnel, military personnel, gun club members going to or from target practice, gun dealers, and persons returning to home or to a business following the purchase or repair of a handgun are not required to have a permit to carry a handgun.) (pp. 621-622)

The Commission concluded that in addition to stricter enforcement of existing firearms legislation enactment of new legislation was an initial first step "to bring to a halt the steady increase in the homicides, assaults and robberies committed with handguns in the District." (p. 623) The legislative action recommended was—

(1) that the laws of various neighboring counties restricting the sale of handguns be bolstered by Federal legislation prohibiting the sale of handguns to anyone who is not a resident of the state where the seller does business. (p. 623)

(2) that the District's laws relating to handgun control be substantially stiffened in an effort to curtail the easy availability and

criminal use of these dangerous weapons. We support legislation
which would . . . require all persons possessing handguns in the District of Columbia to register them with the police . . . . (p. 623)

The Commission further recommended enactment of a handgun licensing
law in the District of Columbia, by which the Metropolitan Police Department would issue licenses to purchase or possess a handgun after a complete
investigation, proof of qualification to use the gun, and "an affirmative. and
specific showing of need to possess a handgun." Examples of the "need"
which must be demonstrated to be granted a handgun license were "persons
who show that their lives have been threatened; or that their dwellings, places
of business, or similar places of business or residences in the immediate neighborhood have been victimized by housebreakings, robberies or other acts of
violence; or that . . . have handguns solely for target practice; or that . . . are
bona fide collectors." (p. 624)

In summary, the Commission concluded:

> We recommend stringent new controls on the possession of firearms
> in the District of Columbia in an effort to reduce the alarming amount
> of handgun crime in this city. In 1965 robberies increased by 50 per-
> cent, while the number of handgun robberies increased over 100 per-
> cent. The District has a much higher rate of crimes committed with
> handguns than does New York, which strictly regulates their posses-
> sion. While cognizant of the many legitimate interests involved in
> owning or using guns, the Commission has recommended the enact-
> ment of a handgun licensing law aimed at severely curtailing the
> purchase and possession of handguns by District residents. (ch. 11,
> "Conclusions")

In response to the District of Columbia Crime Commission recommendations, the District of Columbia enacted a new firearms law which became effective on November 14, 1968. The law regulates the sale of handguns as well as
rifles, shotguns, and ammunition and make felons, drug addicts, persons under 21, persons of unsound mind, and persons with prior firearms violations
ineligible to possess firearms. The new law requires an application to the Metropolitan Police Department prior to the purchase of a firearm and an annual
license to carry a handgun and a 5-year license to possess a rifle or shotgun. It
also requires that all firearms in the District be registered with the police'and
that the registration certificate be displayed before ammunition can be purchased.[17]

Residents of the District of Columbia who attempt to purchase handguns
outside the District are also subject to the Gun Control Act of 1968. Under
this act, sale of any firearm to a person who is not a resident of the state in
which the dealer is located is prohibited, except when the nonresident is from
a bordering state.[18] Such a nonresident may purchase a firearm after execut-
ing a sworn statement setting forth that he is of legal age and that his possession of the firearm will not violate either state or local law of the locality in

---

[17]Arts. 50-56 of District of Columbia Code.
[18]The IRS interprets the act to require affirmative legislation by the states involved
  before bordering state purchases may be made.

which he resides. The dealer must then forward the sworn statement by registered or certified mail to the principal law enforcement officer of the locality where the nonresident lives. When the dealer has received a return receipt and 7 days have elapsed, the firearm may be delivered to the nonresident.

The President's Commission on the Assassination of President John F. Kennedy (Warren Commission)

This Commission was created by President Johnson on November 29, 1963, to investigate the murder of President John F. Kennedy. The only portions of the Warren Commission report which appear relevant to this Task Force are the facts relating to the firearms used by Oswald and Oswald's murderer:

(1) Oswald ordered and received by mail under an assumed name the rifle which the Commission found was used in Oswald's attempt to kill Maj. Gen. Edwin A. Walker on April 10, 1963. (pp. 13, 20)

(2) The Mannlicher-Carcano Italian rifle used by Oswald in killing President Kennedy on November 22, 1963, was purchased on March 13, 1963, by mail from Klein's Sporting Goods Co. of Chicago under Oswald's assumed name, A. Hidell. The rifle, which was ordered on a form clipped from the February 1963 *American Rifleman,* cost $21.45, and was delivered to a post office box in Dallas which Oswald rented. (pp. 118-119)

(3) Oswald used a Smith & Wesson .38 caliber revolver to murder Patrolman J. D. Tippet 45 minutes after the assassination of President Kennedy. He had purchased this revolver from Seaport Traders, Inc., a mail-order division of George Rose & Co., Los Angeles, Calif. Oswald ordered the revolver on a mail-order form dated January 27, 1963. He enclosed $10 as a deposit on the total price of $29.95. In the portion of the form for the signature of a witness, the name D. F. Drittal was written in Oswald's handwriting. The revolver was shipped on March 20, 1963, to A. J. Hidell at a Dallas post office box. Railway Express Co. documents showed that the balance of $19.95 and a $1.27 shipping charge was collected on delivery to Hidell, Oswald's frequent pseudonym. Seaport Traders had received this revolver on January 3, 1963, in a shipment of 99 guns from Empire Wholesale Sporting Goods, Ltd., Montreal. After receiving it, the 5-inch barrel, with which it was originally manufactured, was shortened by Seaport Traders to 2¼ inches. (pp. 171-174) The Warren Commission observed: "The shortening of the barrel had no functional value except to facilitate concealment." (p. 558)

(4) The firearm used by Jack Ruby in killing Oswald was a .38 caliber Colt revolver, which Ruby carried routinely in a bank money bag in the trunk of his car. Before going to the police department on the morning he killed Oswald, Ruby took the revolver from his automobile and placed it in his pocket. (pp. 17, 354)

The Warren Commission report does not discuss the Texas and Dallas laws regulating firearms. Review of these laws[19] indicates that when Oswald bought the assassination rifle and the murder revolver through the mails, no provision of Texas law or the law of the city of Dallas was violated. Neither Dallas nor Texas has subsequently enacted any law relating to mail-order sales. However, it probably was a violation of both Texas and Dallas law for either Oswald or Ruby to carry firearms on or about their person.

In regard to Jack Ruby, it would appear to violate both Texas and Dallas law for him to have a revolver in the trunk of his car. Although Texas law has been construed to allow carrying a handgun on one's person while traveling between his residence and place of business,[20] Ruby was apparently not so traveling, and was, therefore, probably illegally carrying a concealed weapon.

---

[19]The Texas law provides in relevant part:
    "Any person who shall carry on or about his person, saddle or in his saddlebags, or in his portfolio or purse any pistol, dirk, dagger, sling shot, blackjack, hand chain, night stick, pipe stick, sword cane, spear, knuckles made of any metal or any hard substance, bowie knife, switch blade knife, spring blade knife, throw blade knife, a knife with a blade over five and one-half (5½) inches in length, or any other knife manufactured or sold for the purposes of offense or defense shall be punished by a fine of not less than One Hundred Dollars ($100) nor more than Five Hundred Dollars ($500) or by confinement in jail for not less than one (1) month nor than one (1) year. . . ." (Texas Penal Code, Title 9, Art. 483)
    "It shall be unlawful to have in one's posession within the city upon any property owned by the city any firearms, rifle, shotgun, automatic rifle, revolver, pistol or any other weapon designed for the purpose of firing or discharging a shell or cartridge. . . ." (City of Dallas Code § 31-11)
[20]*Boyett v. State,* 167 Texas Cr. R. 195, 319 S.W. 2d 106 (1958).

TYPES OF FIREARMS IN THE UNITED STATES

Shotguns

The shotgun is a smooth bore, long arm designed to fire paper or plastic cartridges loaded with lead pellets.[1] It comes closest to being an all-purpose weapon by virtue of the variations in barrel length and shot loads made to accommodate hunters, sport shooters, farmers, and law enforcement agencies. It also has a long history as a frontier weapon of household defense and has earned notoriety as a weapon of gangsters and some armed robbers.

The shotgun's utility derives mainly from its effectiveness against fleeting targets. Despite its short range and limited penetrating power, the gun's expanding shot pattern greatly increases the likelihood of hits on birds in flight and running game. In police work, where ricochet bullets might endanger bystanders or other officers, the shotgun's short range and limited penetrating power are definite assets. At the same time, it can be an extremely destructive weapon at close range.

Traditionally, the shotgun is a simple and inexpensive firearm whose single or double barrels require reloading by hand after each shot. Although the recent trend has been toward repeating and autoloading[2] shotguns, single shot models still enjoy considerable popularity for certain types of hunting and sport shooting. The great majority of shotguns sold in this country are of domestic manufacture.

Rimfire Rifles

Almost all rimfire rifles are .22 caliber arms suited mainly for target shooting, plinking, and hunting small game. Despite its limited utility as a hunting weapon, the .22 rimfire rifle has always been popular among all classes of shooters because of its low cost and inexpensive ammunition. Despite its relatively low power, .22 rimfire ammunition has sufficient range and accuracy

---

[1]The exceptions are uncommon: shotgun pistols, metallic shot cartridges for use in rifles and pistols, brass shot shells loaded with a single lead slug for large game hunting.

[2]Repeating firearms carry a supply of cartridges in a magazine, but require hand operation of the reloading mechanism between shots; semi-automatic or autoloading firearms utilize gas pressure or recoil to perform this operation and will fire as fast as the shooter can pull the trigger.

for serious target shooting. Its most common use is probably for informal target shooting—plinking at tin cans and bottles.

Almost all rimfire rifles sold in this country are of domestic manufacture. Although rimfire rifles are built with a variety of single shot and repeating actions, the current trend appears to be toward semi-automatics.

Centerfire Rifles

Although some centerfire rifles are .22 caliber, most are larger, and center-fire cartridges, regardless of bullet size, typically have several times the power and range of rimfire ammunition. This greater range and power, together with the generally higher cost of the gun and ammunition, once tended to limit ownership of centerfire rifles to the more serious sportsmen. Since World War II, however, large numbers of surplus military rifles have been sold by the U.S. Army or imported from abroad at bargain prices. Consequently, high powered centerfire rifles have increased in popularity among all classes of shooters to the point where this type of rifle now rivals the .22 rimfire in popularity.

While experienced sportsmen generally prefer a conventional hunting rifle manufactured by an established American firm, many hunters have purchased military surplus rifles to convert them to sporting weapons with new sights, stocks, and finishes more appropriate to civilian purposes. Some surplus military rifles have thus been converted into handsome, high quality sporting arms. Most surplus military arms are poorly suited to any hunting purpose, however, because of their size, weight, obsolete design, poor condition, or use of military ammunition. Some verge on junk and are suitable only for decoration.

In addition to increasing the incidence of centerfire rifle ownership by people who do not regularly hunt or participate in shooting sports, military-surplus rifles and ammunition have increased large bore target shooting, especially plinking, and have greatly stimulated gun collecting as a hobby among younger persons who have limited budgets and who view surplus arms as military antiques.

Centerfire rifles are available in a wide variety of calibers, styles, and actions. A few are single shot, but the great majority are bolt, pump, or lever action repeaters. Surplus military rifles of American manufacture include the 1903 and 1917 bolt action, .30 caliber Army rifles of World War I vintage and the semi-automatic M1 rifles and carbines of World War II, many of which have reached the civilian market through the Army's Civilian Marksmanship Program.[3] Most foreign-made military rifles are of the bolt-action type.

Rimfire and Centerfire Handguns

Virtually all rimfire handguns, like rimfire rifles, are chambered for .22 caliber ammunition. Because of the relatively low power of .22 caliber cartridges and the marksmanship skills required of handgun shooters, such arms

---

[3]Figures provided by the U.S. Army indicate the sale of almost 200,000 .30 caliber M1 rifles and carbines through the Director of the Civilian Marksmanship Program from 1958 through 1966. The program is discussed in detail in App. H.

are rarely used for hunting. Sportsmen may carry pistols and revolvers as sidearms while in the field, but the sporting use of such weapons is confined chiefly to target shooting and plinking. If properly designed for accuracy, the .22 caliber handgun is particularly suited to target shooting by virtue of its moderate price and the low cost of ammunition. In recent years, however, the domestic firearms market has been flooded with imported .22 handguns too cheaply and poorly made to serve even the most casual sporting purpose. Crime statistics indicate that these rimfire handguns are increasingly being used as pocket weapons in the old "$2 pistol" tradition. Because these low-quality handguns have virtually no appeal for the hunter, sport shooter, or collector, it is likely that the million or more sold in the last few years are largely in the hands of persons who own no other firearms.

This flow of cheap handguns from abroad should be substantially eliminated under the Gun Control Act of 1968, which allows importation only of handguns that are suitable for "sporting purposes." Manufacture of such weapons may, of course, begin within this country, but because of higher manufacturing costs they will probably then sell for $15 to $25.

The centerfire handgun ranges from .25 to .45 caliber and is a more powerful weapon than the rimfire handgun. The greater range, power, and cost of centerfire ammunition limits its use for plinking, although a few shooters use centerfire handguns for target shooting and hunting. From all indications, however, most centerfire handgun owners buy this type of weapon at least partly for purposes of personal and home protection. As with centerfire rifles, ownership of centerfire handguns appears to have increased substantially due to the importation of military surplus arms since World War II. Many of these guns are military service sidearms of sufficient quality and historical interest to appeal to serious sportsmen and collectors. However, the mail-order availability and relatively low cost of many of these firearms has doubtlessly led to their purchase by many persons who might not otherwise own a centerfire handgun.

Antique and Hobby Firearms

The Gun Control Act of 1968[4] is not applicable to antique firearms, defined in the act as firearms manufactured in 1898 or before, or to replicas of such firearms so long as they have not been modified to fire conventional ammunition. The act also establishes for the first time a federal license for collectors, defined as persons acquiring, holding, or disposing of firearms "as curios or relics." "Curios or relics" are defined in the Commissioners' proposed regulations as firearms "of special interest to collectors by reason of some quality other than is ordinarily associated with firearms intended for sporting use as offensive or defensive weapons." In order to qualify as a curio or relic, a firearm either must have been manufactured 50 or more years ago, must be certified by a firearms museum curator as "novel, rare, or bizarre," or must be associated with "some historical figure, period, or event."[5]

---

[4]82 Stat. 1213, Public Law 90-618 (1968).
[5]26 C.F.R. sec. 178.

In addition to firearms legally defined as antiques by the 1968 act, many essentially modern firearms qualify as collectors' items in the view of firearms hobbyists. Most German military sidearms of World War II and earlier (such as Lugers and Mausers), certain early model Colt and Browning automatic pistols, and even some of the nickel-plated revolvers are gradually being taken out of circulation by collectors.

The number of serious gun collectors in the United States has been conservatively estimated at 10,000, most of whom belong to one or more of the approximately 75 local and regional collectors associations.[6] In addition, there are probably many thousands of Americans who qualify as gun "buffs" and who simply accumulate sizable collections of firearms without any serious effort to specialize in any one type.

One small, but active, segment of the firearms industry manufactures modern muzzle loaders and replicas of antiques, and several firms manufacture specially designed rifles and pistols that are suited strictly for target shooting.

Paramilitary Firearms

A recent and potentially troublesome gun phenomenon is the appearance of nonmilitary firearms designed primarily for "civilian defense," "home protection," and similar nonsporting purposes. These include semi-automatic pistols with actions and magazines of the M1 carbine rifle, high-powered semi-automatic rifles styled after military "assault" rifles and light machineguns, "riot" shotguns of the type used by police agencies, and such combat accessories as bipods, muzzle brakes, flash hiders, folding stocks, and large-capacity magazines.

Despite appearances, these weapons can be legally sold in this country because they are not assembled from surplus machinegun parts and are not readily modified for fully automatic fire. They are virtually useless for hunting or other sporting purposes, and the advertisements for them in gun publications suggest that their main appeal is to paramilitary groups and to individuals arming themselves in expectation of civil disorders. While the traffic in these guns is difficult to determine, the records of one recently formed company show the sale of more than 4,000 .45 caliber "submachine"-type carbines in the first 4 months of 1968,[7] indicating a demand that is sizable and probably increasing.

Destructive Devices

Since World War II a substantial quantity of military ordnance other than small arms has reached the U.S. civilian market through returning servicemen and dealers of military surplus. This equipment includes mortars, rocket launchers (bazookas), cannon, antitank rifles, mines, bombs, and hand grenades. Sale and possession of such weapons are now regulated by the Gun

---

[6]Robert S. Carr, Ohio Gun Collectors Association, Hearings before Senate Subcommittee to Investigate Juvenile Delinquency, 89th Cong., 1st sess., p. 3490 (1963). Other estimates range from 15,000 upward. See Carl Bakal, *The Right to Bear Arms* (New York: McGraw-Hill, 1966), p. 75.
[7]Information furnished the Task Force by the Alcohol and Tobacco Tax Division.

Control Act of 1968, which requires all such "destructive devices" to be registered with the Treasury Department's Alcohol and Tobacco Tax Division.[8]

The danger presented by private ownership of these devices has been mostly a potential one and probably somewhat exaggerated. The mines, bombs, and grenades sold on the surplus market are defused and deactivated and are not feasibly restored to working order. Bazookas and mortars are simple launching tubes; their ammunition has been regulated by existing explosives laws and is virtually unobtainable. Some cannon and antitank rifles are serviceable weapons insofar as ammunition has been available through surplus arms dealers. Their misuse has never been a serious problem, however, and they appear to be mostly in the hands of "cannon buffs" and collectors of military ordnance.

Of greatest concern has been the acquisition of heavy weapons and explosive devices by certain paramilitary groups such as the Minutemen. However, the further import and sale of this type of ordnance would appear to have been largely curtailed by the Gun Control Act of 1968.

Prohibited Firearms

The National Firearms Act of 1934 and the statutes of a number of states regulate the ownership of sawed-off shotguns and rifles, automatic weapons,[9] handguns made from long arms, and silencers.

Under federal and most state laws, a sawed-off firearm is a shotgun whose barrel length is less than 18 inches, a rifle whose barrel length is less than 16 inches, or any shotgun or rifle whose overall length is less than 26 inches. This includes any shoulder weapon which has been modified into a handgun and any handgun which has an attachable shoulder stock. The usual purpose of cutting down a rifle or shotgun is to increase its concealability, though in the case of shotguns the short barrel length increases the weapon's shot pattern and deadliness at close ranges. The ease with which a conventional hunting shotgun or rifle can be cut down into a "gangster" weapon precludes effective control of sawed-off weapons as such. However, the illegality of sawed-off weapons often provides law enforcement agencies with an arrest and prosecution tool.

Automatic weapons include machineguns (chambered for rifle ammunition), submachineguns (chambered for pistol ammunition, usually .45 caliber or 9 mm), and certain rifles, carbines, and pistols capable of automatic fire (usually by means of a fire-selector switch).

The most common source of illegal machineguns has been the "deactivated" machineguns brought into the country under a Deactivated War Trophy (DEWAT) program instituted by the Alcohol and Tobacco Tax Division of the Treasury Department after World War II. Under this program, owners of prohibited weapons could, without penalty or confiscation, have these firearms rendered inoperable. The program was aimed at returning servicemen

---

[8]82 Stat. 1213, Public Law 90-618 (1968).

[9]Semi-automatic (autoloading) firearms automatically reload after each shot, but each shot requires a separate pull of the trigger. An automatic firearm is a machinegun which fires a stream of bullets with a single pull of the trigger. These two types of firearms are sometimes confused because of the common practice of calling semi-automatic rifles and pistols "automatic."

who were slipping such weapons into the country, either complete or piece by piece. However, several large surplus armament firms soon seized upon the program as a means of selling excess stocks of obsolete or captured weapons to domestic collectors. Before the DEWAT program was discontinued in 1958, large numbers of military machineguns and submachineguns were imported, "deactivated" by steel welding, and sold at prices as low as $10 each.

While the DEWAT program specified deactivation by steel welding in a manner that would make restoration extremely difficult, many collectors and amateur gunsmiths have proved themselves equal to the challenge. In some cases, the companies selling such machineguns were doing less than a thorough job of welding. But even the most carefully deactivated gun can be restored to working order with enough machine shop equipment and determination. Replacement barrels and other parts for most submachineguns have long been available through the mail-order houses. The registration of unserviceable machineguns by the Alcohol and Tobacco Tax Division has presumably discouraged wholesale reactivation of machineguns, but there is no question that many such reactivated guns are in circulation today.

Another source of illegal machineguns was the sale of obsolete military weapons to junk dealers in the early 1960's. The guns were "demilitarized" by means of torch cuts across the receivers and along the chambers, burned to remove the wood, and then sold as scrap metal. A few thousand of these "demils" found their way back into circulation, and some have turned up, reactivated, in the arsenals of paramilitary groups. The military services no longer sell demilitarized ordnance on the commercial scrap market.

Most of the automatic weapons still coming into circulation are those being brought into the country by service personnel on foreign duty. Although the extent of this smuggling is difficult to evaluate, a recent spot check of parcels from Vietnam disclosed that a significant percentage contained arms of one kind or another.

A final source of automatic weapons is the amateur gunsmith. Gunlore has it that semi-automatic weapons can be converted to full automatic by simply "filing down the sear." While some semi-automatics can thus be altered to fire automatically, amateur attempts to do this usually result in a largely useless weapon that fires, if at all, erratically and uncontrollably and at a rate that empties the magazine in one quick burst (unless the weapon stops by jamming). Nevertheless, many amateur gunsmiths have thus "built machineguns" in violation of federal law, usually motivated merely by a desire to see if they could do it. At the same time, however, a skilled machinist with proper equipment and a technical knowledge of firearms can not only convert many autoloading rifles and pistols into automatic weapons but can construct workable submachineguns from metal stock found in any machine shop.[10] Although very difficult to control, the number of illegally manufactured machine-type weapons is probably negligible.

---

[10]According to the Alcohol and Tobacco Tax Division, the Minutemen organization has supplied members with plans and instructions for the home manufacture of a simple submachinegun resembling the British Sten. Although the gun appears to be sound in design and inexpensive in materials, its actual manufacture is probably beyond the capacity of the amateur machinist.

The great majority of illegally owned machineguns are probably in the hands of otherwise law-abiding gun fanciers who have succumbed to the temptation to reactivate their own registered submachinegun or have acquired one for secret target practice with an exotic weapon. The appeal of machineguns to collectors and paramilitary groups has taken them out of general circulation over the last 2 or 3 years and has priced them out of reach of the casual gun buff. Similarly, their high value on the collectors market—often upward of $200—and the fact of their illegality seem to have discouraged their use by other than the most romantic of criminals.

STATISTICAL COMPILATION OF DOMESTIC FIREARMS PRODUCTION AND IMPORTS

To obtain information on domestic production of firearms for the civilian market, the Task Force in August 1968 served subpenas on 68 firms thought to be firearms manufacturers.[1] The subpenas requested information on the number and value of nonmilitary firearms manufactured for sale in the United States each year since 1920. Subsequently, the same information was also requested for the years 1899 to 1919. When precise production information was not available, manufacturers provided estimates based on a variety of records, including factory output, shipping, warranty, and similar records. Although such estimates may not provide accurate totals of domestic production for any particular year, they are the best available information.

The Task Force recognizes that many companies which manufactured firearms earlier this century have now gone out of business, and any information on their production is virtually unobtainable. For example, only eight manufacturers supplied estimates of their production before 1920, even though census data indicate there were about 30 firearms manufacturing concerns at that time. In order to compensate, at least in part, for this omission, information on firearms production was also obtained from the Census of Manufacturers conducted by the Bureau of the Census every other year from 1919 to 1939. Interpolations were made to arrive at estimated total domestic unit production for each of the intervening years from 1920 to 1938. No similar census was made prior to 1919, so the production totals for the years 1899 to 1918 are probably understated.

The other major ingredient in our aggregation of firearms in this country is imports. No figures were kept prior to 1918, but the Bureau of Customs has maintained some records every year since that date. The census data, however, may also understate actual imports. Not only can three firearms be brought into the country by every returning citizen or visitor without being counted, but the census figures also do not include "actions" (the assembly of bolt or lever and trigger). Large numbers of "actions" may have been imported into this country as "parts" and then converted into usable firearms.

---

1. The Treasury Department in 1968 issued 751 manufacturers' licenses. Only a portion of this number are actually engaged in manufacturing firearms; the remainder make parts or are small gunsmithing shops. The Task Force decided to subpena 68 holders of manufacturers' licenses based on information from the Treasury Department, the Commerce Department, and Dun & Bradstreet.

The totals also include the military firearms sold by the Army's Director of Civilian Marksmanship from 1921 to 1940 and from 1958 to 1968. The Army was unable to supply any information on the sales to civilians in the intervening years 1941 to 1957, and no attempt has been made to estimate the volume of such sales.

The aggregation of firearms production by domestic manufacturers for private sale in the United States since 1899 is set forth in Table C-1. The aggregation of reported firearms imports since 1918 for private sale in the United States is set forth in Table C-2. Domestic production (Table C-1) and imports (Table C-2) are combined in Table C-3.

Table C-1—Production of firearms by domestic manufacturers for private sale in the United States

Year	Handguns	Rifles	Shotguns	Total
1899–1945	11,721,901	20,650,672	13,337,675	45,710,248
1946	176,454	728,545	621,173	1,526,172
1947	257,399	952,706	860,425	2,070,530
1948	427,392	1,169,508	1,012,931	2,609,831
1949	255,937	862,249	1,049,636	2,167,822
1950	261,127	846,990	1,324,492	2,432,609
1951	307,023	668,041	1,001,410	1,976,474
1952	398,153	521,166	899,480	1,818,799
1953	354,616	540,949	948,090	1,843,655
1954	326,734	437,231	706,643	1,470,608
1955	362,373	556,380	739,205	1,657,958
1956	450,715	554,143	829,843	1,834,701
1957	460,331	514,024	688,327	1,662,682
1958	439,920	405,734	530,668	1,376,322
1959	518,943	517,275	610,406	1,646,624
1960	474,677	469,162	564,421	1,508,260
1961	447,146	481,697	574,696	1,503,539
1962	430,781	528,585	591,427	1,550,793
1963	452,994	578,528	638,931	1,670,453
1964	491,073	712,840	745,556	1,949,469
1965	666,394	789,906	898,621	2,354,921
1966	699,798	850,031	976,108	2,525,937
1967	926,404	908,683	1,043,854	2,878,941
1968*	1,259,356	1,100,376	1,155,262	3,514,994
Total	22,567,641	36,345,421	32,349,280	91,262,342

*Projection.
Source: Task Force study.

Table C-2–Imports of firearms for private sale in the United States

Year	Handguns	Rifles	Shotguns	Total
1918–45	935,717	70,116	193,102	1,198,935
1946	291	114	6,788	7,193
1947	6,857	122	23,416	30,395
1948	16,642	4,104	28,981	49,727
1949	6,567	4,727	24,313	35,607
1950	16,911	14,070	32,031	63,012
1951	41,350	24,131	44,628	110,109
1952	56,076	26,970	55,806	138,852
1953	61,241	12,856	81,168	155,265
1954	49,721	10,651	81,837	142,209
1955	66,864	14,938	89,323	171,125
1956	84,249	37,734	92,114	214,097
1957	77,701	129,896	110,297	317,894
1958	79,442	198,202	92,975	370,619
1959	129,729	269,307	129,078	528,114
1960	128,166	401,767	124,684	654,617
1961	114,596	309,820	107,596	532,012
1962	167,868	230,607	117,100	515,575
1963	223,068	218,550	119,753	561,371
1964	253,200	181,532	138,692	573,424
1965	346,906	245,243	174,151	766,300
1966	513,019	291,148	191,963	996,130
1967	747,013	239,141	221,667	1,207,821
1968*	1,239,930	263,488	280,650	1,784,068
Total	5,363,124	3,199,234	2,562,113	11,124,471

*Projection.
Source: Task Force study.

Table C-3—Domestic firearms production and imports
for private sale in the United States

Year	Handguns	Rifles	Shotguns	Total
1899–1945.	12,657,618	20,720,788	13,530,777	46,909,183
1946	176,745	728,659	627,961	1,533,365
1947	264,256	952,828	883,841	2,100,925
1948	444,034	1,173,612	1,041,912	2,659,558
1949	262,504	866,976	1,073,949	2,203,429
1950	278,038	861,060	1,356,523	2,495,621
1951	348,373	692,172	1,046,038	2,086,583
1952	454,229	548,136	955,286	1,957,651
1953	415,857	553,805	1,029,258	1,998,920
1954	376,455	447,882	788,480	1,612,817
1955	429,237	571,318	828,528	1,829,083
1956	534,964	591,877	921,957	2,048,798
1957	538,032	643,920	798,624	1,980,576
1958	519,362	603,936	623,643	1,746,941
1959	648,672	786,582	739,484	2,174,738
1960	602,843	870,929	689,105	2,162,877
1961	561,742	791,517	682,292	2,035,551
1962	598,649	759,192	708,527	2,066,368
1963	676,062	797,078	758,684	2,231,824
1964	744,273	894,372	884,248	2,522,893
1965	1,013,300	1,035,149	1,072,772	3,121,221
1966	1,212,817	1,141,179	1,168,071	3,522,067
1967	1,673,417	1,147,824	1,265,521	4,086,762
1968*	2,499,286	1,363,864	1,435,912	5,299,062
Total	27,930,765	39,544,655	34,911,393	102,386,813

*Projection.
Source: Task Force study.

STATISTICAL MATERIALS

1. Polls and Market Research

Much of Part I is based on public opinion polls and market research that had been commissioned by different manufacturers and supplied to the Task Force. This section describes, briefly, the methods and sample sizes of previously unpublished research which is used as source material in the text of the report.

A. Harris Poll, October 1968

This was a national sample of 1,175 men and women over 18, who were asked:
    1. Do you own a firearm?
    2. How many pistols, rifles, shotguns, muzzleloaders, or other firearms do you own?
    3. How many pistols, rifles, shotguns, etc., did you acquire used?
    4. Where do you usually acquire used firearms?
    5. Have you ever disposed of a firearm?
    6. Where do you usually dispose of your firearms?
Table D-1 shows total gun ownership by sex from the Harris data.

Table D-1—Firearms ownership,
United States, 1968
[In percent]

Male	Female	Both Sexes
49	32	41

The high female total was evidently the result of women answering when their husbands owned guns, because the "Female Nonhead of Household" total was nearly double the "Female Head of Household" total—35 percent versus 18 percent—yet "Male Household Heads" outowned "Male Nonheads" nearly 2 to 1—52 percent to 29 percent. Since 1966 manufacturers' research put female ownership at 7 percent of all gun ownership, female Harris returns were disregarded, and the male figures were used as the basis for projecting household ownership.

The average number of guns owned by a person owning any firearms was 2.24. Persons who owned a particular type of firearm were asked how many of that type of firearm they owned. Table D-2 shows the pattern for handgun, shotgun, and rifle owners.

Table D-2—Handgun, rifle, and shotgun owners by number of each weapon owned
[In percent]

	Handguns	Rifles	Shotguns
Own 1............	83	63	75
Own 2	11	24	17
Own 3	4	7	5
Own 4	1	3	3
Own more than 4..	1	3	1
Total	100	100	100

Other data from the survey are discussed in chapters 1, 2, and 3, *supra.*

B. "Manufacturer's Market Research, 1964"

This was an interview poll conducted by an established survey research organization in 1964. By agreement with the organizations which supplied these data, the commissioning and polling organizations cannot be named. The national sample was divided into "shooters" and "nonshooters" to evaluate differences in attitudes between the two groups.

C. "Manufacturer's Market Research, 1966"

A three-stage mail poll involving 35 one-thousand-family panels, supposed to be representative of the nation in social variables. Phase 1 of this poll gave ownership percentages, but these were based on only slightly over 31,000 returns out of the 35,000 questionnaires mailed out. Phase 2 was sent to those in Phase 1 who admitted owning a firearm. Phase 3 was a selection of gun-owning families used in Phase 2 who reported ownership of a particular kind of firearm. In Phase 3, a detailed questionnaire was sent to a subsample of owners of particular types of firearms. Seventy-five to 84 percent of previously identified long gun owners replied to the detailed questionnaire, while 52 percent of previously identified handgun owners replied.

D. 1966 NORC Poll

The data in Chapter 10 on ownership of a weapon in the home for self-defense come from a poll conducted by the National Opinion Research Center for the President's Commission on Law Enforcement and Administration of Justice. The survey was conducted in June 1966. The question on self-defense firearms was asked of a random sample of nonvictims of crime and all victims of crime identified in a 10,000-household survey—the total number of individuals asked the firearms question was 3,787, a disproportionate number of which were crime victims. Because crime victimization was not significantly associated with firearms ownership, the relatively greater amount of representation of crime victims would not appear to distort ownership percentages within racial, social, and economic classes. But, because some groups are more crime prone than others, this relative weighting might have had a slight effect on the total ownership figure. For whites, ownership is positively correlated with income. For Negroes, ownership is negatively correlated with income. Since the sample of victims is made up of a disproportionate number of blacks and poor people of all races,[1] two possible biases, running in opposite directions, can be noted. Both are of relatively small magnitude.

2. Statistical Studies of Firearms and Crime

In addition to a number of analyses based on Federal Bureau of Investigation data, the Task Force attempted to collect detailed information on firearms and crime in 26 cities across the United States. Involved in this effort were 14 of the 16 largest cities in the country, excluding only Milwaukee, Wisconsin, and Chicago, Ill. Milwaukee was excluded on the advice of the International Association of Chiefs of Police, who cooperated with the Task Force in securing the collaboration of the local police departments, and Chicago was excluded from the field study, which began in late August 1968, because that city was experiencing unusual demands on its administrative resources during that period. Ten smaller cities, five of them located in states with generally permissive firearms licensing and five in states which did not have firearms control also were studied. The control and noncontrol cities were matched with respect to region and approximate ethnic concentrations, in an attempt to gage the effectiveness of firearms control strategies with more precision than is allowed by national correlation studies. Unfortunately, in several cities, it was not possible to obtain all the information requested. For this reason, the number of planned small-city comparisons was quickly reduced to three situations in which both cities in a matched pair were able to provide data sufficient for analysis, a number insufficient to generate meaningful conclusions.

With respect to the larger cities, a variety of statistical analyses were made. One of these, mentioned in Chapter 7, involved comparison of knife and firearms attacks and fatalities and the relative deadlines of knives versus firearms in 24 cities for which sufficient data were available. Correlations for the years 1965, 1966, and 1967, and for the 3 years taken together, are presented in table D-3.

Table D-3—Correlations between knife attacks (as a proportion of all attacks) and the proportion of knife as compared to firearms attacks which are fatal, by class of city, 1965-67.

	1965	1966	1967	Sum of 1965-67
14 large cities.................	-.37	-.47	.22	-.31
10 smaller cities...............	-.40	-.58	-.41	-.56
All cities combined	-.39	-.49	-.11	-.44

Source: Computed by the Assist Corp., Annandale, VA.; statistics provided by the FBI.

An earlier analysis had shown that absolute fatality rate from knife attacks did not increase as the proportion of knife to gun attacks increased, but that raw comparison did not control for inter-city reporting differences. On the basis of these data, which do control for reporting differences, it appears that as the number of knife attacks increases in relation to the number of firearms attacks (which presumably happens where guns are less available to assailants), the proportion of knife attacks that are fatal does *not* increase relative to that

---

[1]Ennis, "Criminal Victimization in the United States," U.S. Government Printing Office, 1967, p. 31.

proportion among gun attacks. The small negative correlations in Table D-3 suggest, if anything, the opposite is the case.

FBI and field survey data were utilized further in an attempt to gage the effect of *self-defense firearms* on *crime rates.*[2] This was done in two stages. First, FBI statistics on the *rates of felons killing civilians,* and *rates of civilians killing felons* in 56 cities and robbery rates per 100,000 population in the Standard Metropolitan Statistical Areas of these 56 cities were intercorrelated. Robbery rates are utilized here as a measure of criminality in these cities. The correlations are presented in Table D-4.

Table D-4—Correlations among rates of felons killing civilians, civilians killing felons, and robberies, 56 cities, 1967.

	Rates of felons killing civilians (rate per 100,000)	Rates of civilians killing felons (rate per 100,000)
Robbery rates, SMSA	.48	.12
Rates of felons killing civilians	. . . .	.36

Source: Rates obtained from FBI.

Not surprisingly, robbery rates are moderately related to rates of civilians killed by felons. Rates of civilians *killing* felons are only slightly related to robbery rates, however ($r=.12$). The two types of killing also are moderately related to one another, and this correlation is unaffected when robbery rates are held constant (the partial correlation is .35.) Thus, as the number of felons killed by civilians increases, the number of civilians killed by felons also increases, independent of changes in robbery rate.

In an effort to study this question in more detail, FBI data from the 26 cities originally involved in the field survey were further studied. For this purpose four variables were added to those included in the previous correlation matrix: (1) firearm accident fatality rates of the states in which the cities are located; (2) home robbery rates; (3) burglary rates for the SMSA's of these cities; and (4) the population of the SMSA's. The correlation matrix obtained in this analysis is presented in Table D-5.

Table D-5—Correlation between rates of civilians killing felons and other variables, 26 cities, 1967.*

	2	3	4	5	6	7
1	-.05	-.33	.52	.86	.20	.38
2	. . . .	.25	.46	.02	.33	.35
3	. . . .	. . . .	-.20	-.36	.68	-.08
4	. . . .	. . . .	. . . .	.60	-.22	.71
5	. . . .	. . . .	. . . .	. . . .	-.17	.67
6	. . . .	. . . .	. . . .	. . . .	. . . .	-.07

*Variable 1 = SMSA population.
Variable 2 = Rate per 100,000 of felons killing civilians.
Variable 3 = Rate per 100,000 of civilians killing felons.
Variable 4 = States accidental firearms death rate per 100,000.
Variable 5 = Home robbery rate per 100,000.
Variable 6 = Robbery rate per 100,000.
Variable 7 = Burglary rate per 100,000.

---

[2]See footnote 10 in ch. 10, *supra.*

For these cities the relation between civilians killing felons and robbery rates is much closer (.68) than was the case for the 56 cities. By way of contrast, civilians killing felons bears a small *negative* relationship (-.36) to *home* robbery rates in these cities, general robbery rates *increase*, but the rate of home robberies tends slightly to decrease (accounting for about 13 percent of the variation in such rates). On the other hand, felons killing civilians are unrelated in any systematic way to home robbery ($r = .02$), but they are related somewhat more closely to rates of all robberies ($r = -.33$).

3. Study of Gun Use in Crime

Data on the use of firearms in two closely related crimes—homicide and aggravated assault—are forwarded to the FBI each year from reporting police agencies. The Task Force surveyed 15 major cities on gun use in these crimes and robbery. The robbery data were requested so that gun use in this different area of criminal behavior could be compared with gun use in homicide and assault. The data on assaults, homicide, and robbery by type of gun used were desired to determine the relative importance of handguns and long guns in these crimes.

Usable data on robbery were obtained from 11 of the 14 cities, but the figures in three cities showed firearms robbery as a percentage of armed rather than total robbery, as the following comparison between FBI figures and the Task Force questionnaire figures for 1967 illustrates.

Table D-6—Robbery statistics: 1967.

	Reported to FBI		Reported to task force	
	(a)	*(b)*	*(c)*	*(d)*
	All robbery	Armed robbery	All robbery	Gun robbery
New Orleans ..	2,017	1,453	1,440	1,100
Pittsburgh.....	1,850	897	819	467
San Francisco..	3,879	2,281	2,333	1,438

In these three cases, because columns (b) and (c) were so similar, the percentage of total robbery involving guns was estimated by expressing gun robbery (d) over total robbery reported to the FBI (a).

In three of the 11 major cities where usable robbery data were obtained, data supplied to the FBI and those supplied to the Task Force were substantially inconsistent in reporting either the number of crimes or number of gun-involved crimes.[3]

With these cities excluded, Table D-7 shows the percentage gun involvement and rank of percentage gun involvement for the eight cities.

---

[3]See footnote 7, ch. 11.

Table D-7–Gun use in violent crime: rank order of 8 U.S. cities.

	Homicide		Robbery		Aggravated assault	
	Percent	Rank	Percent	Rank	Percent	Rank
Atlanta.......	78	1	65	3	44	1
Houston......	76	2	76	1	35	2
St. Louis	69	3	70	2	28	3
Los Angeles ...	60	4	46	4	23	4
San Francisco..	53	5	37	5	17	7
Pittsburgh.....	47	6	26	6	19	6
Boston	35	8	19	7	22	5
New York	40	7	13	8	13	8

Rank order correlations:
  Homicide/robbery .91.
  Homicide/aggravated assault .83.
  Aggravated assault/robbery .83.

If the three inconsistent cities are included, by arbitrarily accepting the figures in the police report to the FBI and rejecting those reported to the Task Force, the percentages and rank orders shown in Table D-8 are obtained.

Table D-8–Gun use in violent crime: rank order of 11 U.S. cities.

	Aggravated assault		Homicide		Robbery	
	Percent	Rank	Percent	Rank	Percent	Rank
Cleveland*	49	1	65	5	30	7
Atlanta.......	44	2	78	1	65	3
St. Louis......	28	5	69	3	70	2
Houston......	35	3	76	2	76	1
Detroit*......	27	6	66	4	25	9
Los Angeles ...	23	7	60	6	46	5
San Francisco..	17	10	53	8	37	6
Pittsburgh	19	9	47	9	26	8
Boston	22	8	35	11	19	10
New York.....	13	11	40	10	13	11
New Orleans*..	33	4	56	7	51	4

Rank order correlations:
  Aggravated assault/robbery .63.
  Homicide/aggravated assault .77.
  Homicide/robbery .76.
*Conflict with Task Force figures. See note 7, ch. 11.

The FBI has collected and published data on the types of firearms used in homicide.[4] Table D-9 shows percentage use of handguns in firearms homicide, aggravated assault, and robbery for the major cities surveyed by the Task Force where these data were available.

---

[4]See Fig. 8-1, in ch. 8, and FBI 1967 Uniform Crime Reports, pp. 7, 11.

Table D-9—Handguns as a percentage of all guns used in crime—11 cities: 1967.

	Homicide	Aggravated assault	Robbery
New York.................	87	91	98
Los Angeles	84	80	98
Philadelphia	92	*	99
Detroit.....................	87	83	97
Houston....................	92	89	99
Cleveland	93	94	99
San Francisco...............	90	88	97
St. Louis	93	*	99
New Orleans	95	91	*
Boston.....................	100	*	99
Atlanta	93	98	99

*Not available in comparable form.
Source: Police departments.

4.   Previous Studies of Gun Laws and Violence in the United States

One method of seeking information about the effects of gun laws is to compare rates of gun violence in American states with and without gun licensing. Such comparisons unfortunately are unable to control for the effect of interstate movements of guns, but a number of multi-state comparisons have been made.

Because handguns are so closely associated with violent crime, the significant state laws to be evaluated would seem to be those governing the possession of handguns. Of such laws, two very different forms exist: restrictive laws that attempt to reduce the number of handguns in circulation and permissive laws that attempt to keep such weapons from a small number of high risk individuals but allow most persons to purchase firearms.

Only two American jurisdictions, New York and Massachusetts, have attempted restrictive pistol licensing on a statewide basis. Because the number of restrictive licensing jurisdictions is so small, and because both of them are located in the Northeast, comparing the crime statistics of these states to other states through use of multi-variate correlation techniques is inappropriate. However, a number of states have passed permissive handgun licensing legislation, allowing most individuals to obtain handguns after screening by police or other local authorities to establish that the applying individuals do not have criminal records or suffer from other manifest disqualifications.

A number of inquiries have been made concerning the effectiveness of these state gun laws before the interstate firearms ban in the 1968 Gun Control Act, but the published materials are sparse. The Wisconsin Legislative Reference Bureau noted, in 1960, that states with "gun license laws" exhibited rates of violent crime both higher and lower than the national average.[5] Krug,[6] in 1968, showed that if all states with gun license laws are lumped together and no other factors are considered, the gun law states have crimes no lower than nonlicense states. Because it is difficult to find states that differ in gun laws but are similar in all other respects to use for comparison

---

[5]Wisconsin Legislative Reference Library Research Bull. No. 130, July 1960

purposes, these rough correlations are not of great value. Moreover, since urban, violence prone states are more likely to institute gun laws than other states, a lack of relationship may conceal real differences in violence attributable to differences in gun laws—the problem here is often called self-selection. Also, these two studies do not make comparisons controlling for regional differences that have a profound effect on rates of violent crime.

Unpublished studies of gun law effects are more interesting. The Olin Mathieson Co. conducted a set of multi-variate correlation studies that showed gun license states do not experience significantly less total homicide than non-license states. The correlation matrix obtained is shown in Table D-10.

Table D-10—Firearms laws, other variables, and homicide.

	1	2	3	4	5	6	7
Persons 67/sq mi ...							
Percent urban 60 ...	.5485						
Percent Negro	-.0076	-.1521					
Per capita per income	.4787	.6427	-.4622				
Handguns laws	.0758	-.0653	-.0213	.0405			
Murder rate per							
100,000	-.1713	-.1122	.7507	-.2573	-.1236		
Gun murder rate. ...	-.2668	-.2067	.7204	-.3411	-.1304	.9800	

Because this set of exercises partially controlled for the differences other than gun laws that might condition differences in the rate of homicide, it is of more value than simple correlations between gun laws and crime. However, the comparisons were between states—and thus left a rather large margin of comparative error—and the controls used in this study were not complete. For example, the study controlled for the percentage of a state's population that was "urban" but did not distinguish between degrees of urban concentration, so that Waterloo, Iowa, and New York City are counted equally when. factoring in the effect of the percentage of a state's population that is urban. Yet large metropolitan areas have far higher rates of violent crime than smaller urban areas, so the possibility of self-selection concealing gun law differences remains. Also, while this study controlled for the proportion of Negroes in a state's population, it did not consider the impact of other minority group populations, such as Puerto Rican or Mexican descent groups.

Chism (unpublished honors thesis, University of Chicago, 1968) compared *metropolitan areas* with and without gun licensing laws and concluded that gun laws have a significant effect in reducing violence. The Chism exercise is superior to state-by-state comparisons because it narrows the units compared to metropolitan areas, but this study failed to stratify the areas studied by region.

None of the studies cited above sought to control for factors other than gun laws that might influence rates of violent crime by considering only the percentage of violent crimes that involved firearms. Using percentage gun use as a measure might provide a baseline control for nonlegislative influences. Informative materials might be developed if this approach were combined with comparisons of metropolitan areas rather than states.

---

[6]Alan S. Krug, "The True Facts on Firearms Legislation," three statistical studies, National Shooting Sports Foundation, Inc., 1968.

FIREARMS AND VIOLENT CRIME: CONVERSATIONS WITH PROTAGONISTS

By Donald E. Newman, M.D.

[This paper is based on interviews with 31 inmates of a California prison for youthful offenders. The interviews were conducted by Dr. Donald E. Newman, Director of Psychiatric Services at the Peninsula Hospital and Medical Center, Burlingame, Calif., at the request of the Task Force. The study is designed to provide some insight into the circumstances under which criminals obtain and use firearms and the different roles firearms play in criminal violence.

Of the 31 prisoners interviewed, 18 were Caucasian, 9 were Negroes, and 4 were Mexican-Americans. Eleven were serving terms for assault, 10 for robbery, 6 for murder, and 4 for robbery and assault.

Dr. Newman observed that, although the prisoners differed considerably in temperament and personality, virtually all were victims of low self-esteem and felt a strong need to prove their manliness. Some sought this proof in physical aggression, both in fights and robberies and in the willingness to injure others and risk injury to themselves without feeling or admitting fear. Others sought merely to control, dominate, or intimidate rather than inflict actual injury. For some, self-esteem derived neither from injuring nor dominating others in a fight or holdup, but from being a "successful" criminal with money to spend on girl friends and expensive possessions.

Most of those interviewed exhibited personality disorders ranging from relatively mild to probably psychotic. Almost all showed poor impulse control. Alcohol or other stimulants, particularly methadrine, appeared often to trigger the aggressive impulse or provide the courage necessary to act upon it.

The individuals who seemed especially prone to physical violence almost invariably carried or used firearms. The conspicuous exceptions were those who prided themselves in not needing a gun or those who did not want a fight or assault to end in murder.]

I. How Firearms Criminals Obtain their Firearms

A. Homicide

Of the 31 men interviewed, 6 had killed someone. Of the six, three had used a gun. None of these three provided detailed or reliable information, but two of the men had had guns for 6 months to a year prior to using them. One of the men had a severe addiction to narcotics and used his gun as a means of supporting his habit. The other man stated he had carried a gun routinely for a long period of time, got into a fight at a party, and had used the gun in self-defense against a man with a knife. In the third case, the man stated he was carrying the gun for self-protection against someone who was out to get him, that it fell to the floor in a store, and that he was forced into a situation in which someone was killed. All three had purchased their guns "on the street."

B. Aggravated Assault

Of the men interviewed, 15 were in prison for assault or had committed assaults in the past. Of these 15, 6 committed assault without using a gun. Out of these six, four had consciously avoided using guns, although they were constantly embroiled in street fighting and violence. All were quite specific as to why they avoided the use of guns. They were young men who never backed off and always "went the limit" even in the face of rather overwhelming odds. They were fearful that the gun would lead to killing. In addition, they felt bigger for not needing a gun.

Table E-1 shows that of the 15 men interviewed, 9 used a gun. Only two of the nine obtained the gun within several days prior to the assault. In the other seven cases, the men had guns available for relatively long periods prior to the assault. Most of the histories are similar—that is, once the men and guns got together, difficult situations became potentially lethal.

Table E-1—Obtaining guns for assault

	1	2	3	4	5	6	7	8	9
When prior to crime	1-2 yrs.	Mos.	Mos.	Mos.	1-2 yrs.	Days	1-2 yrs.	Wks.	2 yrs.
How	?	BT	?	B	BT	BT	BT	BT	BT
New/used	?	Used	?	New	New	?	Used	?	?
Acquisition preceded intent	Yes	Yes	Yes	Yes	No	No	Yes	No	Yes
Gun suggested crime	Yes	Yes	Yes	Yes	Yes	Yes	Yes	Yes	Yes
Choice of weapon	Hand-gun	Hand-gun	Hand-gun	Hand-gun	Shotgun	Hand-gun	Hand-gun	Hand-gun	Hand-gun
Crime result of having gun at that moment	Yes	No	Yes	Yes	No	No	Yes	Yes	Yes

Key:
  Yrs. = years,   Mos. = months,   Wks. = weeks,   BT = bought,   B = burglary

The nine men were relatively consistent in how they obtained their guns. Six bought what they believed were stolen guns that were selling from $5 to $35 "on the street." (Although some of these guns are acquired from burglaries of homes, most are new guns acquired through burglaries of sporting goods stores and gunshops, the men reported. If a particularly large cache is involved, it is shipped from one end of the state to the other, where the guns can be disposed of easily "on the street," in poolhalls, or similar places.) In two cases, the source of the gun was vague; in a third, the gun was obtained in a burglary by the interviewee.

As noted above, the guns for the most part were obtained long before the occurrence of the assault. In the two exceptions the intent either to protect or to hurt preceded the obtaining of the gun. The third case where intent preceded acquisition, the cause and effect relationships are less well defined.

This third case involved an intense, cold and bitter young man who had had a variety of weapons readily available for a number of years. His favorite weapon was a shotgun which was always ready for use. In addition, he usually had several handguns. The guns were not only readily available, but used with a fair degree of frequency.

The handgun was clearly the weapon of choice for the assaulters. One exception was a young man who preferred the shotgun because of its greater firepower. His shotgun was usually sawed off and could be hidden in the trunk of a car or on a motorcycle. However, in addition to the shotgun, he always had available a number of handguns to be prepared for any eventuality. This same young man noted that members of his motorcycle gang generally used shotguns and that some were seriously looking for machineguns.

C. Robbery

With robbers, the patterns of gun acquisition and use are less clear, with more room for individual style and circumstance. Table E-2 shows that of the 14 robbers, all but one used a gun.

There was a marked contrast between the men who used guns for assault and the men who used guns for robbery. Those involved with assault had long periods of time between acquisition and use. In contrast, 7 of the 13 men who used guns for robbery obtained them within 1 to 2 weeks prior to the robbery. This group included two men who acquired guns the day of the robbery. Six of the 13 men acquired their guns months or years prior to the commission of the crime.

Again there is a contrast between robbers and assaulters in how guns were acquired. In the assault group, the overwhelming majority had bought weapons they thought were stolen. In the robbery group, however, only 5 out of the 13 bought weapons in street sales. Four others obtained guns in the course of prior burglaries, which generally preceded robbery as the crime of choice for these men. The acquisition of a gun during the course of a burglary played a varying role with respect to when a young man changed from burglary to armed robbery. In the four remaining cases, the weapons were obtained under unusual circumstances. One young man used toy guns which looked real and were purchased in toy stores. A second obtained a gun in the strongarmed robbery of a hardware store run by a very old man. Another young man borrowed guns from friends without their knowledge—despite the fact that he had many of his own. In another case, a man used a gun his wife had owned prior to their marriage.

Of the firearms bought "on the street," half were new, probably stolen from stores. One man used a toy weapon. It seemed to matter little whether a gun was new or used. Only one of the men purchased a new weapon from a store, and he got a defective weapon which misfired during the course of a robbery. The other men found street purchases far easier, less costly, and without risk.

Table E-2—Obtaining guns for robbery

	1	2	3	4	5	6	7	8	9	10	11	12	13
When prior to crime	4 years	Same day	Weeks	Same day	Months	1-2 months	Days	Weeks	Weeks	Months	Weeks	6 months	2 years
How	Wife	Borrowed	Robbery	Burglary	Burglary	Burglary	Toy	Bought	Burglary	Bought	Burglary	Bought	Bought
New/used	Used	Used	New	Used (Father)	Used	New	New	New	New	New	Used	Used	New
Acquisition preceded intent	Yes	No (Friends)	No	No (Father)	Yes	No	No	No	Yes	No	Yes	No	No
Gun suggested crime	Yes	No	No (Friends)	No (Father)	Yes	No	No	No	Yes	No	Yes	No	No
Avoids firing of gun	Yes	Yes	Yes	Yes	Yes	Yes	Yes	Yes	Yes	Yes	Yes	Yes	Yes
Crime result of having gun at that moment	No	No	No	Yes/no	Yes/no	No	No	No	No	No	No	No	No

The robbery group also differs in another way from the men using weapons for assault. The majority of the assault group acquired their weapons with no specific act in mind, whereas 9 of the 13 robbers acquired the weapons after they decided upon their crime.

Handguns or facsimiles of handguns were used by most of the robbers. In addition to the man who used a toy gun, several used unloaded guns or target pellet guns. These men were concerned that a loaded gun might lead to their seriously injuring or killing someone. Most spoke of having a gun that would frighten people, and the usual choice was a big gun. The target gun was apparently one of the fiercest looking of the handguns available. There were, however, a number of men who insisted on having firepower in the event a victim happened to have a gun. Interestingly, these men were also involved in assault and gang fighting. They shared the characteristics of never wanting to be put down, always insisting upon being the masters of a situation.

II. The Role of the Gun

The gun seems to have played many roles, conscious and unconscious, in the violent behavior of these men. Some of these roles could be ascertained from these initial conversations. However, this is a preliminary study involving single interviews. Were we to lengthen the interview process and add psychological testing, we could undoubtedly greatly expand our understanding of the complex significance of this simple device called a gun, not only for the violent offender but for other gun users as well.

A. Assault and Homicide

Of the 15 men charged with assault, 4 spoke of not needing a gun, of being able to rely primarily on their fists and toughness. One of these men prided himself on the use of his knife, which was clearly his choice of weapon.

> The man considered the knife an extension of his hand. It was almost as if it were a part of him. To him, a gun was a foreign body—he could not make it a part of him nor see it as an extension of himself. To use a gun he would have to depend upon something that was not his own. Something he could not (or would not) do. He insisted that all encounters and all victories be his and his alone. He could not share that moment of glory with anyone or anything. In his view, the knife was a part of him. Thus he protested against the increasing use of guns by many of the men involved in violence "on the streets."

One of the men interviewed prided himself on the use of his fists. He too frowned on the use of guns, refusing to depend on a foreign object which would share in the victory. However, he spoke of fighting with his fists as something from the past.

> With the wide use of guns, he feels street fighting without guns is finished. In the past, if you whipped a man with your fists, you knew and he knew who was the stronger. Now, the weakest, most frightened loser can in a single moment become the victor with a gun. He feels that after leaving prison he too will acquire a gun and join a large organization in order to meet this new challenge. There is no defiance when

he states this, but there is more a sense of sadness, for the gun and the organization cannot possibly give him the sense of self-esteem and satisfaction that his fists have provided him in the past. Though he will continue to fight now with a gun and an organization and may win, it will not be his victory, his esteem, and himself. Thus it is with reluctance that he accepts this new dependency on a gun.

This young man makes several points which are echoed in the conversations with the others charged with assault. The process of escalation from fists, tire chains, and knives to guns is more than a numerical progression of hurting power. The gun appears to introduce a number of new elements. As with atomic weapons and small nations, the gun on the street allows the weakest to join the superman club. Whereas there was once a sense of stability, with each man knowing his place in the pecking order, the gun introduces uncertainty. This element of instability in part is corrected by enlarging the gangs, which appears to be the present trend. Five men described this process of escalation. All had used a variety of weapons in the past, but now used guns. Each quite independently picked 1967 as the turning point in the shift to guns, although several of them had used guns previously. Most of them cited deteriorating race relations and outbreaks of racial violence as a major reason for the shift to guns.

John is a handsome young man who is neatly groomed and speaks with some authority. He is at ease and readily discusses his feelings and past history with pride at the insight he has been able to attain by carefully thinking over his life and the events that led to his crimes and imprisonment. The incident for which he is in prison involved his driving into a rival gang's territory and firing over the heads of a number of men who were closing in on him and two of his friends. He spoke of having the weapon in his car, readily available for just such an occasion. He said that when gangs fought in Los Angeles, weapons were always used. He had been shot twice and charged with assault on a number of occasions. The old gang fights using fists, chains, and knives, he noted, were a thing of the past. Now the gun was the favored weapon, and its adoption had led to serious escalation in street fighting.

Guns do not appear to have suggested the crime of assault, but they clearly escalated the violence involved. The men who had guns available eventually used them when the gun, the situation, and the man were all at the right spot at the right moment. Others were able to recognize that this might happen and avoided carrying guns. However, most of the men felt that the situation had progressed to the point where guns were becoming essential, because everyone else had them.

A number of factors are involved in this process of escalation. Guns are readily available. They can be bought cheaply and without delay. They allow a man to attack his victim from a safe distance. In addition, there is an advantage in striking the first blow, and several of the encounters involved assault in order to prevent being assaulted—so-called preventive warfare. The move to guns results in an escalation of the conflicts as well as an escalation of the violence. Whereas fist fighting may have ended a dispute in the past, it is now likely to be settled with a shootout which is usually far out of proportion to the anger involved in the original dispute. With a gun, a moment's anger or loss of control can quickly result in a killing.

The young man who entered the interview room seemed ill at ease during the first part of the interview. He spoke of having a serious drinking problem which had been going on for 4 years. In order to support himself he committed a number of robberies, but had never harmed anyone. He had not been involved in any significant violence in the past. Prior to his coming to prison, he began carrying his gun on his person, even though he was not involved in robbery at that time. He stated that he carried a gun because he was frightened of the police, knew he was wanted, and needed it for protection. He was involved in a 7 day drinking party with a group of friends, playing poker and generally having a big time. There was an acquaintance at the party who challenged him with a knife. After successfully avoiding a fight with this man, he pulled the gun and shot him. He could not explain why, except that he had the gun and was still fearful of the man and his knife.

There is an additional danger in the increasing use of guns. Bystanders are sometimes hurt or killed, which rarely occurs when a fight involves only fists and knives.

Jim described a situation in which he awoke early one morning hearing a commotion across the street. He learned that his sister had been shot and his impression was that she was dying. At the time, Jim was living with his wife. His family had purposefully tried not to involve him because they knew he was easily angered. He became incensed upon hearing of the shooting and possible death of his sister and could think of nothing but revenging her. He suddenly found himself driving a car with four other men, all of whom had guns. They drank and talked of getting the guy, because this same man had been in a lot of other trouble. When they arrived at the place where they found him, they were confronted with three men in the house—all armed with guns. During the fight that followed, a girl was killed. Jim had owned the gun about a year and half without using it. He kept it just in case he might someday need it. The need came, he is now in prison, and a girl is dead. The gun had never been used in a crime, nor had he carried it on the street until the evening of the murder.

Unlike Jim, several other men had carried their guns regularly. For at least one of these men, the actual need for a gun seemed less important than the psychological need merely to be armed.

The man entering the interview room was short, neatly dressed, and confident in his posture and appearance. He smiled readily, though for the first 10 or 15 minutes of the interview he was hesitant and wary. Gradually, he felt more at ease and described how he carried a gun only when he went on the street, dressed and out for a good time, usually with women. This was in marked contrast to when he went to work or when he was not planning to go out socially. On those occasions he never carried a gun. The gun was worn in his belt and was a most important part of his attire. He denied that the gun in any way equalized his lack of height, and he talked about big men falling harder, which made it advantageous to be small. As if to support his contention, he spoke of being good with his fists since the age of 7 when he started defending his manliness. He never allows himself to be pushed around, never backs off, and never takes anything from anyone. He enjoys stealing other guys' girls, and noted that this frequently puts him in a position of having to defend himself. Despite his confident attitude and his prowess with his fists, he has been "wearing" a gun as part of his "dress up for social occasions" for several years now. He spoke of it much as another man might speak of wearing a favorite suit that made him feel better about himself. Whatever he felt he lacked, the gun supplied, and together they were a whole lot more than he was alone.

He did not always use the gun in a tight situation, but its presence allowed him a sense of dignity even when he retreated from several men facing him with a variety of other weapons. He pictured himself backing out of a saloon in an old western movie, covering himself with his gun and telling the "dudes" how he would be back.

B. Robbery

Robbery appears to be a crime made infinitely more possible by having a gun. To rob without one requires a degree of strength, size, and confidence which was lacking in many of the men with whom I spoke. There were, however, four men who said they did not use a gun while robbing. Only two of these had the necessary requisites to carry off a strongarm robbery and they were experts at it. This kind of robbery is performed only when the situation is right—a gas station at night or a single person on the street. For the most part, the men involved in robbery were not very large and not very strong. Some were not very aggressive. Some of these men could not possibly carry out a robbery without a gun. In short, there was a clear reality element in the need for a gun once a man made the decision to rob. The clarity ends there, however, for although the men needed a gun to rob, the converse was also true: they needed to rob in order to use a gun. Some wanted the sense of power and control which robbing with a gun gave them. In each of these cases, it was the gun which provided the power and the opportunity for mastery.

One of the young men with whom I spoke stated he was always the "gunman" in a robbery because he has always been independent. Being in the driver's seat was of prime importance to him. He was not sure he could trust his crime partners, so he elected himself gunman. He notes that this is an easy thing to do because most of the other "dudes" are afraid of guns and would rather drive the car or pick up the money. He showed a real fascination for his gun and spoke of it as if it had an almost magical quality—a key that could unlock any door. As he put it, "it made me king." With a gun he could have anything he wanted—cars, radios, clothes—whenever he wanted.

Another man told me that he was never as powerful as when he had a gun and went into a store to rob.

This young man went on to say that with a gun in his hand he felt as if he were "President or Governor." The feeling was one of absolute power and control. To him it was the epitome of all success; there was nothing to equal it. He spoke of the gun as the instrument that allowed him to have the sheer pleasure and enjoyment of having absolute power. We began to reflect about other weapons that might do this, and he pointed out that this was not possible—only the gun could give him total mastery. As if to complete the parallel with legitimate power, he pointed out that presidents and governors are also dishonest—that they, too, steal and rob, and in this respect he was similar.

One of the young men who had this need to be all powerful appeared to have closed the gap between himself and his gun. He identified with his gun and took on all of its power. Although other men were willing to acknowledge that the power they desperately wanted emanated from the gun, he now saw this power as emanating solely from himself.

I was struck by the childlike appearance of the young man who entered the room with a cocky grin that appeared to reassure him constantly how tough and fearless he was. Although nearly 20, he looked closer to 13. He outlined a life of crime beginning in his early teens, graduating from burglary, car theft, and a variety of minor offenses to armed robbery. At the time of his most recent crimes he was studying college criminology and psychology. He viewed his career in crime much as one views a career in "medicine or any of the other professions." He felt he committed his crimes with intelligence and finesse, and he received a sense of satisfaction from doing it well and fooling the police, especially those who sat in class with him. Although guns were important in allowing him to achieve success with armed robbery, he gave no credit to the gun. He began to speak of accomplishing the same thing with a slingshot or knife, despite his having the size and strength of a boy just reaching puberty. He spoke of himself as if he were a gun. He saw himself as an all-powerful, compelling, frightening giant of a man. Throughout, he remained a babyfaced boy who pathetically wanted to be something he could not be without a gun—a man.

It gradually became clear from these interviews that the most important element in robbery often was not the acquisition of money but the one brief moment in which these men held a gun and forced someone to do anything they commanded. They experienced it as if they were omnipotent, and I often wondered during the course of the interviews if their victims might not represent a significant person from their past. It was difficult to assess how many had become dependent upon or addicted to guns. A number of the men had grown up like many nonviolent, noncriminal men in our culture; i.e., they grew up with guns, were taught how to shoot by their fathers, and had a particular fondness for and fascination with guns. Some kept guns around for no particular reason. Robbery appeared to be almost an excuse to use the gun, giving them both excitement and esteem.

With three of the men interviewed, the gun seemed to play the role of seducer. Its presence suggested and eventually commanded its use, usually to relieve a difficult and frustrating situation. In these cases, the gun was present

prior to the intent to commit the crime. In two of the cases, the gun was acquired in the course of burglary and its possession suggested escalation to
armed robbery. In a third case, it appeared to play an even more important
role as seducer.

> The man who entered the office appeared older than most of the
> others who were interviewed. He had achieved some success in life, was
> educated, and had an air of confidence. It was at first difficult to un-
> derstand why he was here. What came out was a story of a compulsive
> need to gamble in an attempt "to make it big." Throughout his life he
> had preferred taking chances to playing it safe. He gave up several suc-
> cesses, each time gambling on greater rewards. By continually pushing
> the odds, he went downhill financially, until he found himself in need
> of a large sum of money. This sum would enable him to gamble
> once again in a business venture and perhaps "make it big."
> He had never been a violent man, nor had he ever engaged in criminal
> activity. At the time of his marriage several years previously, his wife
> had had a gun, and after their marriage it had always been kept in a
> clothes drawer for their protection. He had done some target practice
> with it several years earlier, but had not thought about it or touched it
> since. Now it was becoming more prominent each time he opened the
> drawer and thought of his need for money. It appeared to act as an
> ever-present suggestion with each new opening of the drawer. He would
> think about it and reject the thought, only to open the drawer and have
> the thought come back again. Eventually, he put the gun to use with
> great fear and trepidation in order to acquire the money he needed.
> This marked departure from his previous life pattern was clearly unac-
> ceptable to him, at least on an unconscious level, and he carefully man-
> aged to get himself caught and imprisoned.

Anger played an important role in the armed robberies committed by several of these young men. In one episode of anger which led to a series of
robberies, the gun played an unusual role.

> One young man related a story of a long history of parental depriva-
> tion. His mother and father had been divorced for a number of years
> and he had alternatively lived alone and with his father whom he de-
> scribed as a "playboy." His father had a number of guns, being an avid
> hunter and gun collector. The boy had been away from his father for a
> prolonged period of time and decided to return in celebration of his
> father's birthday. A fight ensued and his father left the house. Both
> were furious with each other. At this point the son impulsively took
> one of his father's guns and went out to start a series of robberies—
> something he had not done for a rather prolonged period of time. Al-
> though he could not explain all of the dynamics involved, it was clear
> to him the robberies resulted from the anger with his father and that it
> was very important that the robberies be committed with his father's
> gun. It was as if he wanted to have his father along as an accomplice so
> that he could at once be reunited with his father and at the same time
> have him punished as an accomplice in the crime. The closest he could
> come to this was to use his father's gun as his accomplice.

The gun's sharing the guilt as an accomplice is a theme found with a number of the men with whom I spoke. Several felt the need to rid themselves of the gun after a crime as if this rid them of the guilt as well. With one young man, this was a very important theme.

As we talked, I was struck with the overwhelming availability of guns to this man. He had been brought up with guns and now, in his late teens, always had one or two lying around his apartment, and periodically he went target shooting. Although he had plenty of guns of his own, when he needed money and thought of armed robbery, he was careful never to use one of his own weapons. He employed elaborate stratagems to borrow or temporarily steal the gun from a friend, use it in the robbery, and then carefully replace it. He had no good, logical reason for this behavior, but as the previous case, the gun appeared to be an accomplice to share in both the crime and the guilt.

Unlike assaults, the crime of robbery rarely seemed to be inspired by the mere possession of a gun. There were two notable exceptions. One was the young man described above who became angry with his father and took one of his father's guns to use in robberies. However, this young man had robbed in the past. The other case involved a young man who, whenever confronted with a hostile response from a merchant, would pull his gun and "teach him a lesson" by robbing him. This same young man, as in the first example, had also robbed on a number of other occasions which were usually planned in advance and were not the result of possessing a gun at a particular moment.

III. How Would a Scarcity of Weapons
     Affect the Violent Subjects?

Of the men who used guns for assault or robbery, only two felt there was any difficulty in obtaining a gun. The rest not only had no difficulty in obtaining guns but many had guns readily available long before their use or involvement in the crime. Several men mentioned that the delay involved in legally purchasing a gun discouraged them from trying to do so; instead they bought them on the street. In fact, of the men interviewed, only one had purchased a gun through legitimate channels, and this in another state with different laws. Several of the men who committed robbery without guns had found it difficult to acquire one.

One may ask: If guns were not readily available, would the group of men involved in aggravated assault make an effort to acquire guns? With only one or two notable exceptions, the answer seems to be "no" so long as guns were unavailable to either side. Even the two exceptions could get along fairly well with fists, tire chains, and knives. Some of the most violent men would clearly welcome a return to "the good old days."

If one asks the same question concerning those men committing robbery, the answer is less clear. Some of the men would make little effort to get guns. At the same time, there are several men in this category to whom robbery fulfills a significant psychological need; how they would satisfy this need without guns is difficult to imagine. There were several young men who might spend much time and effort in attempting to find weapons; however, this number appears small. Most of the men described a variety of ways they had lived and satisfied needs prior to committing robberies. There were episodes in their lives in which cars were dominant; i.e., they had felt powerful behind a wheel as they now did behind a gun. For a number of young men, engaging in robbery was a way of proving they were not "chicken," and these men had a host of other ways of proving this without resorting to guns and robbery. In short, as with any individual, alternate patterns are sought when the road they are traveling is blocked. Even in a prison setting, they were able to play out their roles and establish their hierarchy.

In speculating with these men on what life in the streets would be like without guns, not one of them could possibly conceive how this could be accomplished and thus found it difficult to speculate on what it would be like. A number of the more violent men assured me this would provide a greater degree of stability in individual and gang relationships.

IV. Summary

The gun to these men is many things. It can in a single individual play a variety of roles and have a variety of meanings. To some it was a source of omnipotent power, while to others it was an equalizer which erased feelings of inadequacy and helplessness. For some, it was a seducer tempting them to an easier and quicker path to success and riches. It was at times a friend, a crime partner, or a fall guy to share the blame.

The gun puts distance between the victim and the assailant. It exaggerates conflict and escalates violence. It is both a source of fear and fascination, and for some it takes on a magical quality. Whatever else a gun may be, it is clearly not simply another weapon, an inanimate object playing a passive role. To these young men it is very much alive.

FIREARMS POLICIES OF EXTREMIST GROUPS

The danger posed by armed extremist groups is difficult to evaluate. Many such groups seem to advocate violence and a few have resorted to it. But extremists tend to attract disproportionate attention; most extremist groups comprise a handful of members, a passionate spokesman, and a busy printing press. Nevertheless, their rhetoric of violence has contributed to the nation's "gun problem" by stimulating fear and the growth of opposition extremist groups.

At the risk of further publicizing these groups, the Task Force has compiled the following excerpts[1] from extremist literature and statements to illustrate the rhetoric at both ends of the spectrum.

Ku Klux Klan

. . .[B]lood will surely flow in the streets. . . .Let it flow! Let us arm our homes to make sure that Negro-Jew blood flows—not ours. . . .[Recommended are hollow-nosed bullets that] go clear through your game, whether two-legged or four. ("Defensive Legion of Registered Americans," *Atlanta Journal,* Apr. 10, 1964.)

———

If you register your gun with anybody, you're a nut! When the conspiracy comes for your firearm, give it to 'em like this grand dragon is going to—right between the eyes. (Robert Scoggins, United Klans of America Grand Dragon for South Carolina, as printed in *Richmond Times-Dispatch,* July 5, 1967.)

———

If it takes buckshot to keep the black race down, Klansmen will use it. (Robert Lee Davidson, Imperial Wizard of the U.S. Klans at Atlanta rally, Nov. 1960.)

National Socialist White People's Party (formerly American Nazi Party)

Whites Must Keep Guns! Gun Control Must Fail!

* * *

More Guns . . .!

If you can spare any kind of weapons, ship them by express. . . . (George Lincoln Rockwell, *White Power,* Sept. 1, 1967.)

———

The National Socialist White People's Party has launched a companion operation. . .NS Arms, which will sell Negro control devices like riot guns, carbines,
and chemical mace to White people who are not yet armed. As soon as NS Arms
has acquired a stock of guns and ammunition from manufacturers, Party members
and supporters will receive a list of weapons which will be available. . . . .

* * *

In August, Party members and supporters are urged to propogandize against
government gun control. Two ways of promoting NS ideas are suggested: letters
to the editor of your local newspapers, and a call to any radio program in your
area which permits people to telephone their opinions in a live broadcast. While
there is always a chance that a letter to the editor will not be published, radio
"talk" shows present a splendid opportunity for blasting gun restrictions.

When explaining the National Socialist viewpoint on gun control, it is essential
to point out that the real issue is not just the protection of the rights of hunters
and sportsmen. The real issue is not even the sanctity of the Second Amendment
to the Constitution, which protects Americans' right to keep and bear arms, although both of these issues are critically important. The *real* issue over gun control is whether or not White Americans will be able to defend themselves against
an uncontrolable, well-armed Black army as soon as the summer riots turn into
all-out race war. Police forces, National Guard and even the Army will be power-
less against twenty million bloodthirsty Blacks who'll have a free hand to burn
and murder unless the White Man is armed and ready to fight. Without guns and
plenty of ammunition, Whites face widespread massacre in every city and rural
community in America. Emphasize the fact that Whites must get their guns and
ammunition and hide them *now,* before gun sales are entirely outlawed. (*Bulletin,*
Aug. 1, 1968.)

———

The following weapons are now available from the Party's new subsidiary,
NS Arms:

Riot Gun. 12 ga., 5 shot, rapid-fire, pump action. The perfect weapon for self-
defense and crowd control. . . .Brand new at $94.95 each.

FN Model 1949 Semi-Automatic Rifle. This is the perfect rapid-fire sniper rifle.
. . .Used . . . at $89 each. Ammunition–$8.50 per hundred.
Madsen Bolt-Action Rifle. . . .With armor-piercing ammunition, this weapon will
penetrate an engine block. Used . . . at $54 each.

The "Volunteer" Semi-Automatic Carbine. Small, compact rifle with nearly un-
limited firepower. Each magazine holds 30 rounds of 45 ACP ammunition, another standard U.S. caliber. Looks just like the old Thompson and shoots as fast
as you pull the trigger. Brand new at $119.95 each. Ammunition at $7.40 per
hundred.

P-38 Semi-Automatic Pistol. . . .This was the standard German sidearm during
WWII. I. . .New, at $89 each. Ammunition at $6.00 per hundred.

Walther PPK Semi-Automatic Pistol. . . .A small, but powerful pocket pistol. Perfect for rapid-fire self-defense. New at $86 each.

Astra .25 Caliber Semi-Automatic Pistol. Seven shots as fast as you pull the trigger, in a weapon smaller than a pack of cigarettes. . . . The perfect weapon for
concealing in a small area. New, at $39.95 each.

High Standard Derringer. . . .Small enough for carrying in purse or under belt.
. . .New, at $39.95 each.

Chemical Mace. . . .The only brand used by thousands of policemen across the
country. Completely disables attackers for several minutes without causing
permanent damage. (*Bulletin,* Aug. 15, 1968.)

Revolutionary Action Movement

Black survival curriculum [presented by Herman Ferguson, former assistant principal of a New York school].

After the morning exercises are over he [the student] goes to physical training where the first part of the period is devoted to target practice on the school shooting range. Following this he reports to a nearby classroom for instruction in weaponry, gun handling and gun safety. (*Guardian*, Mar. 9, 1968.)

Minutemen

Don't overlook the potential of .22 long rifle, pistols or rifles as guerrilla warfare or resistance weapons. These advantages include ready availability, light weight, fast accurate second and third shots due to absence of recoil, and readily available ammunition, good accuracy, simplicity of care and comparatively small report when fired. The .22 can be silenced completely with materials that are always available. Although the .22 lacks killing power, this can be readily increased by filling hollow point bullets with poison. It would be devastating to the morale [sic] of an enemy army to be continuously sniped at by guns that make no flash and no sound but provide sure death from poison projectiles or slow healing wounds from hollow points filled with ordinary household lye. (*Bulletin*, Jan. 1966.)

1. Buy a gun that is new or nearly new . . . .
2. Expect to pay a good price for a good gun. . . .
3. Avoid civilian-made copies of military-made firearms. This especially applies to copies of the .30 carbine. . . .
4. Try to buy your gun in such a way that it cannot be traced to you. If you live in a state or city that requires a permit to buy a gun, go to some other state that does not have such a requirement. Most dealers will ask your name but few will ask for identification.
5. Don't wait—buy your gun now. . . .

* * *

Suppose the reader has no gun at all and is planning to buy one gun only. . . . What shall it be? Though it will surprise many people, my recommendation is a .22 caliber semi-automatic pistol. . . .

It's true that the .22 lacks the "shock" effect of a more powerful cartridge, but this is largely compensated for by the ease of putting a well-placed shot into heart or brain. When needed a second well-aimed shot can be fired quicker from a .22 than from a more powerful weapon. . . .

As a deadly weapon, their effect can be greatly increased by using hollow-point bullets filled with poison. If needed, the hole in the point can be opened up further with a small drill. Sodium or potassium cyanide are two fast acting and easily obtainable poisons. Pharmacists or medical doctors will have ready access to succinyl choline or tubocurarine which are excellent when used in powdered form. If nothing better is available ordinary household lye (thirty cents for a pound can at your local grocery store) will do nicely. . . .

For a small "hideaway" gun, the .25 Browning automatic is unsurpassed. A man wearing slacks and sports shirt can easily carry one of these in his side pants pocket without its ever being noticed. Quality of material and workmanship on all Browning firearms is excellent.

If my one-and-only gun were to be a rifle, once again it would be a .22. First choice would be the Browning semi-automatic which retails at $69.50. This particular rifle can be quickly divided into two parts by just pushing a button and giving the barrel a half twist. The two pieces could then be carried easily in a small suitcase.

The gun can be reassembled just as quickly and is very accurate. . . .

Most of the advantages for the .22 target pistol apply also to the .22 rifle. One advantage not previously mentioned is the ease with which these guns can be silenced. The possession of a "silencer" at this time is illegal but they can be made quite easily and quickly. . . .

Regardless of what kind of gun you have or buy, start at once to buy extra ammunition. Without any public notice, the government has already taken steps to limit the availability of ammunition. Don't wait, when you find it, buy it. If at all possible, keep 1000 rounds per gun on hand at all times. (*On Target,* Dec. 1966.)

Paul Revere Associated Yeomen, Inc. (PRAY)

(1) Join the National Rifle Assn. . . .

(2) Absolutely *REFUSE* to register or give up your arms—under *ANY* circumstances!

(3) Stock up on rifles, shotguns, pistols—all of STANDARD make; with LOTS of STANDARD ammunition. Arm EVERY member of your family who can shoot a gun to protect his own life!

(4) Join "THE MINUTEMEN."

(5) Consult with your next-door neighbors on HOW best to protect your family and home. Arrange to wear certain kinds of caps or shirts for identification; so you won't be firing at one another in the confusion. Do NOT organize the whole block in your neighborhood, as 10% of the people are probably on the OTHER side—trained for "leadership" of such neighborhood groups, to sell you into do-nothing surrender. Be your OWN LEADER of your own household. . . and make it an ARMED ARSENAL!

(6) PREPARE yourself and your sons to fight in the streets—in the alleys—in the parks—in public buildings—around the water works—power plants—City Hall—TV and Radio Stations. . . .while your wife and daughters protect their lives and your home with gasmasks, shotguns, rifles and pistols.

REMEMBER! The Communists CANNOT subdue an ARMED citizenry! (Mar. 22, 1964 letter.)

Breakthrough

Due to the civil disorders and terror that is being planned for the American people by the Communist Conspiracy. . . .the following information is presented to you. . . .for the purposes of defending your home, your family and your neighborhood. In so doing we remind you that that sacred document which is our United States Constitution guarantees every American citizen the right to keep and bear arms.

The most effective weapon for home defense is a 12-gauge shotgun—pump or double barrel. If you are going to buy one, may we suggest a 12-gauge with an 18" or 20" barrel also known as a riot gun. . . .If you are buying one for defense, buy one without a choke.

*   *   *

The above two headings [Ammunition and Rifles] would take a tremendous amount of reading to be able to understand. Therefore, the General Douglas Mac-Arthur Shooting Club has been founded so that interested citizens may join the Club. Instructions on firearms and practice shooting in addition to safety will be taught with the help of the National Rifle Association. The Club will be sanctioned by the National Rifle Association.

Your obligation to provide security for yourself and your family is very great and will probably become greater as time passes. By joining the MacArthur Shooting Club there is much that you can learn to help protect your family. . . . (*Bulletin,* Oct. 1967.)

The Black Panthers

You're all chasing dollars, but there are other people who are chasing dollars to buy guns to kill judges, and police and corporation lawyers. . . .We need lawyers today who have a lawbook in one hand and a gun in the other. . .so that if he goes to court and that. . . .doesn't come out right, he can pull his gun and start shooting.

If I could get two machine guns out of this crowd I wouldn't care if you applauded me or threw glasses at me. . . . (Speech by Eldridge Cleaver, Panther Minister of Information, to a lawyers organization, *Newsweek,* Sept. 16, 1968, p. 30.)

———

It is . . . mandated as a general order to all members of the Black Panther Party for Self-Defense that all members must acquire the technical equipment to defend their homes and their dependents and shall do so. Any member of the Party having such technical equipment who fails to defend his threshold shall be expelled from the Party for Life. (Huey Newton, Executive Mandate No. 3, *The Black Panther,* Mar. 16, 1968.)

———

Every black man should have a shotgun, a 357 magnum or a .38 in his pad to defend it. . . . Every woman should understand that weapon . . . . (Bobby Seale, Panther Chairman, *The Black Panther,* May 18, 1968.)

———

MALCOLM X . . . ROBERT WILLIAMS . . . STOKELY CARMICHAEL . . . RAP BROWN . . . HUEY NEWTON . . . LE ROI JONES . . . these are the people I like . . . CHE GUEVARA . . . FIDEL CASTRO . . . MAO TSE TUNG . . . HO CHI MINH . . . KWAME NKRUMAH . . . FRANTZ FANON . . . I no longer hustle to buy a cadillac but save every coin I can rake, scrape, and borrow for a down payment on a MACHINE GUN . . . . ("I Pledge Allegiance," *The Black Panther,* Nov. 23, 1967.)

———

The Black Panther Party teaches that in the final analysis the amount of guns and defense weapons, such as handgrenades, bazookas, and other necessary equipment, will be supplied by taking these weapons from the power structure . . . . ("In Defense of Self-Defense," *The Black Panther,* May 4, 1968, p. 20.)

———

For the past two weeks we have received reports of your moving against the pig in a revolutionary fashion. You have placed the fear of the gun in them . . . . [H]ere are some things that must be corrected:

One—Target practice is essential so that you can hit what you are shooting at.

Two—You must (repeat YOU MUST) know the effective range of your weapons. ("Message to the Black Panthers of Hunters Point and Potrero Hill," *The Black Panther,* June 10, 1968, p. 3.)

APPENDIX G
STATE FIREARMS LAWS

This appendix is an attempt to describe in brief tabular form the principal provisions of the firearms laws of the 50 states relating to handguns, rifles, and shotguns. No attempt has been made to cover the state laws relating to machineguns and other automatic weapons covered by the National Firearms Act. The assistance of the attorneys general of the various states was requested in an effort to make the summaries as accurate as possible. Although the information in this appendix reflects the firearms laws as they appear on state statute books, this information may not be totally in accordance with the interpretation of these laws in court decisions.

State	Alabama	Alaska	Arizona
Citation of law	Revised Code Ann., Title 14, §§161-186	Stats. Ann., 11-55,010 to 11-55,070	Rev. Stats. Ann., Title 13 §§911-921
Dates of major legislation	1840, 1936, 1947, 1957	1949, 1963	1901, 1939, 1953
Firearms covered	Handguns, firearms with less than 12" barrel	Handguns or concealable arms	Handguns
Persons ineligible to possess	Convicted of crime of violence, drug addict, or habitual drunkard	Convicted of felony or crime of violence, alien, one under influence of alcohol or drugs	Convicted of crime of violence
Ineligible to transfer to	Same as above, minor under 18 and person of unsound mind	No provision	Minor under 18 without parent's consent
Application to purchase required	Yes, sent to Chief of Police within 6 hrs.	No	No
Waiting period required	Yes, 48 hrs.	No	No
License to purchase required	No	No	No
License to possess required	No	No	No
Dealer licensed	Yes	No	No
Dealer must keep record of sales	Yes, for 6 yrs., with serial number	No	No
Dealer must report sales to police	Yes, and must mail copy to Sec. of State	No	No
Registration required	No	No	No

State	Alabama	Alaska	Arizona
License to carry required	Yes, if concealed	No	No
License to carry obtained from	County sheriff	No provision	No provision
Fee and duration	$1 for 1 yr.		
Carrying prohibited	If concealed	If concealed	If with intent to assault
Carrying in vehicle prohibited	Yes	No	No
Unlawful intent required	No	No	Yes
Altering serial numbers prohibited	Yes	No	No
Confiscation on unlawful use	Yes	No	Yes
Penalties for violation:			
Illegal possession	Up to 5 yrs.	To $1,000 and/or 1 yr.	To 5 yrs., $2,000, or both
Illegal carrying	To 6 mos. hard labor	5 to 100 days and/or $10 to $200	10 to 30 days
Other illegal acts	$50 to $500 fine		$20 to $300, or both
Exemptions:			
Persons	Law enforcement officers, military, members or organizations authorized to purchase firearms from U.S.	No provision	Peace officers while on duty, person in self-defense, if not concealed
Firearms	Antiques, rifles, shotguns	Rifles and shotguns	No provision
Municipalities with additional local provisions			

State	Arkansas	California	Colorado
Citation of law	Stat. Ann., §§41-4501 to 41-2525	West's Ann. Calif. Code, Penal Code, §§12000 to 12560; Penal Code, §171a-171e	Rev. Stats., §§40-11-1 to 40-11-11
Dates of major legislation	1837, 1881, 1953	1917, 1925, 1967	1963
Firearms covered	Handguns	Handguns and concealable weapons	Handguns and concealable weapons
Ineligible to possess	No provision	Alien, drug addict, felon using firearm	Felon within past 10 yrs, or convicted of narcotics possession, cannot carry concealed
Ineligible to transfer to	No provision	Same as above and minors between ages 16 and 18 without parent's consent for all firearms and minors under 18 for handguns	No provision
Application to purchase required	No	Yes, and for mail orders	No
Waiting period required	No	Yes; 5 days	No
License to purchase required	No	No	No
License to possess required	No	No	No
Dealer licensed	No	Yes	No
Dealer must keep record of sales	No	Yes	No
Dealer must report sales to police	No	Yes; on date of sale with copy to State Bureau of Identification	No

State	Arkansas	California	Colorado
Registration required	No; repealed prior to 1930's	No	No
License to carry required	No provision	Yes; if concealed or loaded in public place	Yes, if concealed and on the person
License to carry obtained from	No provision	Sheriff, Chief of Police	Chief of Police, mayor, or county sheriff
Fee and duration	No provision	$3 for 1 yr.	No provision
Carrying prohibited	Yes; if used "as a weapon" and other than an Army or Navy pistol uncovered and in the hand	If concealed or loaded in a public place	If concealed
Carrying in vehicle prohibited	Yes	Yes, if concealed or loaded	No
Unlawful intent required	No	No	No
Altering serial numbers prohibited	No	Yes	No
Confiscation on unlawful use	No	Yes	Yes
Penalties for Violation: Illegal Possession		Up to 15 yrs. in state prison; or up to 1 yr. in county jail, or $500, or both	By felon, 2 to 10 yrs.
Illegal carrying	30 to 90 days, or $50 to $200, or both	Misdemeanor—up to 1 yr. in jail; 2d offense is felony if weapon concealed.	By felon, 2 to 10 yrs.
Other illegal acts	Same	Carrying loaded weapon in certain public places	Up to 1 yr.

State	Arkansas	California	Colorado
Exemptions: Persons	Police or military while on duty, and persons while on journey or upon own premises	Peace officers, members of armed forces, guards, or messengers while performing employment duties exempt from carrying laws; antique gun club members exempt enroute to and from meetings.	Peace officer on duty while on or enroute to or from range; licensed hunter or target shooter exempt from limitations on use of firearms by ex-convicts.
Firearms	Army or Navy pistols, rifles and shotguns	Antiques, rifles and shotguns	Rifles and shotguns
Municipalities with additional local provisions		State presumed to preempt local regulation.	

State	Connecticut	Delaware	District of Columbia
Citation of law	Stats. Ann., Title 29, §§27 to 38; Title 53, §§202 to 206A	Code Ann., Title 11, §§461-467; Title 24, §§901-905	Code of, Title 22, §§3201 to 3217, Arts. 50 to 56
Dates of major legislation	1947, 1949	1915, 1939, 1953, 1968	1906, 1932, 1958, 1968
Firearms covered	Handguns	Handguns and concealable deadly weapons	Handguns, rifles, and shotguns
Ineligible to possess	Felon	Alien, felon, convicted of crime of violence, person committed for mental disorder, narcotic addict.	Felon, drug addict, person of unsound mind, person convicted of assault or narcotics offense, person convicted of crime of violence or weapons offense, person with physical defect, person to whom not in public interest, or

State	Connecticut	Delaware	District of Columbia
Ineligible to possess—Continued			person involved in mishap causing death or injury to another; minor 18-21 unless has parent's consent and during daylight hours and with licensed person over 21.
Ineligible to transfer to	Alien, minor under 18	Same as above, and, minors or intoxicated persons	Same as above
Application to purchase required .	Yes	Yes	Yes; dealer must receive permission from police before he can deliver pistol
Waiting period required	Yes; 1 week	No	48 hrs.
License to purchase required . . .	No	No	No
License to possess required	No	No	Yes; via registration of all firearms
Dealer licensed	Yes	Yes	Yes
Dealer must keep record of sales .	Yes; for 6 yrs. with serial number	Yes; with names of 2 persons who identify purchaser to dealers	Yes; with duplicate application to police
Dealer must report sales to police.	Yes; within 24 hrs.	No	Yes; and must forward applications to register rifle and shotguns to police
Registration required	No	No	Yes; all prior possessed firearms and rifles and shotguns as acquired; within 48 hrs. if brought into District

State	Connecticut	Delaware	District of Columbia
License to carry required	Yes; with fingerprints; appeal provided upon denial	If concealed	Yes
License to carry obtained from	Chief of Police	County Superior Court Judge	Chief of Police
Fee and duration	$2 for 1 yr.	$2 for 1 yr.	$2 for registration; $2 for 1 yr. handgun license; $2 for 5 yrs. shotgun or rifle license
Carrying prohibited	Yes; open or concealed, pistol or loaded rifle and shotgun	Yes; if concealed	Yes
Carrying in vehicle prohibited	Yes	Yes; if available for immediate use	Yes; rifles and shotguns must be unloaded and wrapped
Unlawful intent required	No	No	No
Altering serial numbers prohibited	Yes	No	Yes; dealer cannot sell gun without serial number
Confiscation on unlawful use	Yes	Yes	Yes
Penalties for violation:			
Illegal possession	By felon, up to 5 yrs. or $1,000, or both	During commission of felony—not less than 5, or more than 30 yrs., or fine, or both	Up to 10 yrs.
Illegal carrying	Up to 3 yrs. or $500, or both	20 days to 7 yrs. or $25 to $2,000, or both	Up to 1 yr., or $1,000, or both
Other illegal acts		Not less than $500 or more than $2,000, or 90 days to 5 yrs., or both	Not more than 10 days or $300 for failure to register

State	Connecticut	Delaware	District of Columbia
Exemptions:			
Persons	Police, military, travelers, and members of organizations authorized to purchase firearms from the Federal Government	Police, military, and peace officers	Police, military, members of organizations authorized to purchase firearms from the Federal Government; firearms dealers and gunsmiths
Firearms	Antiques, rifles, and shotguns	Hand pistols, rifles, and shotguns	Antiques, toys
Municipalities with additional local provisions			

State	Florida	Georgia	Hawaii
Citation of law	Stats. Ann., Title 44, ch. 790	§§26-1702, 26-4505, 26-5110 to 26-5112, 26-5201, et. seq.; 26-5404, 26-6907, 26-7301, 26-7308, 26-7311, 27-3101, et. seq.; 86-1302; 92A-901 to 92A-911, 92A-9925	Rev. Laws, §§157-1 to 157-33
Dates of major legislation	1927, 1955, 1965	1837, 1882, 1910, 1958, 1960, 1963, 1964, 1968	1927, 1933
Firearms covered	Handguns, concealable arms, and repeating rifles	Handguns	All firearms and ammunition
Ineligible to possess	Mental incompetent, drug addict, alcoholic, vagrant, minor under 18 without parent's consent	Minor under 18	Convicted of crime of violence or narcotic offense; alien; fugitive from justice

State	Florida	Georgia	Hawaii
Ineligible to transfer to.	Same as above	Minor under 18, insane person, felon and convict	Pistol to person without a permit. Rifle and shotgun to minor under 20 without a hunting license
Application to purchase required.	No	No	No
Waiting period required	No	No	No
License to possess required	No	No	Yes; via permit to purchase or registration
License to purchase required	No	No	Yes; from Chief of Police; no fee, valid for 10 days
Dealer licensed	No	No	Yes
Dealer must keep record of sales	No	No	Yes
Dealer must report sales to police.	No	No	Yes; dealer must send permit to police, with serial number, within 48 hrs.
Registration required	No	No	Yes; with police
License to carry required	Yes (also for repeating rifles)	Yes, but cannot carry concealed	Yes
License to carry obtained from	County commission with $100 bond	Local official with $100 bond to Governor	Chief of Police
Fee and duration	For 2 yrs.	$0.50 for 3 yrs.	$10 for 1 yr.
Carrying prohibited.	Yes (also for repeating rifles)	Yes, unless licensed	Yes

State	Florida	Georgia	Hawaii
Carrying in vehicle prohibited. . .	No; if cased	Yes, if on or near person	Yes
Unlawful intent required	No	No	No
Altering serial numbers prohibited	No	No	Yes
Confiscation on unlawful use	Yes	Yes	Yes
Penalties for violation:			
Illegal possession.	3 to 6 mos. or $100 to $500, or both	Misdemeanor	Up to 1 yr. or $500, or both
Illegal carrying.			Up to 1 yr. or $1,000, or both
Other illegal acts		Misdemeanors—shooting on or near public highway, shooting on Sunday without cause, shooting at or in trains or cars, shooting at picnics, carrying deadly weapon in court, and pointing at another without cause; shooting at another without cause: 1-4 yrs.	
Exemptions:			
Persons.	Police; militia; authorized shooting and hunting clubs, en route to or from hunting, camping, or target shooting; bank and armored car guards	Peace officer, military, militia, gun collector (from dealer licensing)	Police, military, and during target practice
Firearms	Rifles and shotguns	Rifles and shotguns	
Municipalities with additional local provisions	Since 1968, Miami Beach requires registration		

State	Idaho	Illinois	Indiana
Citation of law	Code of, Title 18, §§3301 to 3313, Title 36, §403	Stats. Ann. (Smith-Hurd), Ch. 38 §§24-1 to 24-6 and §§83-1 to 83-15	Stats. Ann. (Burns), Title 10, §§4701 to 4755
Dates of major legislation	1913, 1947	1925, 1968	1819, 1925, 1935
Firearms covered	Handguns	All firearms and ammunition	Handguns
Ineligible to possess	Indian	Minor under 18 (pistol), minor under 21 (long guns), felon within 3 yrs., misdemeanant within 5 yrs., narcotic addict, person of unsound mind	No provision
Ineligible to transfer to	Indian and minor under 12	Same as above	Felon, drug addict, person of unsound mind, minor under 21, intoxicated person
Application to purchase required	No	No	Yes
Waiting period required	No	72 hrs.	48 hrs.
License to purchase required	No	Yes; identification card for purchase of only firearms and ammunition	No
License to possess required	No	Yes; ID card	No
Dealer licensed	No	Yes	Yes
Dealer must keep record of sales	No	Yes; handguns for 10 yrs. with serial number	Yes; for 6 yrs.

State	*Idaho*	*Illinois*	*Indiana*
Dealer must report sales to police .	No	No	Yes; within 6 hrs. of purchase
Registration required	No	No	No
License to carry required	If concealed	Yes; ID card	Yes
License to carry obtained from . .	County sheriff	Department of Safety	Police Chief, sheriff
Fee and duration	No provision	$5 for 5 yrs.	$1 for 1 yr.
Carrying prohibited.	If concealed and within city limits; if intoxicated	If concealed or in public meeting	Yes
Carrying in vehicle prohibited . . .	No	If concealed	Yes
Unlawful intent required	No	No	No
Altering serial numbers prohibited	No	Yes	Yes
Confiscation on unlawful use . . .	No	Yes	Yes
Penalties for violation: Illegal possession		Felon—1 to 10 yrs., others up to 1 yr. or $1,000, or both	Felon—up to $1,000 or 1 to 10 yrs., or both
Illegal carrying	20 to 90 days or $25 to $200, or both	Up to 1 yr. or $500, or both	Up to $500; third offense: up to 1 yr.
Other illegal acts			

State	Idaho	Illinois	Indiana
Exemptions: Persons	Peace officers and county officials	Police, military, members of shooting club; nonresident if possesses valid license from own state, nonresident if firearm unloaded and encased, nonresident licensed hunter, nonresident traget shooter	Police, military, traveler, member of target or shooting club
Firearms	Rifles and shotguns		Antiques, rifles and shotguns
Municipalities with additional local provisions		Since 1968, Chicago requires registration of all firearms	

State	Iowa	Kansas	Kentucky
Citation of law	Code Ann., §§695.1 to 695.27, §§696.1 to 696.11	Stats. Ann., §§21-2601 to 21-2617, §§38-701 to 38-702	Rev. Stats. (Baldwin), §§435.170 to 435.235
Dates of major legislation	1935, 1965	1933, 1955	1813, 1962
Firearms covered	Handguns and concealable weapons	Handguns	Concealable weapons
Ineligible to possess	No provision	Felon, drug addict, person convicted of narcotic violation, habitual drunk, minor under 21	Minor
Ineligible to transfer to	No provision	Same as above, and incapacitated person	Minor

State	Iowa	Kansas	Kentucky
Application to purchase required .	No	No	No
Waiting period required	No	No	No
License to purchase required . .	No	No	No
License to possess required . .	No	No	No
Dealer licensed	Yes	No	No
Dealer must report sales to police.	Yes; to county recorder within 24 hrs.	No	No
Registration required	No	No	No
License to carry required	If concealed	No	No
License to carry obtained from . .	County sheriff	No provision	No provision
Fee and duration	1 yr.		
Carrying prohibited.	If concealed	If concealed	If concealed
Carrying in vehicle prohibited . .	Yes; unless unloaded and in trunk or case	No	Yes
Unlawful intent required.	No	No	No
Altering serial numbers prohibited	No	No	No
Confiscation on unlawful use . .	No	Yes	Yes

State	Iowa	Kansas	Kentucky
Penalties for Violation:			
Illegal possession	Up to 5 yrs. or $1,000, or both	Felon, up to 5 yrs.	2 to 5 yrs.
Illegal carrying		Up to 1 yr.	
Other illegal acts		Unlawful sale: $5 to $100 or up to 30 days, or both	
Exemptions:			
Persons	Police, unloaded gun transported to range, hunting, or for collecting purposes		Sheriffs, police, mail carriers, military
Firearms	Rifles and shotguns	Rifles and shotguns	Rifles and shotguns
Municipalities with additional local provisions			

State	Louisiana	Maine	Maryland
Citation of law	Stats. Ann., Title 14, §§91, 94, 95; Title 40, §§1751 to 1791	Rev. Stats. Ann., Title 15, §§391-393, 455; Title 17, §§853, 854; Title 25, §2031	Ann. Code, Art. 27, §§36,406, 442-448
Dates of major legislation	1935, 1942	1955	1904, 1951, 1966
Firearms covered	Handguns and concealable weapons	Handguns and concealable weapons	Handguns
Ineligible to possess	Alien enemy, minor under 21	Felon if released within 5 yrs.	Convicted of crime of violence, habitual drunk, narcotic user, fugitive from justice, minor under 21

State	Louisiana	Maine	Maryland
Ineligible to transfer to.......	Same as above	Same as above. Minor under 16 without parent's consent for hunting	Same as above. Minor under 18: any firearm without parent's consent
Application to purchase required .	No	No	Yes; sent to state police, given 7 days to disapprove
Waiting period required	No	No	7 days
License to purchase required ...	No	No	No
License to possess required	No	No	No
Dealer licensed	Yes	No	Yes
Dealer must keep record of sales .	No	Yes; with serial number	Yes; permanent
Dealer must report sales to police.	No	No	Yes; with serial numbers which are kept in central file
Registration required	No	No	No
License to carry required	If concealed	If concealed	No
License to carry obtained from ..	No provision	Local police chief or 1st selectman and chief of state police for non-resident	Superintendent of state police
Fee and duration		1 yr.	
Carrying prohibited.........	If concealed	If concealed	If concealed

State	Louisiana	Maine	Maryland
Carrying in vehicle prohibited	No	No; except loaded	Yes; if on or about person
Unlawful intent required	No	No	No
Altering serial numbers prohibited	No	No	Yes
Confiscation on unlawful use	No	No	No
Penalties for Violation:			
Illegal possession			
Illegal carrying	Up to 1 yr. or $500, or both	Up to 90 days or $100, or both	6 mos. to 3 yrs.
Other illegal acts			
Exemptions:			
Persons	Sheriff, militia, and military	Police, licensed private detective, guard	Police, person with reasonable apprehension of danger to his person; minor in organized militia
Firearms	Antiques, rifles, and shotguns	Rifles and shotguns	Antiques, rifles, and shotguns
Municipalities with additional local provisions			State presumed to preempt local legislation

State	Massachusetts	Michigan	Minnesota
Citation of law	Gen. Laws Ann., Ch. 140j, §§121-131H; Ch. 296, §§10-14	Comp. Laws Ann., §§28.421 to 28.434, §§750.222 to 750.239	M.S.A. Publ. Health and Safety, §609.66; Game and Fishing, §100.29
Dates of major legislation	1795, 1927, 1957, 1968	1949, 1963	1942, 1950

State	Massachusetts	Michigan	Minnesota
Firearms covered	All firearms	Firearm 30 inches or less in length	Handguns
Ineligible to possess	Alien, felon, convicted of unlawful use, possession or sale of narcotics; minor under 18	Felon, until 8 yrs. after release; minor under 21, person under influence of drugs or alcohol; person of unsound mind	Alien, except when hunting
Ineligible to transfer to	Same as above; all firearms to minor under 18 without parent's consent	Same as above. Resident of less than 6 mos.	Minors under 18 without parent's consent
Application to purchase required	No	Yes	No
Waiting period required	No	No	No
License to purchase required	Yes (handguns); ID card (rifles and shotguns)	Yes; valid 10 days	No
License to possess required	Identification card	Yes (safety inspection certificate)	No
Dealer licensed	Yes	Yes	No
Dealer must keep record of sales	Yes; with permit number	Yes; with serial number	No
Dealer must report sales to police	Yes; to Commissioner of Public Safety	Yes	No
Registration required	No	No	No
License to carry required	Yes	If concealed	No
License to carry obtained from	Chief of Police	County licensing board (with fingerprints)	No provision

State	Massachusetts	Michigan	Minnesota
Fee and duration	$2 for 2 yrs.	$3 for 3 yrs.	
Carrying prohibited	Yes	If concealed	No
Carrying in vehicle prohibited	Yes	Yes; unless unloaded and encased in trunk	Yes; if loaded
Unlawful intent required	No	No	Yes
Altering serial numbers prohibited	Yes	Yes	No
Confiscation on unlawful use	Yes	Yes	No
Penalties for Violation: Illegal possession / Illegal carrying / Other illegal acts	$50 (in vehicle, up to $100) Knowingly issuing license in violation of act—6 mos. to 2 yrs. imprisonment; buying by resident for use of another—misdemeanor—$50 to $500 or prison 6 mos. to 2 yrs.	Up to 5 yrs. or up to $2,500 Alteration of serial number: up to 2 yrs. or $1,000, or both	Up to 90 days, or $100
Exemptions: Persons	Person involved in pistol or revolver competition; nonresident with valid out-of-state permit; gun collectors during meeting	Police, military, member of shooting club or organization authorized to purchase or receive firearms from the U.S. Government	Member of organized shooting club
Firearms		Rifles and shotguns	Rifles and shotguns
Municipalities with additional local provisions			

State	Mississippi	Missouri	Montana
Citation of law	Code Ann., Title 11, §§2079 to 2086; Title 31, §§8621 to 8631	V.A.M.S., §§564.610 to 564.650, 564.490, 564.600	Rev. Code, §§94-3525, 3527, 3579 to 3580
Dates of major legislation	1942, 1950	1929, 1949, 1967	1907, 1947
Firearms covered	Handguns and concealable weapons, high powered rifles	Concealable weapons	Handguns
Ineligible to possess.	No provision	Intoxicated person at public meeting	Prisoner; minor under 14 without parent accompanying
Ineligible to transfer to	Minor under 16, intoxicated person, student on campus	Minor without parent's consent	No provision
Application to purchase required .	No	No	No
Waiting period required	No	No	No
License to purchase required . . .	No	Yes	No
License to possess required . . .	No	No	No
Dealer licensed	No	No	No
Dealer must keep record of sales .	Yes; and of ammunition sales for 3 yrs.	Yes	No
Dealer must report sales to police.	Yes; with serial number	Yes	No
Registration required	Yes; pistols and high-powered rifles, with sheriff	No	No

State	Mississippi	Missouri	Montana
License to carry required	No	If concealed	If concealed
License to carry obtained from	No provision	Sheriff	District court judge
Fee and duration			1 yr.
Carrying prohibited	If concealed	If concealed	If concealed
Carrying in vehicle prohibited	Yes	If on or near person	No
Unlawful intent required	No	No	No
Altering serial numbers prohibited	No	Yes	No
Confiscation on unlawful use	Yes	No; but writ of replevin needed to obtain weapon from police	No
Penalties for Violation:			
Illegal possession	By felon, 1 to 5 yrs.		Prisoner, 5 to 15 yrs.
Illegal carrying	Up to 6 mos., or $100 to $500	Up to 5 yrs. or at least 50 days to 5 yrs. in county jail	6 mos. to 1 yr. or $25 to $100 or both
Other illegal acts	Up to 1 yr.	6 mos. to 5 yrs. imprisonment in county jail or $50 to $5,000, or both	
Exemptions:			
Persons	Police, militia, transient, collector registered with the NRA; person using in self-defense	Sheriff, militia and person traveling in a continuous journey peaceably through the state	Sheriff, police, military
Firearms	Unloaded rifles and shotguns	Rifles and shotguns	Rifles and shotguns
Municipalities with additional local provisions			

State	Nebraska	Nevada
Citation of law	Neb. R.R.S., §§28.1011.07 to 28.1011.10	Rev. Stats. §§202.300 to 202.360
Dates of major legislation	1899, 1929, 1943, 1967	1911, 1925, 1959
Firearms covered	Handguns	Handguns and concealable weapons
Ineligible to possess.	Felon, fugitive, minor under 18; alien (all firearms)	Felon, alien
Ineligible to transfer to.	No provision	Minor under 18, minor under 14 (all firearms)
Application to purchase required .	No	No
Waiting period required	No	No
License to purchase required . . .	No	No
License to possess required . . .	No	No
Dealer licensed	No	No
Dealer must keep record of sales .	No	No
Dealer must report sales to police.	No	No
Registration required	No	No
License to carry required	No	If concealed
License to carry obtained from . .	No provision	County Commissioner
Fee and duration		
Carrying prohibited	If concealed	If concealed

State	Nevada	Nebraska
Carrying in vehicle prohibited	Yes	Yes; if concealed and accessible
Unlawful intent required	No	No
Altering serial numbers prohibited	No	No; handgun without serial number cannot be sold or received
Confiscation on unlawful use	Yes	No
Penalties for Violation:		
Illegal possession	Felony	
Illegal carrying	A gross misdemeanor to a felony for second offense	Up to 2 yrs. or $1,000, or both
Other illegal acts		
Exemptions:		
Persons	Police, military	Police, armed forces, and person using in self-defense
Firearms	Antiques, rifles, and shotguns	Rifles and shotguns
Municipalities with additional local provisions	Clark County, including Las Vegas, requires handgun registration	

State	New Mexico	New Jersey	New Hampshire
Citation of law	Const., Art. II, Sec. 6, Stats. Ann., §§40A-22-15, 15-40-12, 53-2-13 and 14, 67-33-44	N.J. Stats. Ann., §2a: 151-1 through 151-62	Rev. Stats. Ann., Ch. 159, Ch. 570:5, 571:20-20-a (supp.)
Dates of major legislation	1963	1924, 1927, 1966	1923, 1951, 1967
Firearms covered	Concealed loaded firearms	Handguns, rifles and shotguns	Handguns

State	New Hampshire	New Jersey	New Mexico
Ineligible to possess	Felon, alien; minor without parent's consent	Felon, fugitive, person afflicted with mental disorder, convicted of crime, narcotic violator or addict, habitual drunk	Prisoner
Ineligible to transfer to	Same as above; nonresidents without permit, or authority under laws of state of their residence	Same as above, and minor under 18	No provision
Application to purchase required	No	No	No
Waiting period required	No	No	No
License to purchase required	No; except alien or felon	Yes; permit to purchase handgun; ID card to purchase long gun	No
License to possess required	No	No	No
Dealer licensed	Yes	Yes	No
Dealer must keep record of sales	Yes	Yes	No
Dealer must report sales to police	Must report to selectmen of towns or chief of police of cities within 7 days of purchase	Yes	No
Registration required	No	No; but records kept of sale	No
License to carry required	If loaded and concealed	Yes; permit for handgun and ID card for long gun	No

State	New Hampshire	New Jersey	New Mexico
License to carry obtained from	Selectman, mayor, police chief for resident, State police for nonresidents	County court judges for handgun, police chiefs for long gun	No provision
Fee and duration	$2 for 2 yrs. to residents, $4 to nonresidents	$2 permanent	
Carrying prohibited	If loaded and concealed	Yes	Yes, if concealed and loaded
Carrying in vehicle prohibited	Yes; if loaded	Yes	No
Unlawful intent required	No	No	Yes
Altering serial numbers prohibited	Yes	Yes	No
Confiscation on unlawful use	No	Yes	No
Penalties for Violation:			
Illegal possession	Up to 2 yrs.	Up to 3 yrs.	Petty misdemeanor
Illegal carrying	By felon; up to 5 yrs., others 1 yr. to 5 yrs. or $100, or both	Up to 7 yrs.	
Other illegal acts	Selling without license, up to 2 yrs., sale to minor: up to 3 mos., or $100, or both	Up to life	
Exemptions:			
Persons	Sale to person personally known as non-licensed seller	Police, military, members of rifle or pistol clubs with list of their members recorded	Police, sheriff, and deputies; private patrol operators
Firearms	Antiques, rifles, and shotguns	Antiques and ornaments	Unloaded firearms, rifles, and shotguns
Municipalities with additional local provisions			

State	New York	North Carolina	North Dakota
Citation of law	McKinney's Penal Laws, §§265.00 to 265.35, §§400.00 to 400.05	Gen. Stats., §§14-269, 402 to 409, 316	N.D. D.C., chap. 62
Dates of major legislation	1882, 1888, 1911, 1931, 1933, 1963, 1967	1919, 1951, 1965	1923, 1943
Firearms covered	Handguns and concealable weapons, rifles or shotguns possessed by felons or certain misdemeanants	Handguns and concealable weapons	Handgun, firearm with 12" or less barrel length
Ineligible to possess	Felon, minor under 16, mentally ill, convicted of certain misdemeanors	Minors under 12, unless under supervision of parent or guardian (all firearms)	Felon, drug addict, habitual drunk, and minor under 17
Ineligible to transfer to	Same as above		Same as above
Application to purchase required	No	Yes	No
Waiting period required	No	No	No
License to purchase required	Yes	Yes (includes mail-order sales)	Yes; permit to carry required to transfer
License to possess required	Yes	No	No
Dealer licensed	Yes	Yes	Yes
Dealer must keep record of sales	Yes	Yes	Yes
Dealer must report sales to police	Yes, state police	No	No; but must report to Secretary of State within 7 days

State	New York	North Carolina	North Dakota
Registration required	Yes	No	No
License to carry required	Yes but licenses issued outside New York City not valid in New York City	No	Yes
License to carry obtained from	Outside New York City: Judge of court of record. In New York City: Police Commissioner		Judge, sheriff, police chief, or marshal
Fee and duration	Outside New York City: $3 to $5 (valid until revoked). In New York City: $20 for 2 yrs. and renewable $10 for 2 yrs.		1 yr.
Carrying prohibited	Yes	If concealed	Yes
Carrying in vehicle prohibited	Yes	No; if not concealed on or about person	Yes
Unlawful intent required	No	Yes	No
Altering serial numbers prohibited	Yes	No	Yes
Confiscation on unlawful use	Yes	Yes; but may be returned by court order	No
Penalties for Violation:			
Illegal possession	Felony	Up to 2 yrs. and/or $1,000	
Illegal carrying	Felony		Felony, 10 additional yrs. if while committing crime
Other illegal acts	Class A misdemeanor	30 to 120 days; $50 to $200	Misdemeanor

State	New York	North Carolina	North Dakota
Exemptions: Persons	Police, military, person surrendering pistol to police	Police and military	Law enforcement officers; military; certain Federal officials; dealer or gunsmith
Firearms	Rifles and shotguns	Rifles and shotguns	Antiques, rifles and shotguns
Municipalities with additional local provisions	Since 1968, New York City requires registration of rifles and shotguns.		

State	Ohio	Oklahoma	Oregon
Citation of law	Rev. Code (Page's) Title 29, §§2923.01 to 2923.06, 2923.28, 2945.76	Stats. Ann., §1271 et seq.	O.R.S., §§166.210 to 166.480
Dates of major legislation	1953, 1967	1910, 1957	1925, 1933, 1953
Firearms covered	Handguns	Handguns	Handguns and weapons with less than 12" barrel
Ineligible to possess	Minor under 17 and tramp	Minor, felon	Alien, felon, minor under 18
Ineligible to transfer to	Same as above	Same as above	Same as above
Application to purchase required	No	No	No
Waiting period required	No	No	No
License to purchase required	No	No	No

State	Ohio	Oklahoma	Oregon
License to possess required	No	No	No
Dealer licensed	No	No	No
Dealer must keep record of sales	Yes; for 5 yrs.	No	Yes, with serial number
Dealer must report sales to police	No	No	Yes
Registration required	No	No	No
License to carry required	No provision	No	If concealed
License to carry obtained from	No provision	No provision	County sheriff, or head of police department
Fee and duration			$0.50 for 1 yr.
Carrying prohibited	If concealed	Yes	If concealed
Carrying in vehicle prohibited	Yes, if concealed and accessible	Yes	If concealed
Unlawful intent required	No	No	No
Altering serial numbers prohibited	No	No	Yes
Confiscation on unlawful use	No	No	If unlawfully concealed
Penalties for Violation:			
Illegal possession		Felony for a felon	
Illegal carrying	30 days to 6 mos., up to $500; or 1-3 yrs.	Up to 30 days, or $25 to $50	Up to 5 yrs. if felon or alien 5 to 100 days or $10 to $200
Other illegal acts			Up to 1 yr. and/or $500

State	Ohio	Oklahoma	Oregon
Exemptions: Persons	Police, sheriff, special police with bond; person using in self-defense	Police officer, except when intoxicated, person while hunting	Police, military or civil organizations while parading or going to or from meetings, member of target shooting club, hunters and fishermen while going to or from expeditions
Firearms	War trophies in unserviceable condition	Rifles and shotguns	Rifles and shotguns
Municipalities with additional local provisions	Since 1968, Toledo requires ID card to possess		

State	Pennsylvania	Rhode Island	South Carolina
Citation of law	Stats. Ann. (Purdon's), Title 18, §§4416, 4628, 4629	Gen. Laws, §§11-47-1 to 11-47-56	Code of, §16-129, §15-1388
Dates of major legislation	1939, 1953, 1956	1927, 1938, 1956, 1959, 1968	1922, 1952
Firearms covered	Handguns and concealed firearms	Handguns	Handguns
Ineligible to possess	Alien (all firearms), convicted of crime of violence, drug addict, drunk, person of unsound mind and minor under 18	Convicted of crime of violence, fugitive from justice, tramp, drunk, person of unsound mind and drug addict	Convicted of crime of violence, fugitive from justice, drunk, drug addict, mentally unsound person, minor under 21, subversive
Ineligible to transfer to	Same as above and minors under 16 (all firearms)	Same as above, and minor under 21	Same as above

State	Pennsylvania	Rhode Island	South Carolina
Application to purchase required .	Yes	Yes (including out-of-state pur-chasers)	No
Waiting period required	48 hrs.	72 hrs.	No
License to purchase required . . .	No	No (repealed in 1965)	No
License to possess required . . .	No	No	No
Dealer licensed	Yes	Yes	Yes
Dealer must keep record of sales .	Yes, for 6 yrs.	Yes; with serial number for 6 yrs.	Yes; with serial number for 3 yrs.
Dealer must report sales to police.	Yes, within 6 hrs. of application	Yes; within 24 hrs.	No
Registration required	No	No government agency may keep list of privately owned arms	No
License to carry required	If loaded and concealed	Yes	No provision
License to carry obtained from . .	Chief of police or sheriff of county	Police chief, attorney general	No provision
Fee and duration	$0.50 for 1 yr.	$2 for 1 yr.	
Carrying prohibited	If loaded and concealed	Yes	Yes
Carrying in vehicle prohibited . .	Yes	Yes	Yes; if accessible
Unlawful intent required	Yes	No	No
Altering serial numbers prohibited	Yes	Yes	Yes

State	Pennsylvania	Rhode Island	South Carolina
Confiscation on unlawful use	No	Yes	Yes; but city cannot confiscate—only state
Penalties for Violation:			
Illegal possession	Up to 3 yrs. or $3,000, or both	Up to 5 yrs. or $1,000, or both	Up to 1 yr. or $1,000, or both
Illegal carrying	Up to 1 yr. or $500, or both	Up to 5 yrs. or $1,000 or both	10 to 30 days or $20 to $100, or both
Other illegal acts		Up to 1 yr. and 1 day	
Exemptions:			
Persons	Police, military, members of target clubs, and members of organizations authorized to purchase or receive firearms from the U.S.	Police, military, and person carrying firearms to and from target range	Police, military, hunter, and member of shooting and target clubs
Firearms	War trophies, antiques, unloaded rifles, and shotguns	Antiques, rifles, and shotguns	Antiques, rifles and shotguns
Municipalities with additional local provisions	Since 1965, Philadelphia has required a license to purchase a handgun		

State	South Dakota	Tennessee	Texas
Citation of law	Code of, §§13.1609 to 13.1610, §§21.0104 to 21.0209	Code Ann., §39-4901 et seq.	Penal Code Ann. (Vernon's), Art. 483 to 489c; Civil Stats. (Vernon's), Art. 19.01
Dates of major legislation	1919, 1935	1838, 1932, 1955	1887, 1905, 1951, 1968
Firearms covered	Handguns and concealable weapons	Handguns	Handguns

State	South Dakota	Tennessee	Texas
Ineligible to possess	Felon, drug addict, person of unsound mind, minor under 18	No provision	Felon except on own premises
Ineligible to transfer to	Minor under 15 without parental consent (all firearms)	Minor, alien, drunk, convicted of crime of violence, person of unsound mind, drug addict	Minor without parent's consent
Application to purchase required	Yes	Yes	No
Waiting period required	28 hrs.	15 days	No
License to purchase required	No	No	No
License to possess required	No	No	No
Dealer licensed	Yes	Yes	Yes
Dealer must keep record of sales	Yes; with serial number for 6 yrs.	No	Yes; for 10 yrs.
Dealer must report sales to police	Yes; within 6 hrs.	Yes	Must be available for police inspection
Registration required	No	No	No
License to carry required	Yes	No provision	No
License to carry obtained from	Judge of court of record, chief of police, or sheriff	No provision	No provision
Fee and duration	$0.50 for 1 yr.		
Carrying prohibited	Yes	If with intent to go armed	Yes

State	South Dakota	Tennessee	Texas
Carrying in vehicle prohibited . . .	Yes	Yes	Yes; unless traveler
Unlawful intent required	No	Yes	No
Altering serial numbers prohibited	Yes	No	No
Confiscation on unlawful use . . .	No	Yes	No
Penalties for Violation:			
Illegal possession	1 mo. to 1 yr., or $100 to $500, or both; on premises with liquor license: 2 to 5 yrs.		
Illegal carrying.	Up to 1 yr. or $500 to $1,000, or both	$50 and imprisonment at the discretion of the court	1 mo. to 1 yr. or $100 to $500; 2 to 5 yrs. if offense in bar or dance hall
Other illegal acts			Sale to minor without consent: $25 to $200 or up to 1 yr. or both
Exemptions:			
Persons	Member of shooting club or organization authorized to purchase or receive firearms from the United States; person using in self-defense	Police, military	Military, peace officer, person traveling, or on own premises
Firearms	Rifles and shotguns	Army and Navy pistols, rifles and shotguns	Rifles and shotguns
Municipalities with additional local provisions			

State	Utah	Vermont	Virginia
Citation of law	Code Ann., §76:23-1 through §76:23-8	Stats. Ann., Title 13, §§4001 to 4013	Code Ann., Secs. 18.1-258 through 18.1-272, 18.1-344, 18.1-347, 15.1-523 through 15.1-525
Dates of major legislation	1909, 1943, 1959	1892, 1945	1950, 1956, 1968
Firearms covered	Handguns and concealable weapons	Handguns	Handguns
Ineligible to possess.	Aliens	Minors under 16 (all firearms)	Minor under 18
Ineligible to transfer to.	Aliens and minors under 14 without parental consent	Same as above	Same as above
Application to purchase required .	No	No	No
Waiting period required	No	No	No
License to purchase required . . .	No	No	Only in counties with a population density of more than 1000 per sq mi.
License to possess required	No	No	No
Dealer licensed	No	No	Yes
Dealer must keep record of sales .	No	Yes; for 6 yrs.	Yes
Dealer must report sales to police.	No	No	No; but must report to clerk of circuit court
Registration required	No	No	No

State	Utah	Vermont	Virginia
License to carry required	If concealed	No	If concealed
License to carry obtained from	Peace officer's written consent	No provision	Circuit or corporation court
Fee and duration			1 yr.
Carrying prohibited	If concealed and no written consent by a peace officer	Yes; if intent to injure	If concealed
Carrying in vehicle prohibited	Yes; if loaded	No	Yes; if concealed on person
Unlawful intent required	No	Yes	No
Altering serial numbers prohibited	No	No	No
Confiscation on unlawful use	No	No	Yes
Penalties for Violation:			
Illegal possession	Misdemeanor		
Illegal carrying	Misdemeanor	Up to 2 yrs. or $200 or both	Up to 1 yr. or $20 to $500, or both
Other illegal acts	Misdemeanor		
Exemptions:			
Persons:	Peace officer in performance of his duties		Police, jail guards, mail carriers
Firearms:	Rifles and shotguns	Rifles and shotguns	Rifles and shotguns
Municipalities with additional local provisions	Salt Lake City requires dealer to register firearm purchased		

State	Washington	West Virginia	Wisconsin
Citation of law	Rev. Code Ann., Title 9, §§9.41.010 to 9.41.260	Code Ann., §§61-7-1 to 61-7-13	Stats. Ann., §§164.01 to 164.20, §§941.20 to 941.94
Dates of major legislation	1935, 1961	1909, 1925	1883, 1925, 1955
Firearms covered	Handguns	Handguns and high powered rifles and ammunition	Handguns
Ineligible to possess	Convicted of crime of violence, drug addict, habitual drunk, mental incompetent; alien and minor under 14 (all firearms)	Alien; any firearm	Intoxicated person and minor under 18
Ineligible to transfer to	Same as above, except minor under 21	Same as above	Same as above
Application to purchase required	No	No; except for high powered rifle	No
Waiting period required	No	No	No
License to purchase required	No		No
License to possess required	No; except alien	No	No
Dealer licensed	Yes	Yes	No
Dealer must keep record of sales	Yes; for 6 yrs.	No	No
Dealer must report sales to police	Yes; within 6 hrs.	No	No
Registration required	No	No	No
License to carry required	Yes	Yes	Yes

State	*Washington*	*West Virginia*	*Wisconsin*
License to carry obtained from..	Judge, police chief, or sheriff	Circuit court with publication in newspaper	County clerk
Fee and duration	$1 for 1 yr.	$20 and $3,500 bond	
Carrying prohibited.	Yes; if concealed	Yes	If concealed
Carrying in vehicle prohibited...	Yes; but only if loaded	Yes	Yes; unless encased
Unlawful intent required	No	No	No
Altering serial numbers prohibited	Yes	No	No
Confiscation on unlawful use ..	No	No	No
Penalties for Violation:			
Illegal possession	1 to 10 yrs.	First offense, 6 to 12 mos.; thereafter, 1 to 5 yrs.	Up to 1 yr. or $500, or both
Illegal carrying	90 days or $250		
Other illegal acts			
Exemptions:			
Persons	Police, military, and members of organizations authorized to purchase, or receive weapons from the United States	Police, military, sheriff with bond, member of shooting club	Peace officer
Firearms	Antiques, rifles, and shotguns	Rifles and shotguns	
Municipalities with additional local provisions			

State	Wyoming
Citation of law	Stats. Ann., Title 6m, §§237 to 246
Dates of major legislation	1890, 1910, 1920, 1945
Firearms covered	Handguns
Ineligible to possess	Alien (all firearms), minor under 21
Ineligible to transfer to	Same as above
Application to purchase required	No
Waiting period required	No
License to purchase required	No
License to possess required	No
Dealer licensed	Yes
Dealer must keep record of sales	Yes; permanent, signed by purchaser
Dealer must report sales to police	No
Registration required	No
License to carry required	If concealed
License to carry obtained from	Sheriff

State	Wyoming
Fee and duration	For 3 yrs.
Carrying prohibited	If concealed
Carrying in vehicle prohibited	No
Unlawful intent required	No
Altering serial numbers prohibited	No
Confiscation on unlawful use	Yes
Penalties for Violation:	
Illegal possession	Up to $100
Illegal carrying	
Other illegal acts	
Exemptions:	
Persons	Law enforcement officer
Firearms	Rifles and shotguns
Municipalities with additional local provisions	

THE ARMY CIVILIAN MARKSMANSHIP PROGRAM

Statutes passed in the early 1900's directed the Secretary of the Army to support private shooting clubs; sell rifles, shotguns, handguns, and ammunition at cost to members of the National Rifle Association (NRA); and hold annual shooting matches open to both military personnel and civilians.[1] This support rose from the $2,500 appropriated for trophies in 1903[2] to almost $5 million in the middle 1960's.[3] The "Civilian Marksmanship Program," as its elements are nominated, has currently been cut to a minimal level,[4] as it was during World War II.[5]

---

[1]These statutes now provide in relevent part:
  Civilian Rifle Ranges (10 U.S.C. §4308). "The Secretary of the Army shall provide for (1) the . . .maintenance, and operation of indoor and outdoor rifle ranges; (2) the instruction of able-bodied citizens of the United States in marksmanship,. . .; (3) . . .the maintenance . . . of matches . . . in the use of those arms, and the issue of arms, ammunition, targets and other supplies . . . (5) the sale to members of the National Rifle Association at cost, and the issue to clubs organized for practice with rifled armes, . . . of the arms, ammunition, targets, and other supplies and appliances necessary for target practice . . . ."
  Rifle Instruction (10 U.S.C. §4310).
  "(*a*) The President may detail regular or reserve officers and noncommissioned officers of the Army to duty as instructors at rifle ranges for training civilians in the use of military arms.
  "(*b*) The Secretary of the Army may detail enlisted members of the Army as temporary instructors in the use of the rifle to organized rifle clubs requesting that instruction."
  Issue of Rifles and Ammunition (10 U.S.C. §4311). "The Secretary of the Army may provide for the issue of a reasonable number of standard military rifles, and such quantities of ammunition as are available, for use in conducting rifle practice at rifle ranges. . . ."
  National Rifle and Pistol Matches (10 U.S.C. §4312). "An annual competition called the National Matches and consisting of rifle and pistol matches shall be held as prescribed by the Secretary of the Army. The National Matches are open to members of the armed forces. . .and to civilians. . . ."
[2]32 Stat. 941 (1903).
[3]"Fact Sheet" on Civilian Marksmanship Program, undated, announcing actions taken on June 21, 1968, by the Secretary of the Army; testimony of David McGiffert, Under Secretary of the Army, Hearings on the Federal Firearms Act before the Senate Subcommittee To Investigate Juvenile Delinquency, 90th Cong., 1st sess., pp. 737, 738 (1967).
[4]"Fact Sheet," *supra*, footnote 3.
[5]See, e.g., Hearings on Military Establishment Appropriations before a subcommittee of House Committee on Appropriations, 78th Cong., 2d sess., pp. 503-05 (1944).

I. <u>Legislative Background</u>

At the beginning of the century, the Army was of the view that all infantrymen need not be trained to shoot accurately but only to deliver an even volume of fire over an entire area; trained riflemen were apparently expected to concentrate fire on obvious targets, leaving the rest of an opposing force unharassed.[6] A contrary view seems to have been held by Congress, which began support of accurate shooting by authorizing the expenditure in 1903 of $2,500 for trophies and medals for military rifle matches that year.[7]

The support of marksmanship was extended further in 1905 when the Secretary of War was directed to sell to the states, at cost, Army weapons and ammunition for use by rifle clubs.[8] In 1911, civilians were authorized to compete for the national match trophies.[9] In 1914, sale of Army weapons at cost was streamlined by allowing direct sale to members of rifle clubs.[10]

By 1916 the possibility that the United States might need a large Army encouraged preparation for mobilization. In keeping with European practice, the National Defense Act of 1916[11] envisioned an Army composed basically of untrained troops from civilian life stiffened by a cadre of Regular Army personnel. In addition, support of civilian rifle clubs under the Civilian Marksmanship Program was authorized.[12] A Director of Civilian Marksmanship (DCM) was appointed,[13] rifle ranges were built, and personnel were assigned to instruct on the ranges.[14]

The shortage of rifle instructors and untrained riflemen during the mobilization for World War I reinforced the postwar position of the members of Congress interested in appropriating funds for the national matches, the sales program, and support of the rifle clubs.[15] The Army, which by then supported accurate marksmanship for all its personnel and had surplus ammunition, offered no opposition.[16] In 1924, however, opponents of such expenditures managed to strike from the appropriation bill the language supporting the marksmanship program by successfully arguing that such language was in fact substantive legislation unsuited to an appropriation bill.[17] Congress thereupon enacted

---

[6]See S. Rept. 1291, accompanying H.R. 13446, 70th Cong., 1st sess. (1928); Hearings before Senate Committee on Military Affairs, 70th Cong., 1st sess., pp. 3-4, 11-20 (1928).
[7]32 Stat. 941 (1903).
[8]33 Stat. 986-87 (1905).
[9]36 Stat. 1058 (1911).
[10]38 Stat. 370 (1914).
[11]39 Stat. 166 (1916); see Hearings before the House Committee on Military Affairs on H.R. 12766, 64th Cong., 1st sess., pp. 15-16 (1916).
[12]39 Stat. 166, 211 (1916).
[13]39 Stat. 648 (1916).
[14]*Ibid.*
[15]See, e.g., Hearings on War Department appropriations before a Subcommittee of House Committee on Appropriations, 68th Cong., 1st sess., pp. 864-90 (1924); *Report, supra,* footnote 6.
[16]See hearings, *supra,* footnote 15, p. 881; *Report supra,* footnote 6.
[17]See Cong. Rec., Mar. 27, 1924, pp. 5264-65, 5341-46; May 12, 1924, p. 8599.

legislation restating in permanent form the recurring language from the appropriation bills and added an unexplained change whereby the sale of Army weapons to members of rifle clubs was authorized only to NRA members.[18]

A final statutory change appeared in 1928, after the Army announced that the national matches would be held only in alternate years in order to free support units for field training during the summer.[19] However, shooting interests persuaded Congress to require the Army to hold the matches annually and to submit annual reports to the Congress.[20]

II. Growth of the Program

These annual reports and the testimony during appropriation hearings provide some information on the scope of the program for the past 40 years.

In 1929 the National Board's appropriation was $744,750.[21] The major share, $500,000, was to pay the expenses of 4,455 military and civilian participants in the national matches at Camp Perry, Ohio. The pay and subsistence of 1,868 Army personnel who conducted the matches were provided through ordinary Army appropriations.[22] Support for the matches was suspended or greatly reduced from 1931 to 1935.[23] Beginning in 1952, the matches grew to a peak in the mid-1960's, when they cost an estimated $3 million annually.[24] However, Army support was suspended in 1967, due to the Vietnam war and a shortage of funds.[25]

In the last 40 years, the sale of military firearms to NRA members expanded even more, although this, too, was suspended during World War II. In 1929, 14,797 rifles and 408 handguns and 4.8 million rounds of ammunition were sold to NRA members. Weapon sales escalated with the end of World War II, when surplus stocks were enlarged. A witness at the fiscal 1960 appropriation hearings reported sales of approximately 95,000 rifles in the previous year.[26] The peak year appears to have been 1963, however, when approximately 126,000 rifles and 20,000 handguns were sold to NRA members at cost.[27] Since the beginning of the program, approximately 1 million military firearms have been sold to NRA members. The exact figure is unknown

---

[18]43 Stat. 510 (1924).

[19]See hearings, *supra,* footnote 6.

[20]45 Stat. 786 (1928).

[21]Annual Reports for Fiscal 1929 from the National Board for the Promotion of Rifle Practice and the Director of Civilian Marksmanship to the Secretary of War; Hearings on War Department appropriation bill before the Subcommittee of the House Committee on Appropriations, 70th Cong., 2d sess., pp. 967-998 (1928).

[22]Hearings on War Department appropriation bill before a Subcommittee of the House Committee on Appropriations, 74th Cong., 1st sess., pp. 449, 513-522, 656-660 (1935).

[23]Hearings on Military Establishment appropriation bill before a Subcommittee of the House Committee on Appropriations, 80th Cong., 1st sess., p. 1262 (1947); 81st Cong., 2d sess., p. 1197 (1950); 82d Cong., 2d sess., pp. 1440-1443 (1952).

[24]"Fact Sheet," *supra,* footnote 3.

[25]*Ibid.*

[26]Hearings on National Military Establishment appropriation bill before a Subcommittee of the House Committee on Appropriations, 81st Cong., 1st sess., p. 852 (1949).

[27]Memorandum from the Director of Civilian Marksmanship to the Army General Counsel, dated July 24, 1968.

Table H-1–Military Firearms Sold by Army to NRA Members

Year	Handguns	Rifles	Shotguns	Other	Total
1921	4,079	5,877	....	.....	9,956
1922	3,357	10,482	....	.....	13,839
1923	....	5,470	....	.....	5,470
1924	135	5,777	....	.....	5,912
1925	1,449	8,265	....	.....	9,714
1926	2,645	5,319	....	.....	7,964
1927	482	8,766	....	.....	9,248
1928	657	12,764	....	.....	13,421
1929	408	14,797	2	.....	15,207
1930	....	15,135	7	.....	15,142
1931	....	20,111	7	.....	20,118
1932	170	4,167	....	.....	4,337
1933	129	3,268	1	.....	3,398
1934	118	4,051	....	.....	4,169
1935	231	6,141	....	.....	6,372
1936	145	6,616	3	.....	6,764
1937	154	7,032	....	183	7,369
1938	129	6,962	....	.....	7,091
1939	80	6,747	....	35	6,862
1940	81	7,929	....	16	8,026
1941-57 unavailable*	....	....	....	.....	....
1958	88	844	....	.....	932
1959	9	6,071	....	.....	6,080
1960	35,732	71,204	....	.....	106,936
1961	38,806	78,023	4,329	.....	121,158
1962	43,062	77,180	2,343	.....	122,585
1963	19,551	125,574	1,813	.....	146,938
1964	870	54,346	154	.....	55,370
1965	6,874	44,654	10	.....	51,538
1966	7,489	31,841	17	.....	39,347
Total	166,930	655,413	8,686	234	831,263

*The Army has advised the Task Force that regulations between 1941 and 1957 did not require keeping of these records.

because the Army has not maintained records for all years. A tabulation of sales for the years for which information is available is shown in Table H-1.

Support for rifle clubs, including those in schools, has followed a similar pattern in the last 40 years. In 1929, $275,000 worth of shooting equipment, including 2,426 rifles and 10 million rounds of ammunition, were issued to 1,625 clubs and schools. In 1965 approximately $900,000 worth of such equipment was issued to 5,800 clubs,[28] including the new issue of 2,225 weapons and millions of rounds of ammunition.[29]

---

[28]"A Study of the Activities and Missions of the NBPRP," report to the Department of the Army by Arthur D. Little, Inc., dated Jan. 1966, pp. 28-31. The under Secretary of the Army has indicated that this figure is understated by perhaps $500,000. See Hearings, *supra,* footnote 3, at pp. 743-44.

[29]DCM Memorandum, *supra,* footnote 27.

III. Present Program

The Civilian Marksmanship Program has been drastically curtailed since 1967 as a result of Vietnam budgetary restrictions and doubts as to the cost effectiveness of the program.[30]

Support for the national matches has been terminated; equipment is issued only to junior members of rifle clubs and then only for the first 2 years of activity; and only national match grade rifles are being offered for sale, and only to active competitive marksmen.[31] The Army estimates that the cost of the program has thus been decreased from approximately $5 million to $136,750.[32]

In addition, future NRA weapon buyers will be subject to a fingerprint and record check, as will officers of those junior rifle clubs which are eligible for support.[33] The value of this increased vigilance is illustrated by the fact that a spot check during 4 months of 1967 of 9,663 prospective NRA weapon buyers led to rejection of 75 such prospective buyers, largely because of prior criminal records.[34]

IV. Evaluation

Because the statutory basis for the Civilian Marksmanship Program has not been altered and a termination of the Vietnam war may lead to its reinstatement, the program must be evaluated as it was before the recent cutback. Some groups favoring the program believe any program which encourages gun use is good for that reason alone.[35] This judgment is grounded on the general assumption that trained riflemen are needed to defend against outside attack or internal disorder.[36] The principal evidence offered to support this assumption is the extensive civilian programs conducted by the Russians, Chinese, East Germans, and Swiss.[37]

Whatever validity this assumption may once have had, it is difficult to imagine, in light of the present strength of American military forces, a foreign power successfully landing an army in the United States. The fact that the Chinese, Swiss, and East European countries are worried about such a threat may result from their exposed geographical position, their having less powerful military forces, or perhaps from their desire to remind their populace of the possibility of foreign invasion.

The assumption also suggests trained marksmen are a bulwark against internal disorder. Yet proponents of disorder are also armed,[38] and encouragement of gun use is perhaps as likely to escalate as to control disorder, unless the gun owners are part of disciplined groups such as the National Guard or the Swiss militia.

---

[30]See *supra,* footnote 3.
[31]"Fact Sheet," *supra,* footnote 3.
[32]*Ibid.*
[33]*Ibid.*
[34]Hearings, *supra,* footnote 3, p. 765.
[35]See, e.g., statement by Franklin Orth of the National Rifle Association, prepared for presentation to the Subcommittee on Defense Appropriations of the Senate Committee on Appropriations, dated July 15, 1968, and the supplement to this statement, dated Aug. 1, 1968.
[36]*Ibid.*
[37]*Ibid.*
[38]See app. F.

A. Gun Club Program

   The strongest specific argument in favor of support of junior gun clubs is
that it increases the quality of shooters entering the Army. A report by
Arthur D. Little & Co. showed that only 385, or 3 percent, of the 12,859
basic trainees in its sample had gun club training, and yet they provided 40 of
the 131 recruits who qualified on the rifle range with scores within 10 points
of the top.[39] It is unknown whether this 3 percent, which identified itself
as having a special interest in guns, would have scored as well without the Army
sponsored program. The Little study suggests that the higher a soldier scores
on a standard rifle range, the better he is equipped for combat. Yet current
Army "train fire" rifle instruction involves trainees' walking along a path and
shooting at man-size targets which unexpectedly pop up at various ranges and
in different directions.[40]
   In addition, the club program affects only 3 percent of Army trainees, 85
percent of whom are assigned tasks that do not involve their marksmanship
abilities.[41] The Army must insure that the results merit the expenditure—
approximately $900,000 in recent years.
   Similarly, the Army must decide if the club program is needed as a source
for marksmanship instructors, if not riflemen, in time of emergency.[42] Although a shortage of instructors was alleged during World War I mobilization,[43] similar shortages have not been reported during World War II, the Ko-
rean War, or the Vietnam action.

B. National Match Program

   It has been argued that the $3 million spent each year in support of the national
matches increases interest in shooting by both military and civilian personnel[44] and aids the policemen who attend marksmanship schools while at the
matches.[45]
   In addition to a possible question as to the value of increasing civilian interest in shooting, it can also be asked whether the matches provide desirable
training to military personnel, particularly since the military forces already
hold their own annual shooting matches.[46] Moreover, in addition to their
own small arms schools, police may obtain small arms training through the
FBI. There is no apparent need for schools conducted at the matches to train
police.

---

[39]See report, *supra,* footnote 28.
[40]Hearings, *supra,* footnote 3, p. 773.
[41]See hearings, *supra,* footnote 3, p. 744-745.
[42]See hearings, *supra,* footnote 3, 775.
[43]See, e.g., Hearings on War Department appropriations before a Subcommittee of
   house Committee on Appropriations, 68th Cong., 1st sess., pp. 882-885 (1924).
[44]See statement by Franklin Orth, *supra,* footnote 35.
[45]See Hearings, *supra,* footnote 3, pp. 750-751.
[46]See, e.g., Hearings, *supra,* footnote 3, p. 753.

C. Sales Program

The sales program is said to encourage marksmanship. Sales of .45 caliber pistols and shotguns, however, have at most a limited relationship to marksmanship. The most compelling argument for the sales program would seem to be that it allows the government the highest return on surplus military firearms and ammunition.[47] Pursuit of this objective would lead to selling surplus Army firearms at market value, not cost, to anyone who may legally possess them, not just to NRA members.

Summary

The statutes requiring the Army to assist marksmanship among the civilian population are based on assumptions of 50 years ago which may no longer be valid today. These statutes should be re-evaluated in line with current mili-, tary requirements.

---

[47]See, e.g., Hearings on Military Establishment appropriations before a Subcommittee of the House Committee on Appropriations, 80th Cong., 1st sess., pp. 1727-1773 (1947).

"OUTLAWING THE PISTOL"

As far back as 1926, a debate outline entitled "Outlawing the Pistol"[1] set forth many of the arguments on both sides of the handgun issue.[2] The document is reproduced here because of its charm and surprising similarity to recent documents relating to firearms control.

Resolved: That the manufacture, sale, importation, transportation, and possession of pistols and of cartridges to fit them should be prohibited except as needed for army, navy, police, and other official purposes.

Affirmative

I. The pistol has become a menace to society in this country.
    A, The amount of murder in this country is appalling.
    1. More than ten thousand people are murdered each year.
        a. This is more than in all Europe with four times our population.
        b. The murder rate, that is, the number of murders for each hundred thousand of population, is higher in the United States than in any other country in the world, and twice as high as in the second most murderous nation, Italy.
    2. More than three hundred thousand people have been murdered in this country in the past fifty years, 1875-1925.
    3. Some of our greatest and most useful citizens have been murdered.
        a. Alexander Hamilton and Abraham Lincoln, both victims of the pistol, are usually considered the two greatest statesmen this country has ever had.
        b. President McKinley and President Garfield were also victims of the pistol.
    B. The pistol makes these conditions possible.
    1. About 90 percent of the murders in this country are committed by use of the pistol.
        a. It is easy to conceal, making it possible to get near the intended victim before the weapon is displayed.

---

1 Lamar T. Bernan, "Outlawing the Pistol" (New York: H. W. Wilson: 1926).
2 The outline ignores, however, the argument involving the second amendment, arguments about registration, the fifth amendment, "states' rights," and punishing misuse rather than possession.

    b. It is so easy to operate that any maniac or idiot can use it.

    c. It is capable of quick and handy use, so that a murder may be committed with it in a flash.

  2. Armament always causes strife.

    a. It is with individuals just as it is with nations.

    b. A person armed with a pistol often commits a murder in a moment of passion.

    c. There are more murders where pistols are common.

C. The pistol is responsible for much other harm besides murder.

  1. Many are wounded and injured who are not killed.

    a. Among this number was President Roosevelt.

  2. Accidental shootings are frequent.

    a. This is especially true when children happen to get hold of a pistol.

II. The remedy lies in completely doing away with the pistol except for official use.

A. It serves no useful purpose in the society of today.

  1. It is not necessary for protection.

  2. It is of benefit only to the criminal class.

B. The character of our population makes it necessary to outlaw the pistol.

  1. The conflict between the races in this country often leads to murder.

  2. The large number of foreign born, many of them quick and impulsive in temperament, makes possession of a pistol a constant danger.

  3. The great number of feeble minded and mentally unbalanced people at large in this country increases the danger.

C. The argument that prohibiting the ownership and use of pistols is an interference with personal liberty is all sham and humbug.

  1. Nobody should have the liberty to murder another person.

  2. Personal liberty has always been limited by social necessity.

III. To do away with the pistol is a practicable remedy.

A. All other remedies have failed.

  1. This country has always had severe penalties against murder.

  2. Most of the states have made it a penitentiary offense to carry a concealed weapon.

B. When a few people are making money out of what is a great national shame and abuse, only complete prohibition is an efficient remedy.

  1. Slavery, the lottery, the traffic in narcotic drugs are examples.

C. The conditions we propose to establish in America already prevail in England.

  1. The police of London do not carry revolvers.

    a. London is generally recognized to have the best police force in the world.

  2. Not even the burglars or robbers of England are armed.

    a. The natural result is the much lower murder rate than prevails in this country.

Negative

I. The pistol is not the cause of murder.
    A. There have been murders ever since Cain murdered Abel.
        1. In the past all manner of methods have been used.
        2. The pistol is now used more than any other method simply because it is the most convenient instrument.
    B. Even if all pistols were done away with, murders would still continue.
        1. The murderers would then use the next most convenient method.
        2. Booth crept up back of Lincoln where he could easily have stabbed him.
        3. Hamilton and Burr could have fought their duel with swords or daggers, as well as with pistols.
    C. The cause of murder is social maladjustment.
        1. The remedy for every evil lies in removing the causes.
        2. Murder will be removed from our society only when a proper social adjustment eliminates the desire to murder.
            a. Our stereotyped system of education must be made to fit the needs and the capacity of each individual child.
            b. Religion must be vitalized and brought to every person.
            c. The insane and the feeble minded must be cared for and where necessary confined, though tens of thousands of them are now at large in this country without medical attention or police surveillance.

II. It is unwise to outlaw the pistol.
    A. When the next war comes our soldiers will lack training in the use of arms.
        1. The pistol was used extensively by our forces during the last war.
    B. It would be an undesirable further interference with personal liberty.
        1. Restrictions on personal liberty have already been carried so far as to create disrespect for all law.
        2. Every person has the inalienable right of self-defense.
        3. To many people pistol practice is a favorite pastime.
        4. A pistol is a necessity to people carrying or having in their possession large sums of money.
    C. Some people have advised repealing all our present restrictions on the ownership and possession of pistols and letting everybody go armed.
        1. This will place the law abiding on a plane of equality with the armed bandits and the other murderers.
        2. Many people think this will do more to decrease murder and check crime.
            a. This is a law possible to enforce.

III. To outlaw the pistol is an impracticable remedy for crime and murder.
   A. It will not work out as its advocates hope it will.
      1. It does not strike at the root of the evil.
      2. It would disarm everybody except the criminals.
   B. It cannot be enforced.
      1. The criminals are already armed.
         a. A pistol will last and work well for several generations.
         b. One box of cartridges will last a burglar or a robber for several years.
         c. An unloaded pistol in the hands of a burglar or a robber is just as good as a loaded one.
      2. As new criminals are developed they would have no great difficulty in obtaining pistols.
         a. It will be easy to smuggle them into this country from Canada or Mexico.
         b. It is an easy matter to cut down a rifle so as to make a handy and easily concealable weapon of it.
         c. There would be bootlegging in pistols and cartridges just as there is now bootlegging of whisky and morphine.

THE SECOND AMENDMENT AND THE RIGHT TO BEAR ARMS

A well regulated Militia, being necessary to the security of a free State, the right of the people to keep and bear Arms shall not be infringed.
Second Amendment, United States Constitution.

The second amendment is frequently interpreted as prohibiting governmental interference with individual possession of firearms. This interpretation is difficult to defend. In this Appendix the ancestry of the second amendment is traced from the English Bill of Rights through the American Revolution and Constitutional Convention, and the Supreme Court and lower court cases on the subject are reviewed.

The English Bill of Rights

Even before the Norman Conquest in 1066, English landowners were required to have arms and men constantly ready for the defense of the King.[1] These *milites*, or militia, remained the principal method of defense for the Crown until the restoration of the Stuart kings in 1660, when Charles II, having observed during exile in France the power of a king possessing a standing army, organized a large body of soldiers paid out of the royal purse as guardians of his court and person.[2] His successor, the Catholic James II, increased this nucleus into "the largest concentration of trained full-time troops that England had even seen."[3] He appointed fellow Catholics as officers, and deprived many of his Protestant subjects of militia status and the right to bear arms.[4]

---

[1] See Hays, *The Right to Bear Arms: A Study in Judicial Misinterpretation*, 2 W. & M. L. Rev. 381, 384 (1960); Olds, *The Second Amendment and the Right to Keep and Bear Arms*, Mich. S.B.J. 15, 17 (October, 1967); Sprecher, *The Lost Amendment*, 51 A.B.A.J. 554, 555 (1965); Comment, *The Right to Keep and Bear Arms*, 3 Albany L Rev. 74, 75 (1967); Note, *The Constitutional Right to Keep and Bear Arms*, 28 Harv. L. Rev. 473, 474 (1915).
[2] See authorities cited footnote 1, *supra*; Feller and Gotting, *The Second Amendment: A Second Look*, 61 Nw. U. L. Rev. 46, 47-48 (1966); Rohner, *The Right to Bear Arms: A Phenomenon of Constitutional History*, 16 Cath. U. L. Rev. 53, 58 (1967).
[3] Churchill, *The New World*, 2 History of the English Speaking Peoples 409 (1962).
[4] See authorities cited footnote 2, *supra*.

Incensed over these and other indignities,[5] a group of Tories and Whigs dispatched to William of Orange a request for assistance in delivering the realm from James II. Four months later, William landed in England, and marched unopposed to London. The royal army collapsed, and James fled to the court of the Sun King, Louis XIV, never to return.

In the absence of a king, a provisional government was organized by William, and letters were sent to the boroughs and counties requesting them to send representatives to a convention. This Convention Parliament met for the first time on January 22, 1689, and declared the throne vacant. On February 12, 1689, a Declaration of Rights, embodying Parliament's understanding of the proper roles of the Crown, Parliament, and the people, was agreed upon and presented to William and Mary the next day as a condition upon which the Crown would be offered. William announced, "We thankfully accept what you have offered us," and he and Mary were proclaimed King and Queen.[6]

Thus did the Declaration (subsequently "Bill"[7]) of Rights become part of the law of England. Alleging that it contained the "true, ancient, and indubitable rights of the people,"[8] the Bill held, among other things:

> That the raising or keeping of a standing army within the kingdom in time of peace unless it be with consent of parliament is against the law. . . .[9]

and, in the very next clause,

> . . . that the subjects which are Protestants may have arms for their defense suitable to their condition and as allowed by law.[10]

It is this latter provision which is generally asserted to be the progenitor of the second amendment to the United States Constitution.[11] Therefore, it is important to note that the preamble to this act states the grievance to be the disarming of Protestants "at the same time when Papists were . . . armed." As one observer has noted:

> Parliament did not appear to be claiming for the people a right of individual self-defense or self-effacement, but rather the general right, as a populace, to remain armed in the face of impossible military impositions. The resulting guarantee that Protestants might have

---

[5]Some of the most serious of the ofher objections were the use of the royal prerogative to suspend and dispense laws; the reestablishment of the Court of High Commission, with concomitant forcing of the Catholic religion upon the national church; denial of freedom of election and debate in Parliament; and infrequent calling of Parliaments. For a catalogue of these and other grievances, see 1 W. & M., sess. 2, c. 2 (1689).

[6]See authorities cited footnote 2, *supra*; American Bar Foundation, *Sources of Our Liberties* (Perry and Cooper, eds., 1959).

[7]The Bill of Rights, enacted Dec. 16, 1689, established the Declaration in statutory form. See 1 W. & M., sess. 2, par. 2 (1689).

[8]*Ibid.*

[9]*Ibid.*

[10]*Ibid.*

[11]See, e.g., Feller and Gotting, *supra*, note 2 at 48; Olds, *supra*, note 1 at 17; Rohner, *supra*, note 2 at 58; Note, *supra*, note 1 at 475.

arms for their defense necessarily related to the political grievances against King James which resulted in the Act of Settlement requiring the King to be a member of the Church of England. More specifically, the grievance underlying the guarantee was that Protestants had been deprived of weapons "at the same time when Papists were . . . armed." The imposition lay more in the discrimination than in the disarming.[12]

The right granted by the Bill was only such as "allowed by the law," and the law at that time already regulated firearms to some degree. The offense of "going about armed," for example, was founded in the common law. It was expressed in the 1328 Statute of Northampton[13] and in the following statute of Charles II:

> No person who had no lands of the yearly value of 100 pounds, other than the son and heir of an esquire or other person of higher degree, should be allowed to even keep a gun.[14]

Today England has among the strictest firearms laws in the world.[15]

Thus, to the extent one looks to English or feudal history for the source of the American "right to bear arms," it must be recognized that a measure of governmental control over any such right has long been accepted. The first statutory expression of this right—in an age well acquainted with such limitations—was not to assert a right of individuals, but rather to assert the general right of the Protestant populace to remain armed in the face of religiously discriminatory impositions. If it is to be inferred that the second amendment reflects the English Bill of Rights, it must also be inferred that it reflects the limitation that the English "right to bear arms" was "more nominal than real, as a defensive privilege."[16]

The American Revolution

Among the grievances catalogued by Jefferson in the Declaration of Independence, none had greater emotional appeal than those against the oppression of military rule: the peacetime quartering of troops in private homes, the superiority of military to civil power, the court-martialing of civilians, and the seizure of militia arms.

---

[12]Rohner, *supra*, notw 2 at 59; see also Feller and Gotting, *supra*, notw 2 at 48-49. Clause 6 of the Bill of Rights asserts that James endeavored "to subvert and extirpate" by "causing several good subjects, being Protestants, to be disarmed, at the same time when Papists were both armed and employed, contrary to law." W. & M., sess. 2, c. 2, par. 9.

[13]2 Edw. III, c. 3 (1328). See Knight's Case, 3 Mod. Rep. 117, 87 Eng. Rep. 75 (K.B. 1686); R. V. Dewhurst, 1 State Tr. N.S. 529 (1820); R. V. Meade, 19 T.L.R. 540 (1903).

[14]22 Car. II, c. 25, §3 (1670).

[15]"[D]espite the mandate of the English Bill of Rights, that country has enacted, through the gun license act of 1870, the Pistols Act of 1903, and the Firearms Act of 1937, much more stringent regulation on firearms than any in existence here." Rohner, *supra*, note 2 at 62-63. See also Brabner-Smith, *Firearm Regulation*, 1934 L. & Contemp. Prob. 400, 403.

[16]2 Story, Commentaries on the Constitution 678 (3d ed., 1858).

Basic to all these grievances, of course, was the existence of a standing army. Jefferson had already observed that the King had resorted to "large bodies of armed forces" to carry out his "arbitrary measures,"[17] and his indictment of George III for keeping "among us in time of peace, standing armies without the consent of our legislatures" continued this theme.

Rather than standing armies, the colonies preferred to look to their militias for defense,[18] and any action by the King which tended to disarm the militia was viewed as an attempt to destroy the liberties of citizens. The British attempt to seize the militia weapons cached at Lexington and Concord led to the first important battle of the Revolution.[19]

No doubt during this period there was also a considerable body of thought that individuals had an inherent right to have their own weapons, distinct from the rights of states to maintain independent militias. Many colonists were confronted by a wilderness of animals and Indians, and obtaining food often depended on sharpshooting hunters. But disarming of individuals was apparently not one of the grievances leading to the Revolution; there is no evidence that preservation of any individual right to bear arms was one of the purposes of revolution.[20]

The Second Amendment

With the English surrender at Yorktown, the victorious colonies bound themselves together with the Articles of Confederation. These were weak laws, however, based on the absolute consent of all the colonies, and widespread disaffection led in 1787 to a Constitutional Convention, with the predominant mood favoring the creation of a more effective national government.[21]

During these constitutional debates, some delegates urged the adoption of a prefatory bill of rights. Failing in this, they offered piecemeal amendments. Among these was George Mason's unsuccessful proposal that the grant to Congress of the power to "provide for organizing, arming, and disciplining the militia" be preceded by the clause: "That the liberties of the people may be better secured against the danger of regular troops or standing armies in time of peace."[22] No mention has been found, however, of any proposal securing to individuals the right to have weapons. Further, Mason's famed "Objections to the Proposed Federal Constitution," which

---

[17]*A Summary View of the Rights of British America*, reprinted in Essential Works of the Founding Fathers 97, III (Kiegel, ed., 1964), quoted in Feller and Gotting, *supra*, note 2 at 50.

[18]"The true strength and safety of every commonwealth or limited monarchy is the bravery of its freeholders, its militia." James Lovell, quoted in Rossiter, *Seedtime of the Republic* 387 (1953). "The sword should never be in the hands of any but those who have an interest in the safety of the community . . . such as a well regulated militia. . . ." *Ibid.* See also Trevelyan, *The American Revolution* 175, 187 (Morris, ed., 1965).

[19]See, e.g., Clark, *Opening of the War of the Revolution*, 19th of April 1775, at 5-8 (1875).

[20]See Feller and Gotting, *supra*, note 2 at 52-53.

[21]See, e.g., *id.* at 56-57; Has, *supra*, note 1 at 390-391.

[22]IV Farrand, *The Records of the Federal Convention* 59 (rev. ed. 1937), quoted in Feller and Gotting, *supra*; note 2 at 57, and Rohner, *supra*, note 2 at 57, n. 19.

provided the Anti-Federalist rallying cry, "there is no declaration of rights," does not complain of the absence of such a provision.[23] Apparently, Mason was concerned with the existence of an effective militia as the means of guarding against the possible oppression of a standing army, rather than with a right to bear arms for more personal purposes.

The Constitution was submitted to the states for ratification on September 28, 1787, and the struggle between Federalists and Anti-Federalists reached bitter intensity. As a result, several states, although ratifying, criticized the absence of a bill of basic human rights. To remedy this, they proposed amendments to be dealt with by the first Congress.

Massachusetts was the first to propose such amendments, but none of its proposals concerned the right to bear arms. Samuel Adams introduced in the Massachusetts convention a proposal that the "Constitution never be construed to authorize Congress to prevent the people of the United States, who are peaceable citizens from keeping their own arms," but even Adams ultimately voted against this.[24]

New Hampshire, the ninth to ratify, proposed several amendments, among them the provision: "Twelfth: Congress shall never disarm any citizen unless such are or have been in actual rebellion."[25] This probably would have conferred the individual right so often asserted today, had it been adopted.

In Virginia, whose wealth and population were essential to the union, the grant to Congress of power over the militia was the subject of extensive debate. But these debates swirled around Congress' power to disarm the militia, the states' powers to arm it should Congress neglect to do so, and the ways in which Congress could use the militia. Concern with an individual interest in firearms did not appear[26] and is not reflected in the Virginia resolutions dealing with the militia:

> That no standing army or regular troops, shall be raised, or kept up, in time of peace; without consent of two thirds of the members in both houses.

> That no soldier shall enlist for any longer term than four years, except in time of war, and then for no longer term than the continuance of the war.

> That each state, respectively shall have the power to provide for the organizing, arming, and disicipling its own militia, whensoever Congress shall omit or neglect to provide for the same. The militia shall not be subject to martial law, except when in actual service, in time of war, invasion, or rebellion; and, when not in the actual service of the United States: shall be subject only to such fines, penalties, and punishments, as shall be directed or inflicted by the laws of its own state.[27]

---

[23]Feller and Gotting, *supra*, note 2 at 57-58.
[24]Pierce and Hale, *Debates of the Massachusetts Convention of 1788* at 86-87 (1856), quoted in Feller and Gotting, *supra*, note 2 at 56.
[25]Dumbauld, *Bill of Rights and What it Means Today* 182 (1957).
[26]See Hays, *supra*, note 1 at 392-394; Feller and Gotting, *supra*, note 2 at 59-60.
[27]3 Elliot, *Debates 660*, §§9-11 (2d ed., 1836).

North Carolina proposed an amendment identical to the third Virginia proposal,[28] while Rhode Island recommended that "the people have a right to keep and bear arms," for the effectiveness of the militia.[29]

A compromise in Virginia saw the Federalist James Madison rise to champion a bill of rights—perhaps ghosted by James Mason[30]—in the first session of Congress. Among his proposals was the following:

> The right of the people to keep and bear arms shall not be infringed, a well armed and well regulated militia being the best security of a free country; but no person religiously scrupulous of bearing arms shall be compelled to render military service in person.[31]

The language of this early version of the second amendment illustrates Madison's (or Mason's) probable intent. The right to bear arms was intended to assist the militia—to keep it well armed. The last clause, which exempts conscientious objectors, reinforces this contention, for the entire provision must be taken as a scheme dealing with military service, not individual self-defense. Moreover, the last clause is phrased in individual terms, i.e., "no person," whereas in referring to the right to bear arms the proposal uses the collective term "the people." This contrast supports the view that the right to bear arms is for collective, not individual, benefit.

Madison's proposals were referred to a select committee, which reported the above provision in somewhat different form. In this form it passed the House:

> A well regulated militia composed of the body of the people, being the best security of a free state, the right of the people to keep and bear arms shall not be infringed; but no person religiously scrupulous shall be compelled to bear arms.[32]

In the House, debate was confined to the conscientious objector clause, although Elbridge Gerry of Massachusetts did comment that the purpose of organizing and maintaining a militia was to prevent the establishment of standing armies—"the bane of liberty."[33] There was no mention of any individual right to bear arms.

In the Senate, the wording was changed to its present form. While the religious scruples clause was omitted, the final version retains the collective "people." The Senate debates, unfortunately, were not reported.

This history supports the view that the second amendment was designed to protect the state militia, not to promote the individual's use of firearms.

Whether "militia" is defined as organized military units or as all citizens subject to military duty, the "right to bear arms" refers to collective and not individual defense. Moreover, the courts which have interpreted the second amendment have consistently limited "militia" to organized military units.

---

[28]Dumbauld, *supra*, note 25 at 201.
[29]1 Elliot, *Debates 335* (2d ed., 1836).
[30]See Pittman, *The Fifth Amendment: Yesterday, Today, and Tommorrow,* 42 A.B.A.J. 509, 588 (1956).
[31]Dumbauld, *supra*, note 25 at 207.
[32]*Id.* at 214.
[33]1 *Annals of Cong.* 749-750 (1789).

The Second Amendment and the Right to Bear Arms   259

The Supreme Court Cases

Since the adoption of the second amendment, the Supreme Court has had four occasions directly to construe it. In 1876, in *United States* v. *Cruikshank*,[34] the Court, in holding defective an indictment charging a conspiracy to prevent Negroes from bearing arms for lawful purposes, said that the right of the people to keep and bear arms "is not a right guaranteed by the Constitution."[35]

> The second amendment declares that it shall not be infringed; but this, as has been seen, means no more than it shall not be infringed by Congress. This is one of the amendments that has no other effect than to restrict the powers of the national government, leaving the people to look for their protection against any violation by their fellow citizens of the rights it recognizes to the states. . . .[36]

In 1886, in *Presser* v. *Illinois*,[37] the Court held that an Illinois statute which forbade bodies of men to associate together as military organizations or to drill or parade with arms in cities and towns unless authorized by law did not infringe the second amendment:

> [A] conclusive answer to the contention that this amendment prohibits the legislation in question lies in the fact that the amendment is a limitation only upon the power of Congress and the National Government, and not upon that of the States. It was so held by this Court in the case of *United States* v. *Cruikshank*. . . .[38]

In 1894, in *Miller* v. *Texas*,[39] the Supreme Court held that a Texas statute prohibiting the carrying of dangerous weapons on the person did not violate the second amendment, since "the restrictions of these amendments [the second and fourth] operate only upon the Federal power, and have no reference whatever to proceedings in state courts."[40]

In 1939, in *United States* v. *Miller*,[41] the Court upheld the National Firearms Act in the face of a second amendment challenge. In that case, the lower court dismissed an indictment charging interstate shipment of an unregistered shotgun having a barrel less than 18 inches in length. The Supreme Court reversed, holding that the second amendment must be interpreted in light of its "obvious purpose" of assuring the continued effectiveness of the militia. The Court said:

> In the absence of any evidence tending to show that possession or use of a 'shotgun having a barrel of less than eighteen inches in length' at this time has some reasonable relationship to the preservation or

---

[34]92 U.S. 542 (1875).
[35]*Id.* at 553.
[36]*Ibid.*
[37]116 U.S. 252 (1886).
[38]*Id.* at 265.
[39]153 U.S. 535 (1894).
[40]*Id.* at 538.
[41]307 U.S. 174 (1939).

efficiency of a well regulated militia, we cannot say that the Second Amendment guarantees the right to keep and bear such an instrument. Certainly it is not within judicial notice that this weapon is any part of the ordinary equipment or that its use could contribute to the common defense.[42]

These Supreme Court cases establish two conclusions. First, the second amendment does not restrict state regulation of firearms. The states may pass any firearms laws they wish, consistent with their own constitutions, so long as they do not interfere with some other power of Congress, such as the power to arm the military. A state may even disarm its entire population, save for those arms used by the Army, the FBI, or other federal agencies.

Second, Congress may regulate firearms. By deciding *United States* v. *Miller* on the narrow ground of failure of proof, however, the Court permitted the inference that proof of a reasonable relationship between a weapon and the preservation of a well regulated militia might protect that weapon from regulation. But it is common practice for the Supreme Court to decide constitutional cases on such narrow grounds in order to avoid deciding larger, unnecessary questions, and no such inference should therefore be drawn. Lower court cases support this view and indicate that Congress can regulate, even to the point of prohibition, the possession of weapons—short of direct interference with state military personnel in the performance of their official duties.

Lower Court Decisions

A 1942 First Circuit case, *Cases* v. *United States*,[43] called attention to and rejected this implication in *Miller*. In that case, the defendant had been convicted of violating the Federal Firearms Act by receiving a firearm in interstate commerce after having been convicted of a crime of violence. The appeals court rejected a second amendment attack on the ground that the defendant had used his weapon to shoot up a nightclub and an acquaintance, events which permit no "inference that he was advancing his military training or that his weapon was being used for military purposes."[44]

> [W]e do not feel that the Supreme Court in this [*Miller*] case was attempting to formulate a general rule applicable to all cases. The rule which it laid down was adequate to dispose of the case before it and that, we think was as far as the Supreme Court intended to go. At any rate, the rule of the *Miller* case, if intended to be comprehensive and complete would seem to be already outdated, in spite of the fact that it was formulated only three and one half years ago, because of the well known fact that in the so called "Command Units" some sort of military use seems to have been found for almost any modern lethal weapon. In view of this, if the rule of the *Miller* case is general and complete, the result would follow that, under present day conditions,

---

[42]*Id.* at 178.
[43]131 F. 2d 916 (1st Cir. 1942).
[44]*Id.* at 923.

the federal government would be empowered to only regulate the possession or use of weapons such as a flintlock musket or a matchlock harquebus.

But to hold that the Second Amendment limits the federal government to regulations concerning only weapons which can be classed as antiques or curiosities,—almost any other might bear some reasonable relationship to the preservation or efficiency of a well regulated militia unit of the present day—is, in effect to hold that the limitation of the Second Amendment is absolute. . . . It seems to us unlikely that the framers of the Amendment intended any such result. . . .[45]

That same year, in *United States* v. *Tot*,[46] the Third Circuit considered another second amendment challenge to that provision of the Federal Firearms Act which made it unlawful for any person convicted of a crime of violence to receive firearms or ammunition transported in interstate commerce. That court held it abundantly clear from discussions of the second amendment at the time of its proposal, and from learned articles since, that, unlike the first amendment, it was "not adopted with individual rights in mind, but as a protection for the states in the maintenance of their militia organizations against possible encroachments by the Federal power."[47] Stating that "weapon bearing was never treated as anything like an absolute right by the common law,"[48] the court concluded that the Federal Firearms Act was consistent with the history and purpose of the second amendment and affirmed the conviction.

See also *United States* v. *Adams*,[49] where the defendant demurred to charges of violations of the National Firearms Act on several grounds, including infringement of the second amendment. Declaring that the second amendment "refers to the militia, a protective force of government; to the collective body and not individual rights," the district court held that it had no application to the National Firearms Act.[50]

Some of the foregoing cases, particularly the Supreme Court cases, were decided before recent decisions extended federal constitutional guarantees from some of the first 10 amendments to the Constitution to state and local governments.[51] The Supreme Court has never ruled, however, that all of the 10 amendments in the Bill of Rights are applicable to the states through

---

[45]*Id.* at 922.
[46]131 F. 2d. 261 (3d Cir. 1942), *revd. on other grounds*, 319 U.S. 463 (1943).
[47]*Ibid.*
[48]*Ibid.*
[49]11 F. Supp. 216 (S.D. Fla. 1935).
[50]*Id.* at 218-219.
[51]See, e.g., *New York Times v. Sullivan*, 376 U.S. 254 (1964) (first amendment—freedom of speech); *Engel v. Vitale*, 370 U.S. 421 (1962) (first amendment—freedom of religion); *Mapp v. Ohio*, 367 U.S. 643 (1961) (fourth amendment—unreasonable search and seizure); *Malloy v. Hogan*, 378 U.S. 1 (1964) (fifth amendment—privilege against self-incrimination); *Gideon v. Wainwright*, 372 U.S. 335 (1963) (sixth amendment—right to counsel); *Klopfer v. North Carolina*, 386 U.S. 213 (1967) (sixth amendment—right to speedy and public trial); *Pointer v. Texas*, 380 U.S. 400 (1965) (sixth amendment—right to confront witnesses); *Parker v. Gladden*, 385 U.S. 363 (1966) (sixth amendment—right to trial by impartial jury); and *Robinson v. California*, 370 U.S. 660 (1962) (eighth amendment—prohibition against cruel and unusual punishment).

the 14th amendment,[52] although some Justics of the Court have endorsed this view.[53]

Since an extension of the second amendment to the states would probably invalidate many, if not all, of the estimated 20,000 state and local firearms laws in this country and since an extension is not "implicit in the concept of ordered liberty"[54] and would not provide a fundamental procedural protection for the individual dealing with state and local government, it is unlikely that the Supreme Court would similarly extend the second amendment. In *Burton* v. *Sills*, 37 Law Week 2380 (1969), the New Jersey Supreme Court recently rejected the argument that the second amendment invalidates the New Jersey firearms statute.[55] The court said:

> The plaintiffs . . . urge that "a reinterpretation of the effect of the Second Amendment upon the states is due to be made and the time is now with the New Jersey statute to be the basis for reinterpretation.
>
> We have no hesitancy in rejecting the . . . point grounded on the Second Amendment.
>
> . . . Reasonable gun control legislation is clearly within the police power of the state. . . .

---

[52]The Supreme Court has, in fact, ruled that all 10 of the Bill of Rights are *not* applicable to state and local governments. *Malloy* v. *Hogan*, 378 U.S. 1 (1964). See also, *Beck* v. *Washington*, 369 U.S. 541 (1962), where the Supreme Court ruled that the fifth amendment provision relating to grand juries is *not* applicable to state and local governments.

[53]See Justice Black's dissenting opinion in *Adamson* v. *California*, 332 U.S. 46 (1947), and Justice Douglas' dissenting opinion in *Poe* v. *Ullman*, 367 U.S. 497 (1961).

[54]*Palko* v. *Connecticut*, 302 U.S. 319 (1937).

[55]See also, *Oregon* v. *Cartwright*, 418 P. 2d 822, 830 (1966), *cert. denied*, 386 U.S. 937 (1967).

FIREARMS CONTROL AND THE FIFTH AMENDMENT

> No person . . . shall be compelled in any criminal case to be a witness against himself. . . .–*Fifth Amendment, U.S. Constitution*

As discussed in Chapter 13, the fifth amendment privilege against self-incrimination confers a much-discussed,[1] if at times obscure,[2] individual right not to aid the government in securing one's own conviction, regardless of the public interest in effective enforcement of the criminal law. This privilege applies in civil as well as criminal actions, where the evidence disclosed is likely to lead to a criminal prosecution.[3] Thus, it was perhaps inevitable that on January 30, 1968, the Supreme Court should hand down three cases— *Marchetti* v. *United States*,[4] *Grosso* v. *United States*,[5] and *Haynes* v. *United States*[6]—which cast a fifth amendment shadow over gun control proposals.

In *Marchetti* the petitioner was charged with willful failure to register his name, address, and other information concerning his gambling operations with Internal Revenue officials and with willful failure to pay the $50 occupational tax levied on all persons engaged in the business of receiving wagers. In *Grosso* the charge was willful failure to pay the 10 percent excise tax imposed

---

[1]See, e.g., Mansfield, *The Albertson Case: Conflict Between the Privilege Against Self-Incrimination and the Government's Need for Information*, 1966 Sup. Ct. Rev. 103; McKay, *Self-Incrimination and the New Privacy*, 1967 Sup. Ct. Rev. 193; Note, *Required Information and the Privilege Against Self-Incrimination*, 65 Colum. L. Rev. 681 (1965).

[2]Mr. Justice Harlan recently observed, "the Constitution contains no formulae within which we can calculate the areas . . . to which this privilege should extend, and the Court has therefore been obliged to fashion for itself standards for the application of this privilege." *Spevack* v. *Klein*, 385 U.S. 511, 522 (1967) (Harlan J., dissenting). Others have concluded that "the law and lawyers have never made up their minds just what [the privilege] . . . is supposed to protect." Kalven, *Invoking the Fifth Amendment: Some Legal and Impractical Considerations*, 9 Bull. Atom. Sci. 181-83 (1953).

[3]See, e.g., *Watkins* v. *United States*, 354 U.S. 178, 195-196 (1957); *Emspak* v. *United States*, 349 U.S. 190 (1955); *McCarthy* v. *Arndstein*, 266 U.S. 34 (1924). The exceptions sometimes threaten to swallow this rule, however. See, e.g., *Shapiro* v. *United States*, 335 U.S. 1 (1948) (required records exception); *Wilson* v. *United States*, 221 U.S. 361 (1911) (corporate officer exception).

[4]390 U.S. 39 (1968).

[5]390 U.S. 62 (1968).

[6]390 U.S. 85 (1968).

on all wagers.[7] In *Haynes,* on the other hand, the petitioner was charged with knowingly possessing an unregistered firearm in violation of the National Firearms Act.[8] In all three cases, convictions had been obtained and affirmed in lower courts over objections that the particular statutes violated fifth amendment guarantees against self-incrimination.[9]

The Supreme Court reversed each conviction, holding:

(1) That the requirement that gamblers register and pay the $50 occupational tax creates substantial risks of self-incrimination, in that compliance therewith significantly enhances the likelihood of criminal prosecutions under both federal and state laws, and, therefore, noncompliance cannot be criminally punished.[10]

(2) That the requirement that gamblers file special monthly reports as a condition to payment of the excise tax leads to the production of readily incriminating evidence, and, therefore, the fifth amendment precludes a criminal conviction for failure to pay that tax.[11]

(3) That a proper fifth amendment claim provides a full defense to prosecution either for failure to register or for possession of an unregistered firearm under the National Firearms Act, since such provisions require admission of unlawful possession.[12]

The wagering tax scheme has been a useful source of evidence for state and federal law enforcement officials in the prosecution of organized gambling. Prior to 1968, its constitutionality under the fifth amendment had been twice tested and twice upheld by the Supreme Court. In 1953, in *United States* v. *Kahriger,*[13] the Court ruled registration was a valid condition precedent to the payment of the gambling occupation tax. In support of this stand, the Court adopted the rationale of *United States* v. *Sullivan,*[14] where it had held that the fifth amendment did not excuse a taxpayer's refusal to file an annual income tax return, in that "it would be an extreme if not an extravagant application of the fifth amendment to say that it authorized a man to refuse to state the amount of his income because it had been made in crime."[15] Equally important, the Court in *Kahriger* narrowly restricted the prospective application of the privilege against self-incrimination by reasoning that it related "only to past acts, not to future acts that may or may not be committed."[16]

---

[7]Int. Rev. Code of 1954, §§4401-4423. Briefly, the statutory system operates as follows: Sec. 4401 imposes a 10 percent excise tax on all wagers placed. In addition, Sec. 4411 imposes a $50 annual occupation tax on all those subject to taxation under Sec. 4401. Pursuant to Sec. 4412 all persons liable for these special taxes must register with the appropriate revenue official, while Sec. 6107 requires revenue officials to maintain lists of those who have paid the taxes and to furnish copies of those lists to local prosecutors upon request. Sec. 4422 provides that payment of the special taxes does not exempt the taxpayer from penalties arising under any state or federal law prohibiting gambling.

[8]Int. Rev. Code of 1954, §§5801-5862.

[9]See *Haynes* v. *United States*, 372 F. 2d 651 (5th Cir. 1967); *United States* v. *Grosso*, 358 F. 2d 154 (3d Cir. 1966); *United States* v. *Costello*, 352 F. 2d 848 (2d Cir. 1965).

[10]*Marchetti* v. *United States*, 390 U.S. 39 (1968).

[11]*Grosso* v. *United States*, 390 U.S. 62 (1968).

[12]*Haynes* v. *United States*, 390 U.S. 85 (1968).

[13]345 U.S. 22 (1953).

[14]274 U.S. 259 (1927).

[15]*Id.* at 263-264.

[16]345 U.S. at 32.

Two years later, in *Lewis* v. *United States*,[17] the Court further reasoned that "there is no constitutional right to gamble," and that consequently those who chose to gamble could not avoid payment of the tax.[18] The necessarily implied result, of course, was a fifth amendment waiver, with the choice to gamble implying the choice to register.

The National Firearms Act had also previously been considered by the Court. In 1937, and again in 1939, the Court upheld the act as a valid regulatory tax, although no fifth amendment issues were raised or considered.[19] By January 1968, however, several lower courts had held the registration requirement of the act unconstitutional on the ground that it required an admission of unlawful possession.[20]

Further, it is significant that in *Albertson* v. *SACB*, the Court in 1965 nullified the Communist registration requirements of the Subversive Activities Control Act.[21] It reasoned that, despite immunity from prosecution under that act, compliance with its registration provisions would necessitate the disclosure of information which would establish a *prima facie* violation of the membership clause of the Smith Act and would supply federal prosecutors with "investigatory leads" to violations of that act. This created a "substantial risk" of self-incrimination.[22] The Court distinguished *Sullivan* by ruling that the questions on the income tax return were neutral on their face and not designed to elict admission of criminal acts,[23] while the SACB dealt in "an area permeated with criminal statutes" and with persons "inherently suspect of criminal activities."[24]

The Court approached *Marchetti, Grosso,* and *Haynes* in much the same way as *Albertson*: it analyzed the type of information required by the statutory scheme and the probable effects of its disclosure to law enforcement officials. Since the home states of Marchetti and Grosso had outlawed gambling, the Court held registration would have served to incriminate them, both by providing an investigatory link to past activities and by serving as evidence of intent and conspiracy to gamble in the future:

> We see no reason to suppose that the force of the constitutional prohibition is diminished merely because confession of a guilty purpose precedes the act which it is subsequently employed to evidence. . . .

---

[17]348 U.S. 419 (1955).

[18]348 U.S. at 423.

[19]*United States* v. *Miller*, 307 U.S. 174 (1939); *Sonzinsky* v. *United States*, 300 U.S. 506 (1937).

[20]See, e.g., *Dugan* v. *United States*, 341 F. 2d 85 (7th Cir. 1965); *Russell* v. *United States*, 306 F. 2d (9th Cir. 1962); *United States* v. *Fleish*, 227 F. Supp. 967 (E. D. Mich. 1964). *Cf. Lovelace* v. *United States*, 357 F. 2d 306 (5th Cir. 1966), where a conviction of unlawful possession was reversed because the indictment stated that the defendant had personally failed to register.

With these lower court cases in mind, the government carefully fashioned its prosecution in *Haynes*. At trial, those counts in the indictment which charged Haynes with failing to register were dismissed on motion of the U.S. attorney, who proceeded to trial under the only remaining count: unlawful possession. See *Haynes* v. *United States*, 390 U.S. 85 (1968).

[21]*Albertson* v. *SACB*, 382 U.S. 70 (1965).

[22]*Id.* at 79.

[23]*Ibid.* Several commentators did sound the alarm. See Mansfield, *supra*, footnote 1, 114-116, 158-159 n. 95; McKay, *supra*, footnote 1, 218-221.

[24]382 U.S. at 79.

Moreover, although prospective acts will doubtless ordinarily involve only speculative and insubstantial risks of incrimination, this will scarcely always prove true. . . . It is not true here.[25]

Therefore, the Court overruled *Kahriger* and *Lewis.*

The problem presented in *Haynes,* however, concerned internal statutory defects rather than the extrinsic incrimination of *Marchetti* and *Grosso.*[26] The incriminatory effects of registration under the National Firearms Act were subtle.[27] The act outlined numerous requirements which must be met for a person to legally acquire, transport, import, or make certain firearms and criminally punished any failure to comply with these provisions. Further, the act provided that one who possessed a firearm acquired by him in violation of these requirements must register.[28] Compliance with the registration provision thus compelled an individual who acquired a firearm to admit that he had violated some other section. Haynes' conviction was based on unlawful possession, not on failure to register. But, one could lawfully possess a firearm under the act only if all of the requirements had been complied with or if one registered the weapon. Thus, if one *acquired* a firearm illegally, one could lawfully *possess* it only by registering, which necessarily disclosed the unlawful acquisition. The Court reasoned that the practical effects of both the registration and unlawful possession sections were, therefore, identical and that neither section could be enforced over a fifth amendment objection: "The possession of a firearm and a failure to register are equally fundamental ingredients of both offenses."[29]

However, the Court recognized—

> that there are a number of apparently uncommon circumstances in which registration is required of one who has not violated the Firearms Act; the United States points chiefly to the situation of a finder of a lost or abandoned firearm.[30] . . . We agree that the existence of such situations makes it inappropriate, in the absence of evidence that the exercise of protected rights would otherwise be hampered, to declare these sections impermissible on face. Instead, it appears, from the evidence now before us, that the rights of those subject to the Act will be fully protected if a proper claim of privilege is understood to provide a full defense to any prosecution either for failure to register . . . or . . . for possession of a firearm which has not been registered.[31]

---

[25]*Marchetti* v. *United States,* 390 U.S. 39, 53-54 (1968).
[26]An internal statutory defect in the fifth amendment sense exists where a statutory scheme is so constructed that compliance with one section compels admission of a violation of a related section of the same statute. Extrinsic dangers lie in the fear that the disclosure of the required information might result in prosecution for violation of an unrelated statute. For another example of an internal statutory defect in the fifth amendment sense, see the federal statutes imposing taxation and registration on those who deal in narcotics or marihuana. Int. Rev. Code of 1954, §§4701-4707, 4721-4726, 4741-4746, 4751-4757.
[27]The act has since been amended. See 82 Stat. 1227-1236, Public Law 90-618 (Oct. 22, 1968).
[28]Int. Rev. Code of 1954, §5861.
[29]*Haynes* v. *United States,* 390 U.S. 85, 91 (1968).
[30]"Again, we note that these registrants might be confronted by hazards of prosecution under state law, and that those hazards might support a proper claim of privilege. . . ." *Id.* at 99 n. 13.
[31]*Id.* at 94.

These three opinions, unfortunately, give the misleading impression that it is essentially a simple matter to decide when a fifth amendment privilege applies—that it is merely a question of whether a compelled disclosure tends to incriminate. However, more than one commentator has observed, "the law and lawyers have never made up their minds just what [the privilege] . . . is supposed to protect."[32]

A simplistic approach would invalidate many of the information-gathering activities of government. For example, the Supreme Court has held that the fifth amendment does not excuse a taxpayer's refusal to file an income tax return; the taxpayer must content himself with refusing to answer those questions on the return which incriminate him.[33] Clearly, filing a partially complete return will attract attention and thereby tend to incriminate,[34] but the Court has not extended the privilege this far.

This simplistic analysis might lead to a fifth amendment objection to the annual federal registration of aliens[35] or to state statutes which require motor vehicle accident reporting.[36] It is possible that the courts may eventually sustain fifth amendment objections in these and other areas.

On the other hand, it may be unrealistic to read *Marchetti* narrowly as invalidating only legislation specifically designed to entrap criminals into admissions of guilt. If the privilege turns on the intent behind a particular statutory scheme, it should be noted that the Supreme Court went out of its way in *Marchetti* and *Grosso* to note that "the principal interest of the United States [in the wagering tax scheme] must be assumed to be the collection of revenue, and not the prosecution of gamblers."[37] It seems likely that a more balanced approach must be taken, such as that suggested by one commentator in 1967:

> A large number of factors beyond the question of tendency to incriminate must be considered. Among these are the purpose of the disclosure requirement, the importance of the governmental objective sought to be achieved, and the necessity of self-disclosure as a means of achieving this objective. Also of relevance are the questions whether disclosure is conditioned upon engaging in an activity deemed basic to freedom, whether disclosure is conditioned upon engaging in an activity that is independently criminal, whether incrimination is prospective or retrospective. Finally, there is the question whether the purpose of the disclosure requirement can be achieved without the use of the information for criminal prosecution.[38]

---

[32]Kalven, *supra*, footnote 1, at 182-183. See also *Spevack* v. *Klein*, 385 U.S. 511, 522 (1967) (Harlan, J., dissenting): "The Constitution contains no formulae with which we can calculate the areas . . . to which the privilege should extend, and the Court has therefore been obliged to fashion for itself standards for the application of the privilege."

[33]See *United States* v. *Sullivan*, 274 U.S. 259 (1927).

[34]Filing no return when everyone else is filing will attract attention also, and thereby tend to incriminate, but presumably there is no compulsion inherent in not filing.

[35]See Mansfield, *supra*, footnote 1; McKay, *supra*, footnote 1.

[36]*Ibid.*

[37]*Grosso* v. *United States*, 390 U.S. 62, 66 (1968). See also *Marchetti* v. *United States*, 390 U.S. 39, 42 (1968).

[38]Mansfield, *supra*, footnote 1, at 160.

Perhaps more light will be shed on this subject by future Supreme Court decisions,[39] but for the present the most realistic approach is to assume that fifth amendment objections to gun control statutes will be sustained when raised by those persons whom the statutes require to furnish information which might incriminate them. Any proposed gun control law must be carefully examined with an eye to at least minimizing possible fifth amendment objections, possibly through one of the methods outlined in chapter 15.[40]

---

[39]In *Leary* v. *United States* 37L. W4397 (May 19, 1969) the Supreme Court invalidated the conviction of Dr. Timothy Leary on the ground that registration under tax provisions of federal narcotics laws violated his fifth amendment rights.
[40]See ch. 15.